FEB -- 2008

# EMPTY CASING

# EMPTY

**A SOLDIER'S MEMOIR** OF SARAJEVO UNDER SIEGE

**Fred Doucette**

# CASING

Douglas & McIntyre
*Vancouver/Toronto/Berkeley*

Douglas & McIntyre Ltd.
2323 Quebec Street, Suite 201
Vancouver, British Columbia, Canada v5T 4s7
www.douglas-mcintyre.com

*Library and Archives Canada Cataloguing in Publication*
Doucette, Fred
Empty casing : a soldier's memoir of Sarajevo under seige / Fred Doucette.

ISBN 978-1-55365-291-5

1. Doucette, Fred. 2. Sarajevo (Bosnia and Hercegovina)—History—
Siege, 1992–1996—Personal narratives, Canadian. 3. Yugoslav War, 1991–1995—
Participation, Canadian. 4. United Nations Protection Force.
5. Soldiers—Canada—Biography. I. Title.
DR1313.32.S27D68 2008   949.742   C2007-905047-6

Editing by John Eerkes-Medrano
Jacket and text design by Peter Cocking
Jacket photograph courtesy of Fred Doucette
Printed and bound in Canada by Friesens
Printed on acid-free paper that is forest friendly (100% post-consumer recycled paper)
and has been processed chlorine free.
Distributed in the U.S. by Publishers Group West

We gratefully acknowledge the financial support of the Canada Council for the Arts, the British Columbia Arts Council, the Province of British Columbia through the Book Publishing Tax Credit, and the Government of Canada through the Book Publishing Industry Development Program (BPIDP) for our publishing activities.

The quotation on page vii is excerpted from Department of National Defence (Canada), "Operation Palladium"; online: www.forces.gc.ca/site/operations/Palladium/index_e.asp, accessed October 4, 2007. The quotations on page 25 are excerpted from Dzevad Karahasan, *Sarajevo, Exodus of a City* (New York: Kodansha, 1994); Carol Off, *The Lion, the Fox and the Eagle: A Story of Justice and Generals in Rwanda and Yugoslavia* (Toronto: Random House, 2000); and Rebecca West, *Black Lamb and Grey Falcon: A Journey through Yugoslavia* (London: Macmillan, 1942). The quotations on page 169 are excerpted from Tobias Wolff, *In Pharaoh's Army: Memories of the Lost War* (New York: Knopf, 1994); Department of National Defence (Canada), "The Reality of Operational Stress Injuries," *Canadian Forces Personnel Newsletter*, October 19, 2005; online: www.forces.gc.ca/hr/cfpn/engraph/10_05/10_05_osiss_stress-injuries_e.asp, accessed October 4, 2007; and Ishmael Beah, *A Long Way Gone: Memoirs of a Boy Soldier* (Vancouver: Douglas & McIntyre, 2007).

TO JANICE,

and to soldiers past, present and future

you are in the most honourable of professions

*Pro Patria*

CANADIAN TROOPS first came to the Balkans in February 1992 as part of the United Nations Protection Force (UNPROFOR), which was formed to protect non-combatants during the wars that tore apart the former Republic of Yugoslavia. With the signing on December 14, 1995, of the General Framework Agreement for Peace at Paris, after negotiations conducted at Dayton, Ohio, NATO entered Bosnia-Herzegovina with the 60,000-strong Implementation Force (IFOR) to ensure that the belligerent parties complied with its terms.

SFOR [Stabilization Force, as IFOR became known in 1996] is part of a major international effort to help Bosnia-Herzegovina reshape itself as a democratic European nation. The SFOR mission is to deter or respond to violence and, thus, provide the safe and secure environment necessary for the consolidation of peace in Bosnia-Herzegovina, with the goal of promoting a climate in which the peace process can make progress without the presence of NATO forces. Specifically, SFOR troops patrol so people can go about their daily business without fear.

DEPARTMENT OF NATIONAL DEFENCE (CANADA),
*"Operation Palladium"*

# Contents

# Foreword

WHEN I was asked to provide a foreword to an account of a soldier injured in Sarajevo, I was hesitant, as I do not have any experience in that theatre of operations. However, part two of Fred Doucette's story tells of a battle in which I have a great deal of personal experience—living with an injury to the brain caused by traumatic operational stress.

*Empty Casing* makes it possible for others to understand the effects of traumatic stress. The experiences are so vividly described that they enable the reader to get the feel of situations and understand that it is impossible for anyone to experience such daily terror and not be unchanged or damaged, as individuals do not possess the tools to handle the haunting images and terrifying memories. The vivid descriptions of fear and "living on the edge" make us understand how "boring" normal life back home then seems, and why returning soldiers question what is real and feel the urge to return to operations to get the rush of living dangerous situations.

For soldiers who are exposed to battle and are subsequently diagnosed with operational stress injuries, some not as serious as post-traumatic stress disorder (PTSD) but still requiring professional help, this book is of enduring value, as it shows that PTSD is treatable. It is an encouraging testimony of one soldier's battle and gives invaluable hope and encouragement to other injured soldiers and their loved ones.

ROMÉO DALLAIRE, LGen (Ret'd)
*Ottawa, Ontario · December 13, 2007*

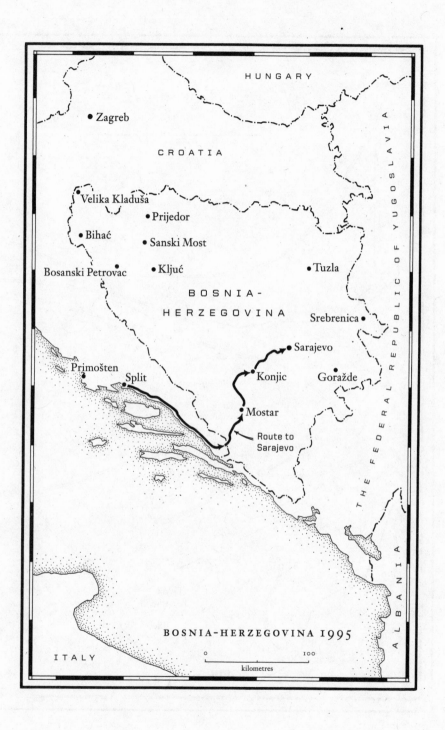

HUNGARY

• Zagreb

CROATIA

• Velika Kladuša

• Prijedor

• Bihać

• Sanski Most

Bosanski Petrovac

• Kljuć

• Tuzla

BOSNIA-
HERZEGOVINA

Srebrenica •

THE FEDERAL REPUBLIC OF YUGOSLAVIA

• Sarajevo

Primošten

Split

Konjic

Goražde

Mostar

Route to
Sarajevo

ALBANIA

ITALY

BOSNIA-HERZEGOVINA 1995

0        100
kilometres

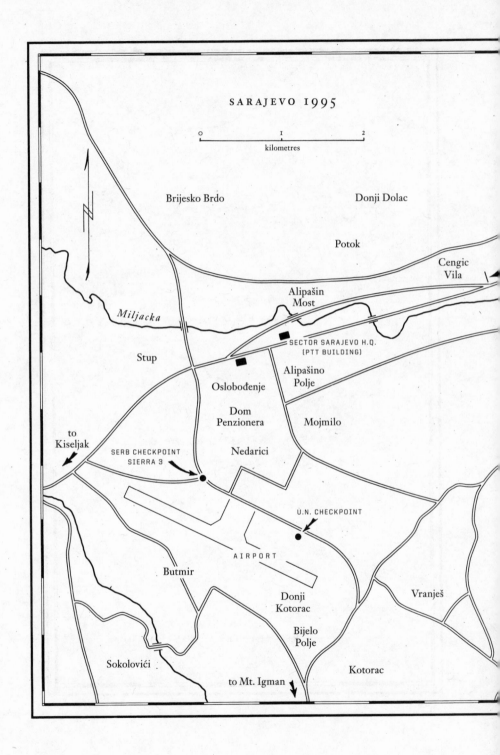

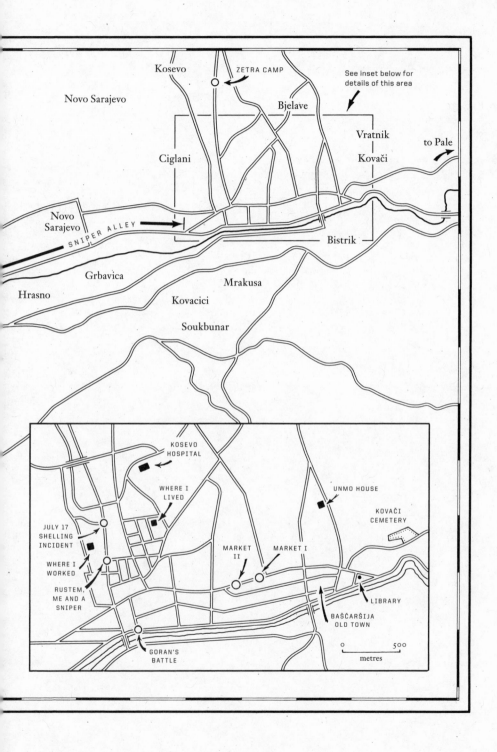

# LOST BOY

**AN IMAGE THAT HAUNTS** my dreams and invades my waking hours is of the children of Sarajevo. The healthy children I see in Canada sometimes trigger memories that either disturb me immediately or later return to haunt me in dreams that are a kaleidoscope of situations and places. Don't get me wrong; not every child I see evokes an image or event from the past. It is much more subtle. Occasionally some small detail—a child's eyes, dishevelled hair, a runny nose, the cry of a voice or a look of vulnerability—catches my eye and sets me off.

The dreams, though they're often terrifying, are a *safe* way to relive some of the trauma I experienced. Safe because they take place at home, in bed and in the dark. But when I'm away from home, the innocent, day-to-day antics of kids often catch my eye. And sometimes seeing these things requires immense self-control just to keep my emotions in check.

I was sitting in the food court at a local mall, sipping coffee. All was well; the crowd was small, I felt safe and in control. Looking up from my coffee, I caught sight of a boy about eight years old. His hair was messed up, his coat hung off his bony shoulders, his eyes were big and dark and he was looking for someone. My eyes locked on him. I felt my heart leap into my throat, my mouth was dry and tears began to well up in my eyes. He was one of those images of innocence but panic filled his eyes and quickened his movements as he searched for his mother or father. Then, in a second, his expression changed to joy as he spotted his mom walking towards him with a McDonald's tray. His eyes brightened, he smiled and ran towards her.

But this incident launched me on an emotional roller coaster. The young boy's look had stirred up images of other children looking and straining to see a familiar face, fearing that they were alone. I had seen their faces in Bosnia and could do nothing to help their hopelessness and fear. In Sarajevo I had been unable to help or care for those hopeless, unknown children caught in the turmoil of war. My chest ached; the tears overflowed and ran down my cheeks, and I hung my head so that no one would see them fall.

My coping technique that day at the mall was to take a napkin and, in the motion of cleaning my glasses, wipe my tears away, get up and find an exit, fast. Once I was safely inside my truck in the parking lot, I put the seat back and stared at the sky. I tried to block out everything so that I could deal with the images. I took deep breaths, gulping in the air like a drowning swimmer, all the time sobbing, letting the tears come. The pain would run its course and turn to the anger and guilt that came from hopelessness.

*Breathe deep, pull the air in, use your diaphragm, fill your lungs, concentrate, hold it in, hold it now, let it out slowly, exhale every bit of air, pause and repeat.* This is how I try to ground myself during and after a moment with the demons. This is a coping skill I call a drill, from my army experience. When we do something as a drill, we do it instinctively. In the army this has a much more sinister purpose: it is done to instill instinctive obedience in a soldier. It is the same with weapons drill or battle drill; it gives you a basis to start from. So when all goes to shit in war, you fall back on those instinctive drills to carry on. This takes the thinking out of a lot of what we do.

Hundreds of books have been written on how soldiers are conditioned to endure the horrors of war. Unfortunately, only a few of them deal with how to recondition soldiers when they return.

# Prologue | **Becoming a Soldier**

I **LEFT OUR HOME** in Oromocto, New Brunswick, on September 22, 1973, only three days after my son Ben was born. Janice, my wife, was in a lot of pain from an abscessed tooth, and her left cheek was swollen. I was scheduled to leave the house at five in the afternoon. Someone was giving me a lift to the drill hall. As things would have it, the phone rang at four. "There's a delay in the flight; report at eleven," was all I was told. This was not a reprieve; I would be leaving for Cyprus regardless of the time, and I wouldn't be back for six months. All the delay did was give us six more hours to feel sad and miserable.

By the time I left, we had cried ourselves dry. Every time I looked at Ben, I got choked up. I was feeling guilty: I was leaving Janice alone with a new baby, no car and a New Brunswick winter just around the corner. Yet we'd both known that the day would come when I would have to serve overseas. My first trip away was to join the United Nations peacekeeping mission to Cyprus. I would not return until March 1974.

My mind was too caught up with the sadness of saying farewell. I hadn't had time to get excited about deploying to Cyprus and wearing the UN blue beret. Yet for as long as I can remember, I had always wanted to be a soldier. I had served in the militia for two years and worked at odd jobs as a labourer. With only a high school education and no job skills I saw no future for myself as a civilian, so I followed

3

my dream: in November 1970 I enlisted in the military, in Montreal. I was recruited into the infantry as an infantryman. I was to be a basic soldier, also known to the uninitiated as a ground pounder, grunt or dirt person or, as the World War II soldiers termed it, the PBI, the Poor Bloody Infantry. What I did as an infantryman is best summed up in the army's definition of the role of the infantry: "To close with and destroy the enemy." For the next thirty-two years, I would train to close with and destroy the enemy.

I WAS THE SECOND in a family of four children. I have an older brother, Neddy; I'm in my fifties and also have a younger brother, Larry, and sister, Marie. We were each born four years apart, and I believe my mother miscarried twice in the late 1940s and once in the early '50s. Raymond, my dad, came from a family of twelve that lived in a New Brunswick village called Collette. He was a hard-working father and loving husband who had a strong sense of responsibility for his family. He was working in the woods, cutting pulp, when World War II broke out. He enlisted as a private in the infantry and had a rough time of it. He spoke no English and could neither read nor write. While waiting to go overseas, he fell in with a bunch of soldiers from Quebec who had no time for "the English war." Relying on some bad advice from the soldiers, he decided to go home and get married. Problem was, he was absent without authorized leave, "on the loose," and had no permission to get married. So in 1941 he married my mom, Winnifred Gould, and decided that since he was AWOL he might as well take an extended honeymoon.

That decision would end up costing him dearly. He was caught, court-martialed and sentenced to two years in detention in a military prison. This may seem a harsh sentence, but there was a war on. Dad was sent to Newfoundland to do his jail time. He kept his nose clean, and with good behaviour he was released after eighteen months. He was a changed man when he returned to the army. He regretted his mistake; he had been naïve and had fallen in with the wrong crowd. From what he told me and from what I heard from relatives and friends, the remainder of his time in the army was exemplary. Dad was demobilized in 1946; he was always proud to have served in the army and was doubly proud of me when I joined the army.

Mom was a loving, caring person. Born on the Fredericton Road in New Brunswick into a family of ten, she was a small woman who made it to grade six in a one-room schoolhouse during the Great Depression. She left school at the age of fifteen to work in Nova Scotia's Annapolis Valley as an apple peeler. I don't know how she met my dad, but I think they met in the village of Minto, New Brunswick. They were married in a small church just outside of Minto. The church is gone but the graveyard is still there, and many of my relatives who attended the wedding in 1941 have found their final resting place there.

My earliest childhood memory is of living in Amherst, Nova Scotia, around 1955. My dad worked at Brookfield Dairy, washing milk cans and tending to the horses that hauled the milk wagons. Amos and Annie, my grandparents on my mom's side, lived with us at the time and stayed with us, off and on, for the next twenty years or so. My grandfather couldn't work; he lost his right arm in a coal-mining accident in the mines in Minto in the 1930s. I don't have many memories of my time in Amherst, but I do remember feeling safe, contented and loved.

In 1956, not long after my brother Larry was born, we moved to Montreal. This was one of many moves my family would make so that my dad could find work. The job he went to was at a car dealership where his brother Benoit worked. My dad cleaned and polished cars, and in the winter he shoveled snow. His lot in life would be as a labourer; he would always earn just above the minimum wage, which in 1956 would mean take-home pay of about twenty-five dollars a week. In the early 1980s, when my father was in his late sixties, he was mopping floors in a tavern. He finally retired and returned to New Brunswick in 1982.

We were Catholics: I remember at my first communion at Holy Cross Church in Montreal, sitting there in my little blue suit, behung with various religious ribbons and not really understanding what it was all about. My mom was seated off to the right with the rest of the families. I glanced over to her, and she caught my eye and smiled back. I can say that is the first time I was overwhelmed with a lump-in-the-throat kind of love. It was also the first time I felt the pain of what it might be like to lose somebody, especially her. You'd think that as you grow older, feelings and thoughts of love would mature—but they don't. My mother died in 1991, well before her time, and my father died in 2000. The pain and anguish of losing them could not have been imagined. When my mom died, I stood in the shed behind the house crying alone so that no one could see this soldier cry.

My life until I went to school was carefree, full of fresh air and adventure. From day one I hated school and feared the teachers, whose attitude was that if you couldn't be taught, then they would beat it into you. My sense of justice and fairness was shattered at the age of six, in grade one at Holy Cross School in Côte Saint Paul, Montreal, where I was strapped along with several others because I did not have the proper slant in my writing. There we were, six of us, lined up outside the classroom, and coming towards us, down the hallway with a strap in his hand, was the principal. First he spoke to us, then yelled at us and the beatings began. He walked up to the first kid, grabbed him by the wrist, raised the strap above his head and started swinging. I heard the strap hitting the tiny hands, all of us crying, some pleading "I'm sorry, I won't do it again," to no avail. I had to be punished, strapped, because my fucking writing didn't slant? Then we were rammed back into the classroom crying and howling so that the others would benefit from our humiliation.

I remember seeing that fucking strap always hanging out of the principal's back pocket as he swaggered around the school, always ready to beat some kid. For nine years we endured slaps in the face, rulers broken over our heads, hair pulling and verbal abuse. These were our teachers. That Catholic school was a poisoned place: you couldn't learn, you didn't want to learn. I can honestly say that other than learning how to read and write, I did not learn anything at the school. I hated it and saw no use for it, and I quit in 1968. I was tired of being abused by the teachers of the Roman Catholic School Board of Montreal.

I had several good friends as a kid and teenager. What made our time together great was that we were all explorers. I lived in a part of Montreal known as Pointe Saint Charles. Back then this area was considered a slum, but for us kids it was an adventure land, with its rail yards, the Lachine Canal, heavy industry and a large city dump along the St. Lawrence River. We were free spirits, putting on miles and miles each day, always on the prowl for something new or for trouble to get into, dreamers who could easily spend a day lying in the sun on top of a lumber pile along the canal, watching the boats go by, imagining where they came from and where they might be going. We were amazed at the flocks of pigeons swirling around the grain boats like a grey cloud, wondered why they didn't crash into each other. We often imagined what it might be like to stow away on one of the boats and see where we would end up. But deep down we knew that our moms would be shattered, and we couldn't hurt them by disappearing like that. Little did we know that in a few short years we would all go our separate ways and, in doing so, we would end up hurting our moms despite our best intentions.

A defining moment in my childhood came when I was nine or ten years old. It was during the Lent period, when you have to abstain from certain things. I gave up eating candy. It seems strange that here we were with nothing, and we were being asked by the Church to give up more. At that time, being a devout Catholic, immersed in faith—or should I say the mysteries of the Church and all that blood and gore of the martyrs—I happily took on my duty and gave up candy and attended church every morning. Because the mass was so early, I was allowed to bring some food to school for breakfast. My mom would put some milk in an old jam jar with wax paper over the top and screw on the lid, wrap a couple of slices of bread in used wax paper and put a small jar of molasses in my lunch bag. She would always tell me to make sure I brought the jars and the wax paper home so that they could be used again.

The interior of our church, Saint Gabriel's, was always dark and had a musty smell of incense. Each morning during Lent I would sit there listening to the prayers and incantations, which were all in Latin. *Mystery and faith is what it is all about*, I kept telling myself. The service, with all its kneeling and standing and not much sitting, was always too long for my young mind and knees, but I was told that it would be all worth it—my faith and all my pain and boredom would get me into heaven. Father MacDonald, all 250 pounds of him, always said the early morning mass. His huge belly, covered by his vestments, reminded me of the Friar Tuck I'd seen in the *Robin Hood* TV shows. Father MacDonald was fat in a part of Montreal where the only people with bellies were the pregnant women. To me, he seemed to want for nothing. His sermons always included a good dose of Catholic guilt and of course emphasized the need for us to do more for the Church. Deep down I sensed that my faith was not as strong as I thought it was. I think I was being devout and pious for my mom, who still had faith.

On this day, when the mass finally ended, I was up and out before the words "The mass has ended, go with the grace of God" were barely out of Father MacDonald's mouth. Outside, in the blinding glare of the morning sun, I paused on the steps and let my eyes adjust to the light. (I often felt that the reason they kept the church interior so dark was that when we stepped outside we would be dazzled by the light and experience this poor-man's miracle of being blinded by the light.) Anyway, I was standing at the top of the stairs, rubbing my eyes, and as my vision cleared I was presented with my poor-man's miracle and with what would be my loss of faith and departure from the Catholic Church. Back then, Centre Street was a grubby street lined with small shops, secondhand stores, grocery stores, churches and rows of three-storey flats. The doors to the ground-floor flats opened right onto the street, and inside these flats a hallway stretched from front to back. And there across the street, sitting on a doorstep, was a barefoot mom dressed in shorts and a T-shirt with a cigarette dangling from her lips. Her hair was ratty and her face was pale. She looked beat, and probably was. In front of her on the sidewalk were two small children in diapers, playing in the dirt; behind her was a bare-assed toddler trying to climb over to play with the other kids. She, like many women in the Pointe, had become a mother when very young. I wondered if there was a father in that family. Today it seems odd to me that at such a young age I would realize that my "adventure land" was full of unfortunates who were worse off than my family.

Why did this scene hit me so hard? As I think back to those days and my years living in the Pointe, I don't remember anyone who was helped out by the Church. On that sunny spring day in 1959, my trust and faith in religion ended. I had just come from a place that preached caring and compassion, in a place that was run by fat priests, and here across the street was this extreme poverty. I shook my head, went down the stairs and turned to go to school. And there, making his way over to the rectory, was the bulbous Father Mac-Donald about to sit down to a hearty breakfast prepared by his maid. To me it was a simple injustice: the Church has it all, the mothers don't, so help them out.

TO BE A TEENAGER in the mid to late 1960s was eye-opening, but I find it difficult to nail down that period of my life. My interest in the army was nurtured by joining the army cadets and then the militia when I was sixteen. In 1967, the Canadian centennial year, I travelled on an army cadet exchange to Ontario, and then in 1968 to the national army cadet camp in Banff. Yet in these years I was also affected by the changes taking place among young people. Everyone was doing their "own thing," trying in their own way to make the world a better place to live. I loved the music that came out of the 1960s, especially as it was played by guitarists like Jeff Beck, Jimmy Page, Alvin Lee and Jimi Hendrix. I did a bit of drugs and didn't see anything wrong with a little grass, hash and the odd chemical now and then. Some kids thought I was weird because I could say no when I didn't feel like doing any drugs. I met some amazing people, a lot of freaks and young people burnt out on drugs. Yet here I was, drawn to the army while coming from a generation that was rebelling against authority.

I think that what drew me to the army was a need for a sense of belonging, security and challenge. In 1969 my prospects, especially relating to my jobs—dish washer, delivery guy, factory worker—were all dead ends. They all paid minimum wage, which at that time was seventy-five cents an hour. So I could stay in Montreal, work as an unskilled labourer and earn the minimum wage working for some asshole—or, "Hello, Army. Where do I sign?"

Enter a beautiful, dark-haired woman, Janice. Although I'd known her brother Jim from the army cadets in 1967–68, I didn't know he had such a rare beauty of a sister. It was December and I had been on a tasking at the military camp in Farnham, Quebec, clearing roads in the training area. On the Sunday when we arrived back at the armory, the kids' Christmas party had just finished. We were hanging out on the stage where Santa had been when Jim, Janice, her niece Jean and her friend Heather came down the stairs from the Sergeant's Mess. *Bang*, I was hooked from the first time I saw her. I had to get to know this woman with long hair, deep-set eyes and a mysterious air. She had a dignified way about her, especially in the way she dressed. The bright scarf around her neck made her look very classy; it also made me feel that she was way out of my league! Little did I know that later that day Janice told Heather, "That's the guy I'm going to marry." I wish I'd known that; it would've made my courting of her a hell of a lot easier.

I was awfully shy when it came to women. It came from attending an all-boy's school; even in high school, the boys and girls occupied separate sides of the school. I was robbed of the boy–girl interaction that should have happened at school (bloody Catholics). So I avoided Janice like the plague, always shying away, until May 1970 when, filled with liquid courage at a dance, I got up the nerve to ask her to dance and then for a date. In my semi-inebriated state, I asked her— a woman who'd lived her first twenty years in Montreal—if she had ever been to Mount Royal Park, which was known to Montrealers as "the mountain." (Is the pope Catholic, do bears shit in the woods? Everyone who lives in Montreal has been to the mountain.) Lucky for me, she understood "drunk"—and that I was making what even I knew was a feeble attempt to get a date with her. To my joy and delight, she said she'd love to go to the mountain with me. We have been together ever since.

The pattern for our future was set that summer of 1970, and for the next thirty-four years we would spend lengthy periods apart. That first summer was spent away at a militia training centre, and when I came home in September I applied for the regular force. I left in November, and we quickly learned to hate goodbyes. The first one was at Central Station in Montreal, on November 16, 1970. I was leaving for my recruit training in Nova Scotia, and I was so in love that I had serious doubts about going. I was devastated; in fact, in January 1971, after Christmas leave, I almost requested my release from the army. But Janice, with wisdom beyond her years, set me straight, so I stuck with it.

Janice and I were married on August 19, 1972, in a small church in a part of Montreal called Verdun. As fate would have it, I was away on a mountain warfare course in the Rocky Mountains of Alberta and wasn't able to go on leave until August 17. Janice was beginning to wonder if I was still committed to getting married. My commitment was there, but the army didn't seem to be in too much of a hurry to get me home. Despite the complications the day was beautiful, as was my bride.

The next day we left for New Brunswick with my dad and younger brother Larry. This was all the honeymoon we could afford, a marathon of visiting in-laws and outlaws, with a bit of camping thrown in, which ended with Janice catching pneumonia. After two weeks, we headed back to Montreal and I returned to the army, in Oromocto. We would have to wait another three months before we could afford for Janice to move down to New Brunswick.

In November 1972 Janice and I were finally together in Oromocto. Our married quarters were located in a court of row houses that housed about forty families. Our possessions consisted of a table, two chairs, a frying pan, a pot, two plates, two forks, spoons, knives and two glasses. Our bedroom was furnished with a single mattress on the floor and a twelve-inch TV at the foot of the bed. What made this austere home livable was love: we were finally together. But even then I spent most of that year in the field (that is, on manoeuvres) or away from home on taskings. Janice luckily met the wives of some of my friends, and they formed a bond unlike the ones soldiers form: those friendships still exist today.

The lives of army wives are lonely and challenging. They endure long separations as well as the extra workload of maintaining a household alone, raising their kids alone and dealing on their own with the many family disasters that only seem to occur when hubby is away. The old saying, "The army makes a man out of a boy," has a parallel in another saying: "A girl becomes a woman when she marries a soldier." Army wives are a cut above other women, and sometimes they are stronger than their husbands. They seem to have the dogged inner fortitude to make things right, to carry on with the conviction that someday things will be better. Their contribution over the years to the success and prosperity of our country is taken for granted or, usually, just ignored.

Janice's strength, patience and common sense throughout my years of service were an anchor for me. I owe her more than I can ever imagine. She showed strength when I was weak, compassion when I was sad and unconditional love for me and our children. I have always felt that we are a team, each bringing something unique to our marriage and filling in wherever and whenever the other needs support. We faced the challenges and threats to our marriage and family head on and dealt with them, and with each success we could feel our bond growing stronger.

Of all the challenges we faced, the separations were the worst, especially the departures. I always felt that the farewells should be done in the privacy of our home, not in a drill hall or airport departure lounge. Our first of many separations came at 2200 hours on that September day in 1973, when my lift arrived to take me to the drill hall on the base. I would be travelling to Cyprus for a seven-month United Nations tour. As I busied myself with moving my luggage from our porch to the car, Janice stood in the hallway, alone and uncomfortable, watching. Ben, our son of just three days, was asleep in his crib. I had gone up earlier to see him and say goodbye. He was so tiny and beautiful, so unaware of the anguish his mom and dad were going through. "Do you have everything?" Janice asked as I stepped back into the doorway. Both of us struggled to hold back the tears that filled our eyes again. We hugged and kissed and I walked down the sidewalk to the car. As I glanced over my shoulder at Janice, who was framed in the light of the doorway, I kept telling myself, *Be strong. Soldiers don't cry.* I took one last look as we drove out of the court. Janice was still there, alone, her hand raised in farewell. She later told me that when I left she went upstairs to Ben's room and cried.

Later that night, as our bus made its way through the sleeping countryside to Moncton to catch the military flight to Cyprus, my thoughts settled down. I allowed them to roam back home. I was only a few hours away from Janice and Ben, but already I missed them so much. I turned my head towards the window and the tears came to my eyes. It was dark and everyone was sleeping, or so I imagined; at least in the darkness no one would see a soldier cry. When I think back to that night, I doubt that I was the only one shedding tears in that darkened bus.

THE WARM NIGHT AIR felt good and smelled like a spicy pizza as I stepped off the plane at Nicosia airport. Cyprus, my first foreign country, my first UN mission—it was all new to me. The flight had been a long one, with a stopover in Germany for an aircrew change. I was glad it was over. The manning or rotation of UN troops was done in stages that related to flights: advance party, main one, two, three and four. We replaced our counterparts man for man, so as we drove from the airport to the camp an equal-sized and much happier group headed to the airport for their flight home.

A short bus ride and we were deposited at Camp Maple Leaf (quite an original name; it seems that every UN mission has a Camp Maple Leaf) with our luggage. I was welcomed by fellows from my platoon. It was nice to see familiar faces and to be congratulated on being a new father. There was a short processing routine—ID card, meal card and other administrative necessities—and then my mates helped me with my gear and I was shown to my accommodation. We slept in huts with corrugated tin roofs and sandstone walls two feet thick with a door at each end. The layout inside these huts was like a traditional barracks: one row of bunks down each side, with a locker acting as a divider. No privacy here, just a bed space. Over the years, by sacrificing a bit of bed space, the platoons occupying these buildings had built small rooms at one end. These rooms were our living rooms, furnished with scrounged furniture such as an old sofa, chairs, a table and a refrigerator. We were not allowed to have any food in the barracks because of the cockroaches and rats, so the refrigerator held only liquids.

Our refrigerator was always stocked with beer, hard liquor, a few soft drinks and a huge two-gallon jug of wine wrapped in wicker. The wine was red, about a week old, and so dry that it made you pucker. The fellows said it was an acquired taste. On my first night there I did the manly thing: I went to the junior non-commissioned mess and got pissed on brandy sours. I was feeling fine, flying high, until the next morning, when I went to our sun-baked outhouse. It smelled of urine, beer shits, disinfectant and creosote, which brought on the gag reflex. I puked like a retching dog until my gut touched my spine. This was going to be a long six months.

There were some World War II and Korean War veterans in the platoon. I was the youngest and the only one who had not been here before, so I had a lot to learn about Cyprus and the UN. I was told that the two players on the island were the Greeks and the Turks. There was a line (the green line) between the two former warring factions, and our job was to keep them apart and prevent them from going to war again. The UN was here to maintain the line between the two nationalities.

I had spent two years in a rifle platoon as a rifleman and had asked to go to a support company, specifically Pioneer platoon. Much to my amazement, I was sent there. Normally Pioneer platoon is made up of the older soldiers, so why they sent me was a mystery. In wartime we were the mine-clearing, mine-laying and explosives guys. We were all infantrymen and could fight as a rifle platoon when called upon to do so.

Our job on this mission was pretty mundane; we were the construction maintenance guys. We maintained the observation posts, oversaw the security lighting along the green line and fixed, repaired or jury rigged anything and everything. Being in Pioneers saved me from the very boring job of manning observation posts. We had free run of our area of responsibility—the city of Nicosia and an outlying outpost in the village of Louroujina. I was teamed up with Corporal Leonard Ivan Piercey, from Newfoundland. We had a Jeep, some tools and work orders that we picked up each day. After sorting them out, away we would go. We'd do about 50 per cent work and 50 per cent touring and shooting the shit with fellows along the green line.

Leonard knew everyone. He had about fifteen years in, and this was his second tour. His plan was to keep busy for the first couple of months, cruise for the next three, and finish off the last month by being extra busy to make the last bit of the tour seem faster. It worked.

I found that the best thing to do was keep busy. I ran, went to the gym and wrote lots of letters. These letters were the only way to reach home, as there were no phones for the troops to call home. I made one call in seven months. To call home, you used the Cypriot telephone system. You would book a time for the call in advance, show up on the chosen date, report in and sit in the waiting room. At the appointed time your name would be called and then you would be told to go to a certain booth. The booths, which lined the walls, were pretty soundproof and had a stool to sit on. At that time (1973) there were only fifty lines off the island to Greece. I sat and listened as they connected to Athens, then London and finally Canada. The line was clear as a bell, and it was fantastic to hear Janice's voice, especially when I knew that I would be home in about a month.

I missed home, but I took comfort in knowing that all was safe and secure there. On that first tour I quickly found out how lucky I was to live in Canada. The poverty in Cyprus was ethnic—the Turks had a lot less than the Greeks. There was a different standard of living when you crossed the green line from the Greek side to the Turk side. I guess that being a new father made me notice the kids and see their plight. No one was trying to kill them; they were just dirt poor. I identified with these people, with their dogged work ethic that focused on surviving from day to day. But the images of those barefoot, runny-nosed, poorly clothed kids burrowed into my memories of Cyprus.

When I had time off, the island was a delight to explore. It seemed that every culture had at one time occupied Cyprus—Egyptians, Phoenicians, Greeks, Romans, Crusaders, Ottoman Turks and lastly the British. So you would see a Greek amphitheatre next to a Crusader castle. It was all very exotic and quite an adventure for me. My future missions would be adventurous in other ways.

I felt that I grew up in Cyprus—I became a man, if there is such a thing. As a soldier in Pioneer platoon, I was among my elders. I slowly, cautiously, learned when and how to open my mouth. It is all about credibility and TI (time in), and I had none. I was the new guy, so a lot of ribbing, shit jobs and at times abuse fell on my shoulders. The time-honoured way for me to deal with my "initiation" was to keep my mouth shut, listen and learn.

But I could not match, or even come close to, my buddies' ability to drink. I saw drunkenness on a level that would shock a civilian; in fact, it would even shock other soldiers. Everyone was a hard drinker, capable of getting pissed to incoherence in the evening and then able to get up, eat a large greasy breakfast, work all day in the Mediterranean heat and get back into the booze again that evening. Although I could match them in getting piss-eyed drunk, I paid dearly for it the next morning. Waking up sick as a dog, stumbling to an outhouse that stank of sun-baked urine and retching like a cat bringing up a fur ball did me in. And my agony did not end with emptying my guts into the urinal. No, lucky Fred would heave all day—dry heaves, in which my guts would retract to the point where my navel would touch my spine. My body craved water, but I was terrified to put anything into myself, for fear of retching it up.

My misery was always the focus of attention for my fellow hard-drinking soldiers. There was no sympathy; in fact, a soldier loves spotting a weakness in another, because it is payback time. Once, he too felt the pokes and prods of his mates. They had all been where I was—young, weak of gut, naïve and trying to impress someone else. Some would look at me and just shake their heads in an "I told you so" sort of pity.

Through exploding headaches, gut-wrenching dry heaves and promises to God that "never again" would I drink, I realized I was not a drinker. It was a hard-learned lesson, but once I admitted it, life became better. My mates respected my weakness and ability to say no. I know that they knew that I would have to decide on my own that alcohol and Fred did not mix. I have stayed off the piss since then, except for a few occasions when I had to drink.

EARLY IN 1974, we could sense that the situation in Cyprus was tense. Several government buildings were bombed, and threats were made to local politicians and authorities. Oddly enough, the tension was among the Greeks, not between the Turks and the Greeks. I witnessed a bombing of the law courts in Nicosia from the roof of our commanding officer's headquarters. Corporal Leonard Piercey and I were patching a leak in the roofing tiles when we heard the awful BOOM! in the next compound. A car bomb had gone off outside the law courts. Smoke and fire is all I remember of the scene. A lot of people were running about; it was very uninspiring to see our officers acting like chickens with their heads cut off. Len and I had a front-row seat to view the confusion and panic of our officers, who until then had led a quiet life. Finally someone noticed us, and we were made to come down from our perch. Not keen on getting caught up in the "defence" of the HQ, we beat a hasty retreat to our camp by the airport.

Our tour ended in March 1974. While I was still on leave at home, the Turks invaded Cyprus. Our replacements, the Canadian Airborne Regiment, had a rough go of it, losing several troops during the invasion. But the regiment did a great job, and when the "new" green line was established, they began patrolling and waving the UN flag. I was glad to be at home with Janice and Ben, watching the war on television.

After a few weeks' leave it was back to training for war and the monotony that training brings. Down at the "coal face," the art of war fighting is not complex. Find, fix and destroy the enemy is the drill. Being proficient with my weapons, physically fit and up to speed with my fighting drills is what it boiled down to for me, the infantryman.

I was not happy then, and it showed in many ways. I was not close to anyone, not even the members of my family. I kept Janice and Ben at a distance. There was no spontaneity, I wasn't a dad. I wanted to run away, and thought a change would make it better. So I took my family—which now included our one-month-old daughter, Erin—on a roller-coaster ride that led to a new trade in the army, one that took us to British Columbia, then Quebec. That change didn't work. Then I figured it was the army, so I got out, we moved to New Brunswick and I attended forestry school. What followed was a move to Prince Edward Island, borderline poverty and a very confused and directionless Fred, with his loving family in tow.

The work on the Island was all part time and short term, and the chance of full-time permanent work in forestry was almost nonexistent. This situation I had put us in really ramped up the stress level, not only for me but for my family. I did not relish the thought of chasing part-time work and relying on unemployment insurance cheques to survive. What was missing was the security of full-time employment, which brought with it sick days, medical benefits, vacation time and pension—which, ironically, had been part of my benefits in the army.

In 1983 Janice decided to return to school, enrolling in the mental rehabilitation counsellor program at Holland College in Charlottetown. She worked hard and was rewarded with a diploma and strong recommendations from the college, and then moved right into full-time employment, managing a group home for mentally handicapped adults. Her job provided the secure wage in the household, which made her the breadwinner and brought a feeling of failure on my part. I could feel myself lacking any initiative to move forward; I missed the army and the life of a soldier. I decided that to suppress the need to soldier I would join the local militia unit, the Prince Edward Island Regiment. My cunning move only increased my yearning to be back in the army as a full-time soldier.

There were times when I felt I was deliberately sabotaging my life as a civilian. I would amplify every little setback or failure and rant and rave, never blaming myself but only others for my failures. I could not and would not put the energy into making a go of my newly chosen life. I was surrounded by Islanders who were no better off than I was, yet I envied them and their perceived happiness. I wallowed in self-pity and felt embarrassed at having to wait for an unemployment cheque, yet I realized how dependent I was on that money. Meanwhile, Janice was excelling at her new profession and Ben and Erin were enjoying school, their friends and living in the country.

My last job as a civilian was working as a silviculture instructor at Holland College—a twenty-four-week contract to manage and instruct about twenty men in how to be woodsworkers. I loved teaching and being outside with the class, but it was a term position and would end in the spring. Looking at the prospect of unemployment in the spring, I sucked up my pride, went into the Armed Forces Recruiting Centre in Charlottetown and asked to get back in the army. I was lucky to go in when I did, because I was within a year of the cut-off age for re-enrollment, and my previous militia service boosted my chances of getting back in. In May I received a call offering me direct entry into the infantry, with the rank of corporal in 3 RCR (Royal Canadian Regiment) in Winnipeg. So the Doucette clan was on the road again. Uprooting my family was not easy: Janice had a good, established job, and Ben and Erin loved the Island; only selfish Fred was keen to move on. So in the fall of 1985, with me weighed down with guilt, and Janice, Ben and Erin saddened at leaving their friends behind, we headed for Winnipeg.

Within a year I was back in Cyprus as a section commander with the UN again. At the time, I thought that UN tour was a busy one. We had several "incidents," but they were nuisances, not really scary. I was commended by the UN force commander, and later by the army commander, for my actions at a riot. I took a few good punches but managed to get my passengers to safety. I did my job, I had a good section and we worked well together.

Returning home was great, but lingering traits came back with me, adding to those from my first UN tour. Anger was now part of my make-up—good for a soldier, not so good for a husband and father. Time to run again. I applied and was accepted for officer training, which took us back to Oromocto. I was commissioned as an officer to the RCR in 1988, took over a rifle platoon (thirty men) in Hotel Company, 2 RCR, and guess what we did? Yup, we trained for war. The challenges and responsibilities of being an officer were greater, but they did not quell the uneasiness inside me.

In 1990 Hotel Company was sent to Montreal to provide armed assistance in the standoff now known as the "Indian Wars at Oka." Because of my French-language ability, I was deployed forward as a liaison officer. I reported directly to the commanding officer on the situation of the other units that were also deployed forward. 2 RCR was held in reserve as the "hammer." Unbeknownst to most Canadians, we came within a couple of hours of letting the hammer fall. It was surreal to see young soldiers writing letters to their loved ones and giving them to the padre, in case they didn't make it. After a couple of weeks as a liaison officer, I ended up replacing Lieutenant Steve Nash as a platoon commander in G Company.

Our politicians had totally fucked up, and they turned to the Canadian army to sort out their mess. Our training for war was going to be used against our fellow Canadians. We all knew that if it worked out and the standoff was resolved, the politicians would breathe a sigh of relief. We also knew if it went to shit, they would have a scapegoat in the soldiers—who would have "failed." In the end, the soldiers' cool-headed, no-nonsense professionalism paid off. Other than enduring minor scuffles, cuts and bruises, we all went home none the worse for wear and were promptly forgotten about. We went back to training for war.

When the Gulf War broke out, we were all bitter and questioned what our government wanted from us. We were left at home, not committed to the land battle—the war we had trained for. Like the rest of the world, we watched the war on television. I finished my time at the battalion and was posted to the Western Area Headquarters in Edmonton to manage full-time reservists. Other than giving me a chance to work with great people, the job was a yawning bore. I was not cut out for HQ paper-pushing. I hated it and the world that pumped out that paper. I plodded to work each day and was very unhappy.

Janice tried to be responsible for my happiness, and for her efforts I dragged her down with me. I was depressed, I wasn't sure what I wanted or where I was going.

I howled loud and long enough that I was placed on standby to be deployed overseas as a UN military observer. I was supposed to go to Western Sahara, Mozambique, Rwanda, Bosnia, Dominican Republic/Haiti, then Bosnia again. There are many reasons why I never went on one of those six missions, ranging from not knowing the right people to "mission reconfiguration." But in the end, I flew to Bosnia on July 5, 1995. This was the beginning of the end of the Fred I had been for forty-three years.

# PART ONE

# SARAJEVO

Sarajevo, the capital of Bosnia and Herzegovina, is the country's largest city. Founded by Isa bey Ishakovic in 1440, it is also a typical Bosnian city. Surrounded by mountains, Sarajevo is enclosed and isolated from the world ... cut off from everything external and turned wholly toward itself.

DZEVAD KARAHASAN, *Sarajevo, Exodus of a City*

On April 6, 1992, Canada, along with the European Community, recognized Bosnia as an independent state. The United States followed suit the next day. It was clear—or it should have been clear, given the shootout of the day before—what the consequences would be, but the international community went ahead anyway ... There were more gunshots in Sarajevo the afternoon of the EC declaration; this time, the snipers opened fire from the top of the Holiday Inn, killing six people and injuring dozens more. Sarajevans would soon get used to seeing pools of blood on their streets.

CAROL OFF, *The Lion, the Fox and the Eagle:*
*A Story of Generals and Justice in Rwanda and Yugoslavia*

... this was the one time when staying in Sarajevo was not purely agreeable.

REBECCA WEST, *Black Lamb and Grey Falcon:*
*A Journey through Yugoslavia*

# 1 | Lucky Me

SARAJEVO IT IS. Our United Nations Military Observer (UNMO) team assignments had just been announced, and I was surprised and shocked. I'd been posted to an UNMO team in "the Javo." It was not my first choice of where to serve the first half of my year in Bosnia. In fact, it was my third choice. I had no interest in serving in the besieged city. The policy for UNMOS with the United Nations Protection Force (UNPROFOR) was that you served your first six months in Bosnia, then you came out and spent the next six months in Croatia or Macedonia. There were about thirty-five UNMO teams in Bosnia, of which five or six teams were within the UN Protected Area (UNPA) of Sarajevo.

So lucky Fred, who never wins anything, had the dubious luck of going to Sarajevo. Sitting in the untouched-by-the-war city of Zagreb, Croatia, I was to form the opinion that only the "I want to experience war" types actually wanted to go to Sarajevo. My experience of war had been my two tours of UN duty in Cyprus, in 1973 and 1986. So I was a bit shocked when I was told, "Away you go. You'll be there in four days."

I kept telling myself, *No need to fret. It can't be all that bad.* I could not figure out why all the military observers who had been "in country" for a while kept wishing me luck.

I should explain what UNMOS in Bosnia were expected to do. Put simply, they were to observe the military activity of all warring factions and forward the information to headquarters in Zagreb. The information was sorted by importance and then distributed both to the UN in New York City and to UN commanders in Bosnia. UNMOS were like spies in uniform, supposedly unbiased and posing a threat to no one.

The dubious thing about observers' work is that they were paid the much-envied MSA (mission subsistence allowance). The money, in good old U.S. dollars (tax-free), was the envy of other UN personnel because it was lucrative, especially in a place like Sarajevo. The idea behind the money was that the UN supplied the teams with vehicles and communications gear but that food, accommodations and so on were not included. That's what the allowance was for. Unlike the case in the UN contingents, there was no administrative or logistical support for the observers; you paid as you went.

So it was up to me and Major Mark Douglas, another unfortunate, to find a way into Sarajevo from Zagreb. It didn't take long to sort out our overland route. There was only one way into the besieged city then: over Mount Igman.

The journey began on July 13, 1995, with our first leg from Zagreb to Split, Croatia, on a UN cargo aircraft. Split, a resort city on the Dalmatian coast, was untouched by this so-called civil war. After landing in Split, we began a practice common among UNMOS: bumming a ride. Although there were many UN vehicles, none were going into Sarajevo. Some people wondered why we would even want to go there. I had a feeling of dread about the days ahead.

We eventually managed to find a ride to the Canadian Support Unit at Camp Primosten, about forty-five kilometres from Split. Our ride to the start point into Sarajevo at Malo Polji would be with a Norwegian UN contingent mini-bus that wasn't scheduled to leave for another twenty-four hours. So off we went to the Canadian Camp, where, with any luck, we hoped to find accommodation for the night and some food.

The ride on the bus, full of Canadians returning from leave, was quiet. Everyone was facing the realization they were back "in theatre." I secretly envied them. All I could think of was that it was July and they'd be home in September. By then I'd still have ten months to go.

When we arrived it was hot and dry. We dumped our gear in

the shade. Mark headed off to see if we could stay the night while I guarded our gear. Being inquisitive, I eyed my surroundings and strolled about. I soon realized that this camp was luxurious.

Before the war, the camp had been a beachside camping resort. It was nestled in a pine forest next to a bay on the Adriatic Sea. The isos (the trade name for prefabricated sea-container-size rooms built to accommodate two to four people) were tucked in the shade of the pine trees. If you had a high-enough rank, you would rate an iso right on the water, one with a small deck complete with lawn chairs and a table with a beach umbrella. Lower ranks would have a short walk to the water. For an infantryman it was impressive, even by Canadian standards.

Major Mark returned from his quest for a room and was actually pissed off; this was rare for him. Like me, he was in awe of our surroundings. I asked him about his change of mood, and he replied that we were almost refused a bed for the night. The duty staff had thrown out all kinds of excuses about why there was "no room at the inn." It wasn't the first time we'd encountered this attitude from our fellow peacekeepers. They felt that since UNMOS were given extra cash for food and accommodation, we should find a hotel and eat in a restaurant. What they gave us was a piece of a tent with no end on it and two beds. Not bad, actually: the lack of an end for the tent gave us a lovely ocean view, and with luck it wouldn't rain. So we had accommodation, at least. Now, where was the food?

Mark said that we were invited to the officers, sergeants and warrant officers' combined mess for a barbecue. We obliged and were treated to a typically Canadian feast, lots of food and beer. The view overlooked a bay where jet skis, Zodiacs and wind surfers were available for use. But everyone seemed tense. We noticed people moving in cliques in what seemed to be very distinct parts of the mess: they were not overly friendly to each other. Later I heard that there were plenty of petty jealousies and poor leadership in the Canadian Logistics Battalion. This mix made for a very unhappy unit.

But I had other things on my mind. Mark and I ate our fill and wandered back to our tent to sort out our gear. We didn't speak much. I guess we were both anxious and a bit scared about our trip the next day. I fell asleep with the sound of water lapping at the shore and the moon beaming into our tent. This would be my last uninterrupted sleep for some time to come.

We started our day with a big breakfast—typical Canadian army type, lots of grease. It took more time than we expected to get a lift back to Split to meet our Norwegian ride. So, by the time we were on our way, we had forty-five minutes to cover forty-five kilometres of coastal roads. During the ride I chatted up our driver about the situation at Camp Primosten.

The driver, a young corporal, was eager to talk. He told us that drivers were the only ones who ever left the camp. They drove the vehicles in the convoys that supplied the two Canadian battalions, one in Croatia, the other in Bosnia. They faced long hours, dangerous roads and the ever-present warring factions. But they got through. The drivers were a minority; most of the troops at Camp Primosten were considered "campers" who were there just living the good life. Oddly enough, the campers earned the same danger pay as the drivers, as did the support staff at Canadian Contingent HQ in Zagreb. True to his profession, our driver delivered us to the Norwegian Camp safe and sound, with five minutes to spare.

### OVER MOUNT IGMAN

The Norwegian Camp was small and very busy, and it seemed to have soldiers from all over the world. Our ride was a small, but luxurious, air-conditioned Toyota, which had all its seats packed with troops and equipment. We squeezed in with our gear and headed off for a trip I will never forget—or should I say, I'd sooner forget.

The initial part of our trip was uneventful. We drove through Croatia, which in this part of the former Yugoslavia was relatively untouched. We made a quick stop to put on our body armour and helmets, and then, much to my surprise, made a quick unhindered "border" crossing from Croatia into Bosnia. Once we were in Bosnia, things changed drastically.

The sights, sounds and smells that greeted us were ones I would become familiar with but never get used to. Destroyed homes, roads, bridges, dams and fields—all void of life. People stared at us with either indifference or anger. *You are the* UN *Protection Force, why didn't you protect us?* was obviously running through their minds. We were all quiet, some asleep; others stared out at the surreal world flashing by them as we made our way to Mount Igman.

We finally reached the village of Tatina, about ten kilometres from the pickup point for the trip to Malo Polje, on the west side of Mount Igman. Here we transferred to French APCs (armoured personnel carriers) for the ride over Mount Igman and down into Sarajevo. At this change-over point, we were immediately surrounded by begging women and children. The French soldiers were jumpy, hurrying us with our unloading and loading, telling the beggars to "Piss off." These solders had been here awhile and had seen it all. For them the trip was just another spin of the roulette wheel, a ride into hell. The moms and kids wanted "paquets," French army ration packs, which contained enough food for one soldier for a day, or for a Bosnian family of four for two days. It was all very hard on the senses; I looked at them and imagined my wife and children in this place. I felt their hopelessness and despair. A feeling soon to be familiar to me crept up—helplessness.

The French APC carried nine passengers and a two-man crew, so in we got. Eleven sardines, all boxed nice and tight, no windows, no air. I was reminded of a CNN news report of eleven French soldiers killed on Mount Igman a few months earlier, and here I was—same mountain, same type of vehicle, with eleven soldiers on board.

Mark and I were amazed at how fast we were moving. The French drivers wasted no time. The worst thing about being closed in the back of the APC was the sensory deprivation, not knowing about the outside surroundings. A person has to see what threatens him; it makes these threats and fears easier to handle. In a metal box, doing ninety kilometres an hour, fear and imagination take over.

My fellow passengers were Danish soldiers who were part of the UN Headquarters (UNHQ) Security Company in Sarajevo. They were returning from leave and their six months in Sarajevo would be done in less than a month. How I envied them. There was a Spanish pilot heading in to work at the UNHQ. In time, I would get to know him quite well. What finally struck me was that the Danes and the French were armed. Maybe I've failed to mention this, but military observers are unarmed. The powers that be said it made us less threatening to the warring factions.

We bounced and jolted along our unseen road, totally ignorant of where we were. Hot and bored, we were soon lulled into a semi-sleep. Then silence. We had stopped. The doors finally opened, fresh air and sunlight rushed in. We were at Malo Polje, the convoy assembly point on the west side of Mount Igman, just below the top. It had been the site of the 1984 Olympic ski-jumping facility; a French infantry company, whose sole purpose was to keep the upper part of the Igman road open, now occupied it. This road was the only lifeline into the besieged city of about two hundred thousand. It was no bigger than a woods road, mostly single-lane and steep, with numerous switchback turns.

We spent a couple of hours sorting out the convoy. Well, actually we didn't; the French did. It all seemed so confused and loud in a way that only the French could manage. Regardless, out of the racket and confusion the convoy formed, armoured escort leading, United Nations High Commission for Refugees (UNHCR) trucks full of supplies for the city, us, then the ominous armoured ambulances, which I hoped we wouldn't have to use. Behind all of us were the daredevil civilian entrepreneurs in their trucks, people willing to risk everything to get a truckload of whatever into the city for the black market. Their method involved using the dark of night, trailing the UN convoy. They hoped to be mistaken for part of the authorized convoy and not be fired upon. Sometimes it worked, but most times it didn't: the UN got fired on, regardless. We were a big convoy and, in my military mind, a big target. The French soldiers were buzzing around, trying to get people back into their vehicles. They were tense and nervous; they didn't like their task, and I would soon know why.

By the end of the night I'd experienced my first "two-way range." This term needs a bit of explanation. In peacetime, an army trains on ranges that are "one way": you fire at targets that don't shoot back. In a war, you shoot and in all likelihood someone shoots back; thus, "a two-way range." For me this was a reality check in the art of soldiering.

Once we were mounted and ready to go, I was surprised at the speed at which we took off—fast! We were moving; hatches down, body armour and helmets on, everyone quiet and anxious. The ride down Igman started in a thick forest of large pines, tall and dark. The road switched back and forth and the grade in places was steep, especially at the hairpin turns. The road had been carved away by the thousands of vehicles going up and down the mountain. The roadsides were littered with the remains of broken-down and destroyed vehicles, which had been scavenged for parts because they'd been left unguarded too long. No tires, fuel, doors, windows or engine parts. All "liberated" and brought into Sarajevo, where they would fetch a nice price on the black market.

The chatter on the radio network never stopped; the term "minimize"—the official term for "Shut the fuck up" on military radio communications systems—didn't seem to exist on French radio nets. I sensed the nervous chatter, things like "Where are you?" "Don't fall back too far." One question that struck me was: "How far to the exposed part?"

Igman is a large ridge, wooded on the upper reaches, but for a few kilometres on the lower part the road ran out of the trees onto a bald-ass side hill. On this stretch of the road, any vehicle going up or down the mountain was exposed to both Serb and Bosnian guns. The French mortar crews were usually aimed at both sides whenever a convoy was moving up or down the mountain. Their job was to fire on whoever fired on the convoy, but—and this is a big "but"—they needed permission to fire.

### THE FIRST MORTAR ATTACK

Igman did not have one safe piece of road on it. In fact, we quickly found out how unsafe it was. The lead elements of our convoy had made their way out onto the open slope. By this time, we were using the cover of darkness to hide our movement. The gunners (Serb or Bosnian, we didn't know) held their fire until the large, ten-ton

UNHCR trucks lumbered onto the open road. Then *boom*, they let
fly with 120 mm mortars and 30 mm cannons. I heard the French
screaming on the radio, yelling orders: "Pull back, move forward, do
fucking something, but get off the hill and under cover." These words
were amazing to hear, because in twenty-five years of peacetime soldiering all I'd ever heard was "Contact, wait out," on hundreds of
exercises. "Contact, wait out" means that you have seen or are being
fired at by the enemy. On exercises in Canada the commanders are
always calm, cool, collected. But not here in the real world, on the
"two-way range." We stopped just inside the tree line and listened to
the radio chatter: three trucks hit and burning, three wounded, Belgian drivers. No one moved. We stayed hidden until early morning
and waited for the road to be cleared, to give the French some time
to build up the nerve to try again.

I was not even in the city yet, and I had already had my first taste
of what was to come. It was all so impersonal. We were just a line of
vehicles moving down the road; someone decided to shake us up a bit.
I've often wondered if anyone had issued orders or if it was just some
guys, drunk, bored, who knows: "Yahoo, here they come! Let's fuck
some UN." After several months in the city and numerous incidents
similar to my first, I realized that very little control was exercised
over the besiegers and besieged of Sarajevo. I could only imagine the
mindset: *Will I kill someone today? Maybe yes, maybe no. Let's see how
I feel. Will someone catch my interest, or is there a house that catches my
eye? Will someone piss me off?* It's all so impersonal, cold, cruel and, for
the uninitiated, quite impossible to comprehend. I come from a nice,
ordered world, we know who the bosses are, police have the guns, we
can go anywhere, do anything, no fears, or at least the threats are
so minimal that they are not even thought about. In Bosnia the gun
ruled. If you had one, you were a boss in your little world. If you were
a warlord, then you were a giver or taker of life.

Sitting in the woods on Igman in the dark, I wondered what I had
gotten myself into. How could I last six months in a place like this? I
felt fear, yet it would be a few more days before I felt terror.

Before first light we were hustled into our eleven-man metal cof-
fins, and our dash into the city was renewed. It's a good thing that

we couldn't see our route; I would see it a month later and be amazed that we survived the ride in. With all the jolting, breaking, crashing and bashing we knew we had more of a chance of dying in a vehicle crash than from enemy fire.

My helmet saved my life twice on that sprint into the city. Once we hit a bump and my head smashed into the roof of the vehicle, driving the head of a retaining bolt into the Kevlar helmet and gouging a chunk out of it. Then I was sent smashing into the engine wall and caught a metal fixture in the side of my helmet. Examining the helmet later, I realized that without it my skull would have been punctured on both occasions. Thank-you to the maker of Kevlar, the synthetic body armour made from space-age fibre, I think. Great shit, whatever it is.

## COMING INTO THE CITY

Finally we came to a halt in Glavogodina, a hamlet southwest of Sarajevo. Outside I heard those familiar words: "Paquets, paquets." Looking through one of the tiny armoured-glass ports, I could see that we were surrounded by more begging mothers and children. The unfortunates we'd seen on the other side of Igman were living large compared with this ragged, starving rabble, ravenous for some form of handout. "Paquets, paquets," they pleaded, making the universal gesture for food, fingers to the mouth. No one offered anything; we had nothing to give. The experienced French troops ignored them. They were already anxious to get to their secure compound and the safety it afforded. In the crowd I saw a handicapped boy of about ten, dark hair, hollow cheeks, no shoes and ragged clothes. He was looking for handouts from the beggars, living on the edge of the edge. Thinking about it now, still vivid, so real, I wonder, did he survive? He must have; he had already spent three years surviving. I hope he made it. I saw my children in him, I felt the need to help, protect, to care. In a flash we were off, almost running the beggars over. Suddenly the boy was gone.

We didn't hesitate long at the checkpoint, which funneled the convoy over a small one-lane bridge that spanned the Zeljeznica River in Butmir. We were still buttoned up in our metal box. It was hot, I was craving something to drink and my only view of the outside world was an occasional glimpse through the small vision ports. What I saw was destruction. We were moving fast through the Serb-controlled side of the front line, following the well-used paths to the UN checkpoints that allowed access to the UN-controlled Sarajevo airport. I caught only a quick glimpse of the airport as we skirted the east end of the runway and arrived at the French UN checkpoint that led to Bosnian front line in the suburb of Dobrinja.

The French sentry opened the back door of the APC to check our UN identification cards. Fresh air flowed in, along with the blinding midday sunlight. The sentry didn't like being exposed outside his bunker and wanted to see our IDs: "*Vite, vite*—fast, fast." I quickly learned that the UN ID card was the only pass accepted by the UN in Sarajevo and, like the commercial says, we should "never leave home without it."

The scene framed by the door of the APC was like nothing I had ever seen. All the buildings were windowless, gutted, burnt, pock-marked and full of holes from direct-fire weapons. A direct-fire weapon is one that allows the gunner to look through the sight at his target, then pull the trigger and watch the projectile hit the target. Unlike the case with aerial bombardment, it takes a lot of direct fire to destroy a building made of reinforced concrete. As the French sentry checked our IDs, I looked at the buildings, imagining the volume of fire required over a long period of time to reduce them to empty shells.

Dobrinja was a place that I came to know quite well once I began the job I was sent there to do. This area of the city was one where the Bosnian and Serbian lines were less than a kilometre apart. There had been intense fighting by the Bosnians outside of the city to try and force their way into it, in order to create a corridor to the outside of the city and break the siege. It was under this strip of no man's land that the besieged citizens (black marketers, more likely) had dug a tunnel. There had been many media reports and rumours about the tunnel and about who and what passed through it. Myself, I'd been to the entrance on the Sarajevo side. It was small and dangerous, especially around the entrance. Its location was known to the Serbs and was frequently targeted by their gunners.

Once the checks were done, the French drivers wasted no time and raced through the dusty streets of Dobrinja and Nedarici. Like horses heading for the barn at the end of the day, these guys wanted the safety and refuge of the Sector Sarajevo HQ. I was totally disoriented, tired, hungry, thirsty and nauseous from all the bumps and turns. I just wanted to get out of this fucking sardine can.

From Dobrinja we headed to the old telephone exchange building. I say "old" because it had had its fair share of impacts and direct fire, and it looked older than it was—like most things in Sarajevo. The building, the headquarters for the UN Sector Sarajevo, was where the sector commander, a French general, resided with his staff and security element. In all, about two to three hundred troops, mainly French, lived in this warren of old offices and basement facilities. It included a bakery, a hospital, living quarters, operations rooms and the famous UN briefing room, which was seen almost daily on CNN during the height of the war. It was a place I avoided because to me it symbolized the UN bureaucracy and what I perceived as its failure in Bosnia.

On our way to the exchange building I caught glimpses of Dobrinja. This high-rise section of the city had been specifically built for the media at the 1984 Winter Olympics. Now the warring factions occupied blocks of flats across the street from each other. When ammo was plentiful and the homemade cognac locally known as rakia or slivovic (slivo) was flowing, the war would rage across twenty metres of open street. Buses were piled two and three high as anti-sniper barricades so that people could scurry about and eke out some semblance of a life. I eventually learned that although the walls of the buses hid us from snipers, they didn't protect us from the ever-present mortars, for centuries the weapon of choice for siege warfare. I would eventually be able to recognize, by sound, the various weapons used to kill and terrorize the inhabitants of Sarajevo.

Finally we arrived at the exchange building and the end of our wild ride with the French. We were dumped in the building's vehicle compound. I found out that I would have to bum a ride into the heart of the city to meet my team. Mark Douglas and I moved into the cover of the building and said our "see you later." We were a bit dazed, confused and disoriented from our wild ride. The lack of sleep and food was on both our minds. However, we did promise to take our first ninety-six-hour pass together and maybe go to Budapest. I envied him: his trip was over, he was going to meet two members of his team and move to a house somewhere in the hills overlooking Sarajevo.

Left alone for a while, I had an opportunity to take in the lay of the land. I found it hard to believe that I really was in this now famous but notorious city. I never imagined that I would end up here. The setting would have been beautiful if not for the war. Mountains and hills surround Sarajevo. It sits in a long bowl formed by the convergence of five valleys, like the hub of the spokes of a wheel. The hills, I was told, were Serb dominated, and anything or anybody in the city was a potential target.

I felt very vulnerable in my body armour and helmet as I looked at all the signs of artillery and machine gun impacts around where I stood. It was hot and I heard familiar sounds, but they were out of place here, in a city. I was used to hearing those sounds back home on training ranges. Here the rattling of machine guns, the booming of outgoing and incoming shells and the crashing noises made by their impacts filled the air. I was scared and wished I were somewhere else, anywhere else.

I often felt naked in that place, as if someone was watching me. Despite all the protective gear and equipment—the helmet and fragmentation vest, the armoured cars and bunkers—I felt vulnerable. I had visions of being shot or ripped apart by shrapnel. I feared how I would react, how it would feel. Would I be brave enough? It was as if the gun sights were lined up on me all the time, but this was just not my day to go.

# 2 | **Welcome to Hell**

**R**IDING THROUGH SARAJEVO, I was oblivious to the danger that surrounded me. I'd managed to get a lift from a Danish guard and the UNPROFOR Forward HQ, and my senses were absorbing everything. The city was wrecked. No water, sewage, electricity, food, gas—it was all gone. The people were visibly beaten. Three and a half years under siege had left them hollow shells of themselves. Their eyes were vacant. I soon found that behind those eyes were images of the past, a good life of family, friends and prosperity. But now there was only fear in a city whose inhabitants played a deadly game of Russian roulette just to survive from day to day. Garbage, wrecked vehicles, fire, smoke and dirt were everywhere.

It was July, and the humidity and heat were unbearable. I was wearing an armoured vest and helmet, and sweating from fear. The spray-painted graffiti in the battle-ravaged suburb of Stup said: "Welcome to Hell." Our driver weaved his way through the back streets behind sniper barricades, all the while trying not to expose us to the eye of the sniper and his "Is it your day to die?" attitude. People didn't walk, they scurried, their heads down, clutching a satchel or a water jug. If you ventured out in Sarajevo it'd better be for a good reason.

Everyone was lean from lack of food; I never saw a fat person in Sarajevo. It was all subsistence living. Every available piece of land safe from snipers was now a vegetable garden. Everywhere there were steep hills, terraced green, with quick-growing vegetables, the sustainers of life. There was a hint of pride in the people, as if they were saying, "You've not beaten us yet." After I'd been in Sarajevo a while, I thought of an ironic couple of books to publish: *Miracle Gardening in Sarajevo* and *The Carts of Sarajevo*. Everyone had some sort of cart for hauling the vast array of multi-coloured water cans. These carts were the innovation of people who risked their lives when they ventured out. They didn't want to have to make a second trip. So they learned to improvise: a baby carriage now carried plastic jugs of water, and roller skate wheels nailed to a board made it easier to move precious bundles of firewood through the streets.

All around were anti-sniper walls, burnt-out, roofless buildings with missing windows that looked like gaps in a fine set of teeth. So many people moved about, daring anyone to upset the bit of normalcy they tried to maintain. Young couples, hand in hand, scurried about. Rusted hulks rotted in the railway yards, burnt, destroyed; no more holiday trains to the Adriatic or the Dalmatian coast. Would they ever come back? Small black-market stalls were set up in the lee of a building. Bananas in Sarajevo were sixteen Deutschmarks (about sixteen Canadian dollars) a kilogram, and a litre of diesel fuel in a bottle was twenty-five Deutschmarks. Garbage either burning in the bins or piled high in the cul de sacs. It had been well picked over— not a trace of anything edible or useful.

People were already worrying about next winter in the city, even though it was only July. Only 27 per cent of the aid had made it over Mount Igman into the city for the month of June. Most of it had been looted by the Serbs or by the black marketers in the city.

The streets I was travelling would soon become familiar to me, even though as we moved into the heart of the city I felt totally disoriented. I was a soldier, I had to know where "the enemy" was; I was trained to focus on who the enemy was. After being in the city for a few hours, however, I was identifying with the Bosnians. The Serbs were definitely the "bad guys" here. I was now one of the besieged, just another target; in fact, I was a prime target, in the hated "blue helmet" of the UN.

We finally arrived at the UN compound, which housed UN Headquarters in Bosnia. It was very small because it was the Forward HQ of the much larger HQ about eighty kilometres east of Sarajevo, in Gornji Vakuf, which because it was the real HQ was known as Gornji Fuck Off.

. Trees! My first impression of the HQ compound was that the trees had not been cut down for firewood. They were safe in a UN compound—at least the UN was protecting something! Our Danish driver explained that this place was one of the villas former Yugoslavian president Marshal Tito used when he visited Sarajevo in the old days. Days not so long ago, when he had ruled with an iron fist and a police force of thousands.

Soldiers do not like HQs, yet I would have to work in and out of this place for the next six months in the UNPROFOR Forward HQ as part of British Major General Rupert Smith's UNMO liaison team. From here I would see the whole picture of what Bosnia was and had been. I'd deal with Serbs, Bosnians, Croats, the whole mess. Deep down I was thinking, *I don't want to be here.*

The helpful Danish driver guided me to the UNMO container, an office the size of a sea shipping container. They were expecting me. I met smiling, welcoming faces: João Lionel, a tall, lanky Brazilian captain; Major Jean Bruyere, a jovial Belgian, on his second tour of the former Yugoslavia; and Major Zilule Haque, from Bangladesh. He looked so young. This was the part of our ten-member team that manned the small-operations centre, which monitored all the UNMO team activities in Bosnia.

There was a lot of handshaking and welcomes, and I immediately felt at home with these guys. "Doucette," Jean Bruyere said, "vous êtes Québécois?" "Non, je suis Canadian." This was the first of many similar discussions I had with my peers. Bosnians, Croats and Serbs, you name it, everyone knows of our unity tensions in Canada. And everyone who spoke about Quebec and Canada could not understand *why* someone would want to split from Canada. What are the reasons? I was always at a loss to explain why, because I honestly did not know the answer.

I was given a quick overview of our place in the scheme of things, and then João gave me a tour of the compound. The Forward HQ housed the commander of UNPROFOR in Bosnia, his immediate staff (half a dozen), operations and intelligence. There were the Joint Commission Observers, made up of the British ultra-commandos from the famed Special Air Service, the United Nations High Commission for Refugees (UNHCR) and a small personnel services section. The UNMOS and the Danish guard contingent rounded out the players in the compound. The compound was about a hundred metres square. Water was trucked in, a generator system supplied electrical power, and as I was soon to find out, there was plenty of food. From my first impression, the HQ compound was an island of normalcy in a sea of deprivation. And it was seen by many as a hated symbol of an already failed UN mission.

João was an enthusiastic and very knowledgeable artillery captain. Young, married, with a daughter back in São Paulo, he had been in Sarajevo for just over a month. He was originally in an UNMO team on the Serb side. After the Serbs would not remove their artillery from around Sarajevo, the UN had American aircraft bomb some Serb gun positions. The bombs were too few, and totally ineffective. The Serbs openly mocked this vain attempt to bring them to heel, and in retaliation they took UN troops hostage. João, along with four hundred other UN personnel, was taken prisoner. Some were chained to Serbian facilities and military positions to act as human shields, a crude but simple tactic that made the UN back off its feeble attempt to use force on the Serbs. João spent ten days as a captive of the Serbs. He was threatened, shoved around and used as a bargaining tool in what was a very tense and dangerous situation. Finally he was released, after having all of his equipment stolen. He made his way to Belgrade and then to Zagreb, where he was given a week off and sent to Sarajevo. No sympathy, just get back in there! João was my kind of soldier—hardworking, honest and with a sense of humour.

The tour of the compound took only a few minutes. There were showers and toilets, and we had a second container that became our "hiding place." I was starved; I'd not eaten in about forty-eight hours.

True to British form (the commander and staff were British), supper (dinner) was not served until six-thirty. We UNMOS were lucky to be allowed to use the dining facility at two American dollars per meal. The previous commander, General Sir Michael Rose—fondly referred to by his own troops as "Shithead"—seemed averse to UNMOS and allowed them nothing. General Rupert Smith didn't seem to care; he had other concerns, like peace in Bosnia. We finally ate. The dining room was full of officers; troops had an adjoining room. The dining room was split in half by a long table running down the middle. Tucked away in the remaining space were a few tables of four. There was always a table reserved for the commander. I was amazed to see waiters in white shirts. How British, I thought. We sat, and the menu was recited to us in clipped English by the Bosnian waiter. Soup, vegetable, chicken, rice; bread, white; water, wet; coffee, hot, and so on. It reminded me of a *Fawlty Towers* skit with Manuel, the waiter. I didn't want anything fancy, just give me food. There was plenty of thin soup and French bread. The bread, I was told, was baked by the French in the basement of the Sector Sarajevo HQ and trucked in to our HQ each day. I would eventually learn to live on a daily diet of one piece of French bread in the morning and a hot meal with my landlord at my accommodation (a routine I came to enjoy immensely).

The dining room was a busy spot. There were Frenchmen, Britons, Turks, Spaniards, Malaysians, Belgians, Egyptians, Dutchmen, Norwegians, Swedes, Russians, Czechs, Canadians and, even though they were *officially* not here, several Americans. I devoured my food and it did the job: I felt full and "food drunk," ready for a long sleep. But I hung around chatting with my teammates, a very interesting bunch. They were glad to have a Canadian on the team.

Now I was exhausted mentally and physically—I needed sleep. At around 2300 hours, after transmitting the daily situation report, João was ready to drive me to my "accommodation." The city was black. As we made the short drive, I noticed the faint glow of candles, well screened from view because light drew bullets. Every now and then I could see and hear the soon-to-become-familiar tracer bullets criss-crossing through the night sky.

### A SECOND HOME

João brought me to 8 Rizaha Stetica, a four-storey block of flats not far from the Kosevo hospital. (The hospital was the site of many CNN reports from Sarajevo; the images of human suffering at the hospital, transmitted by CNN to television screens in North America, had done little to stop the war.) I had no sense of where I was going—it was just too dark. We took my bags up the four flights of stairs. A dog in an apartment barked at our steps. There were no smells—not like in an apartment building in Canada, where you smell everyone's cooking.

Once in, I was shown my room, small but clean and with a roof window overhead. Then I was alone. Three UNMOS occupied the top-floor flat. We rented our rooms for five American dollars a day. João lived downstairs; my housemates were working or away on leave. I found some candles and sat on the edge of my bed exhausted, but tense and alert.

The sounds of a city under siege moved in again. The rifle and machine gun fire was constant, and I pondered the saying that what goes up must come down. The "booms" of incoming and outgoing artillery and mortars were almost continuous. Most of the shells were incoming; the Bosnians in Sarajevo had very few artillery pieces to fire back with. They relied on mortars to return fire on the Serbs. I felt the worm of fear creeping in on me. The situation, the sounds and the loneliness fuelled my fear. I imagined that every weapon in Bosnia was pointing at me.

My roof window framed the black sky with the streaks of light from the tracers. It was clear that this was a very deadly place. I needed sleep. Exhausted, I collapsed onto the bed. In blissful ignorance of what I had got myself into, I slept like a dead man.

I was awake before my alarm clock sounded. It was warm and humid, and the city was quiet. I suppose even the "warring factions" needed sleep—or was this a lull between shift changes? I didn't want to miss my ride to the compound, because I had no idea where I was, and I was starving and didn't want to miss breakfast. Food would become an all too important part of my day, first as needed energy, then as a time marker.

First thing in the morning, Jean Bruyere and I kitted up with helmet and armoured vest to make the short drive to the UN compound in one of our team vehicles. Our team had five vehicles, two of which were supposed to be with a liaison team in Pale, the Bosnian Serb capital, just east of Sarajevo. But this team had not deployed since the hostage-taking by the Serbs in May, so we had plenty of transport. The team vehicles were four Toyota Land Cruisers and a small Nissan pick-up. Two of our Land Cruisers were armoured, which was a blessing. The other two and the pick-up were what we called "soft skinned" vehicles. The drive to the HQ would take all of two minutes.

During the drive I saw my surroundings in daylight for the first time. I could see that I lived on one of the hills that encircle Sarajevo. Unfortunately the geography of the hills and the way they surround the city were what made Sarajevo a good killing ground. Serb gunners had positioned themselves in these hills. In military terms, the Serbs held the "key terrain" that dominated the whole city below. I would soon find out that not much went on in the city without the Serbs seeing it.

I could also see now that the block of flats I lived in was set back from the street. The building was grey with age and grime, as were most of the buildings in the city. But what set this tiny area apart from its surroundings were the trees. Almost all the trees in Sarajevo had been hacked down for firewood, yet here was this small bit of green in a city of grey. Later the trees were explained to me as a symbol to the building's residents of what once was and again is normal to them: green living things, a symbol of hope.

From a soldier's point of view, the building was well protected just because of its location. The way it was tucked away, with taller buildings around it, afforded good protection. However, my fears were not put to rest—there was evidence of impacts all around. The pockmarks of bullets dotting the walls, shell craters from the mortars and artillery, and the ever-present UNHCR plastic on the glassless windows told me this area was as vulnerable as anywhere else in the city. Over the next several months this building became as safe as any bunker to me. I came to call it my home.

### WORKING AS AN UNMO

First day on the job. After the two-minute drive to the "Residency," the most difficult task was to find a parking spot in the compound. (Some things never change.) UNPROFOR in the vernacular of the soldier was a "Fat," or "Cadillac," mission; this was evident from the number of high-priced vehicles in the compound. Everybody and his dog had a vehicle, especially the UN civilian employees. I had got a good look at the "Fatness" at the UN headquarters in Zagreb, where secretaries and typists drove to and from work in $40,000 vehicles while some UNMO teams were struggling to cope in dilapidated vehicles. I had already started to form the opinion that the "Fat Cat" civilian bureaucrats ran the whole show, even the military side.

Jean had his morning routine, something he had established to make life a little more comfortable for himself. He'd head for the UNMO container and find out how the war had been going over the past twelve hours. This info he'd get from the duty UNMO. Once he had found out that the war was still on and little had changed, he would set off for breakfast in the HQ dining room. Everything was laid out prim and proper, a waiter hovering about to take your order like in a British officers' mess. Jean would always get his money's worth by ordering the "full English breakfast" of eggs, sausage, fried tomatoes, you name it. I opted for coffee and French baguettes. I did not have much of an appetite; must have been my nerves.

The scene was so strange, considering the state of the city and its people just outside the compound. The collection of multinationals who wandered in for breakfast seemed bored, yet as I watched them go through their morning ritual it was not boredom I saw but stress and fear. Two weeks earlier the compound had been deliberately targeted by Serb gunners and there had been a 120 mm mortar impact at the entrance to the building. The 120 mm bomb, a large and lethal weapon, had claimed hundreds of lives in Sarajevo. But luck was with everyone that day: amazingly, no one had been killed, though several had minor wounds. For everyone who worked in—especially those who lived in—the compound, the knowledge of how large, important and vulnerable the HQ was must have weighed heavily.

I met a couple of fellow Canadians serving at the HQ. Lieutenant Colonel Rick Hatton, who was there as the G3 (operations) officer for UNPROFOR, was like me an infantry officer in the Royal Canadian

Regiment. Captain Mark Conrad was also on staff as the G3 plans officer. We had been on course together in Canada less than a year ago. The postal clerk also was a Canadian. His nerves were fried; he had been one of the people wounded by the 120 mm impact and was counting his days left to serve in Sarajevo. There were also the personnel clerk, an engineer sergeant major and a major who worked for the UN in the city. So I was not the only Canadian in the city. But as time went by I realized I had little in common with these fellows because of the nature of my work. Other than the engineer major, who worked in the city, they rarely if ever left the compound.

Morning brief was an UNMO ritual. It began with eight or ten of us crammed into the container, door closed for some unknown reason, smokers puffing and non-smokers hacking and bitching. There the operations officer would summarize the overnight events in the former Yugoslavia.

Before I go any further, I should talk about how the UNMOs were organized and where they fit in the UN food chain. In Bosnia the UNMOs were organized into sectors in our area of responsibility (AOR). Sarajevo, because of its activity and population, was a sector of its own. There was Sector South, Southwest, North, East and Bihać, which was a pocket of Bosnians surrounded by Croats and Serbs. There were three UN Protected Areas (UNPAS), two of which were overrun by the Serbs and "cleansed" during the summer of 1995. Srebrenica and Zepa fell in July and August 1995; their stories are books in themselves. The Serbs used all their tried and true methods in dealing with the population of these enclaves.

The third enclave was Goražde, which unlike Srebrenica and Zepa also had an UNMO team. This city of about fifty thousand Bosnians was surrounded by hills that were held by the Serbs. I made it to Goražde several times. Because of its remote location, less UN aid made it there, and these people suffered a lot more than the Sarajevans. Again, it was the children with swollen bellies, dirty, shoeless yet curious, kids in a very horrible place. I remember the little girl we managed to evacuate who was hit in the leg by a fifty-calibre bullet, which is designed for anti-vehicle use. This seven-year-old girl barely clung to life and would probably lose her leg. I often wonder about the sick son of a bitch who deliberately targeted her.

Each sector had several teams. For example, in Sector Sarajevo there were five to seven teams at one point. The teams lived "on the economy," meaning with the people. Typically a team would rent accommodation (a house) and use it as a patrol base and in some cases an observation post. UNMOS would cook for themselves, maintain communication logs, submit daily reports, patrol their AOR and conduct liaison meetings with the local commanders, mayors, nongovernmental organizations and UN troops in their AOR. UNMOS were unarmed; as I said earlier, the theory behind this was that the warring factions would feel that we were less of a threat and so would meet freely with us. Nice theory. In practice, it meant that anyone with a weapon could barge into your accommodation or pull your vehicle over and rob you and it.

Robberies of UNMOS were a weekly occurrence. The best defence was to not resist or argue, just give it all to them and get away with your life. Luckily no one was ever seriously injured. One incident even had a humorous ending: an UNMO who was pulled over and robbed then had the balls to ask his assailants for a lift "home" before they stole his vehicle. The thieves obliged.

UNMO teams were truly multinational; no country had more than one member on a team. The theory behind this was that if the national balance was maintained, no two countrymen could form a power base and promote their national interests. How typically UN. Team leaders were not always the senior rank. It was not uncommon for a captain to command a team with majors or lieutenant colonels. In reality, there was no rank in an UNMO team. Teams could be quite busy; if they were well run, there was always plenty of information to gather if you were willing to go after it. When a team was identified as being unproductive, it would usually get a visit from the sector senior military observer. In most cases the visit was sufficient to motivate the team leader to get on with the job, yet in some cases the ineffective member(s) may have been removed. The nationality of the team leader had nothing to do with a team being strong or weak.

There were good and bad leaders from all countries, including the big peacekeeping contributors like Canada, France and Britain.

Regardless of the anomalies, the UNMOS provided invaluable information both to UN field commanders and to the UN brass in New York. UNMOS were the eyes and ears in any situation. In fact, the most credible piece of information that could be passed was one with the words "UNMO seen," which meant an UNMO had verified his report by physically being on site and had counted the guns, the dead and the wounded or recorded the nature of the incident. The warring factions referred to us as "tank hunters" because we were always counting vehicles or troop movements in our AOR. We reported what we saw regardless of which side we were working on. We prided ourselves on our impartiality. This did not always hold up, especially when we were being shelled or shot at by one side, as was the case in Sarajevo or Goražde.

On this particular morning the duty operations officer was my new friend, Major Jean Bruyere from Belgium. He went through the previous day's incidents sector by sector. We all had to know the situation in Bosnia, and the situation with our teams. We were the advisers to the commander of UNPROFOR and could be called upon to brief him or his staff at any time. My interest was grabbed when I heard "Sector Sarajevo," because this was where I would be spending the next six months. A term that came up often in the briefing was "impacts," which is what resulted when an artillery or mortar shell hit something in the city. This morning, the number of impacts was still in the thousands per day. How we counted the impacts was quite simple. Strategically positioned in the city were UNMO observation posts (OP) manned twenty-four hours a day by observers who counted and tried to determine the type, direction, time, place and extent of damage caused by the shelling. True to the balance of power, the incoming log was much larger than the outgoing log.

The impacts in Sarajevo and their locations were clear indicators of warring-faction activity. A concentration of shelling in a certain area could in theory be an indication of an upcoming offensive in that area. However, when you looked at the pattern of the impacts, it soon became clear that there was no military gain behind the shelling. The random shelling was pure terrorism, plain and simple.

## MEETING THE TEAM

With morning brief completed, I got a chance to meet the rest of my team. Colonel Mohatarem, from Pakistan, was the regional senior military observer (RSMO). He was switched on, politically astute and very aware of the situation in Bosnia. However, he was also pompous, arrogant and overtly aligned with the Bosnian (Muslim) cause. I would accidentally become very aware of his hidden agenda in Bosnia.

Major Zilule Haque, the young Bangladeshi I mentioned earlier, was naïve and very friendly. But I soon suspected that he was only doing 50 per cent of what was required of him. It didn't take much to realize that he was the colonel's personal aide and toady. Regardless, he was a pleasant fellow.

Major Einar Johnson, a big Viking from Bergen, Norway, was efficient, experienced and very professional—what a career soldier should be. He was about six foot two, blond with blue eyes—a true Nordic. His hard-nosed military bearing was offset by a great sense of humour and a real joy for life. Married with two young children, he had a great laugh. We would eventually become close friends and share accommodation and some great adventures. We worked together until late November, when his time in Bosnia was up and he was transferred to Sector East, an area between Croatia and Serbia.

Major Rustem Zarbeeve, the "Russian bastard," as I would affectionately call him, was an excellent fellow, proud and very professional. I would have some great times with him, including long discussions about his side of the Cold War and life in Russia. I felt privileged to serve with him.

Lieutenant Colonel Miroslav (Miro) Lysina, from the Czech Republic, arrived about a week after I did and would become like a brother to me. He was short, very athletic and intelligent, with a mischievous grin and boundless energy. Miro had been in Canada to attend the Pearson Peacekeeping Centre, where they teach high-level negotiation techniques, humanitarian relief on the national level and so on. He had loved his time in Canada, and he and I hit it off immediately. He had served in Angola and Libya and had been in Bosnia before, as deputy commanding officer of a Czech battalion on duty with UNPROFOR. Miro, like Rustem, was very professional and experienced and had an honest concern for the people of Bosnia. He and I would share many adventures, some frightening and some just all-out fun. Miro truly cared for everything in and about Sarajevo.

Miro was supposed to be the leader of the UNMO liaison team in Pale. This team would move into Pale if and when the UN had the balls to re-establish the teams on the Serb side. The UN had had a bad go of it in May 1995, when NATO conducted the token bombing of Serb positions in retaliation for Serb operations. However, the Serbs took various UN soldiers hostage, including many unarmed UNMOS. They then positioned them at key Serb positions as human shields. Since that fiasco, the UN big boys were too terrified to deploy troops, including UNMOS, on "the Dark Side"—the Republic of Srpska, or Serb Republic. So Miro was stuck in our team, waiting to deploy and get the job done. This would prove difficult because he was mired, as was the whole mission, in the UN bureaucracy.

Captain Palo Gonsalves, a Portuguese air force officer, had a great sense of humour and keen sense of duty and honour. I enjoyed working with him because it seemed we could always share a joke about the absurdities of life and war. Palo was a talented artist; he had a sketch book of cartoons he had drawn that clearly depicted the failures of the UN in Bosnia. I used one of his cartoons as my Christmas card home to friends and family. And he was also a great cook, capable of brewing up a great meal from almost nothing. He was a solid soldier—one I trusted, respected and enjoyed working and relaxing with.

Captain Max Van Dorth, "the Dutchman," was older than most of us. He had the calm demeanour that sometimes comes with experience. Max looked like he'd stepped out of a painting by one of the Dutch masters; his well-worn, bony face had the ruddy colour and texture of someone who had been out in the weather a lot. He always had a smoke in his mouth, and he rolled his own. We all felt his tobacco was made from cow shit because that is what it smelled like.

I think the only time I saw him without a cigarette between his lips was when he slept—although I had seen him nod off with a slowly burning cigarette hanging from his lips. An unpretentious guy who had the philosophy that what you see is what you get, he had a cutting wit and a fine sense of logic that he used to bring sense to our sometimes senseless work.

Max was also our self-appointed social director and could organize a gathering at our UNMO house at a moment's notice. Somehow he could get the invites out, organize booze and food and be the gracious host when we all arrived. These were not fancy gatherings; mostly they were what you would call a drunk. Regardless, they were social and enjoyed by all who attended. Max was a boost to our team's morale when it sorely needed a boost.

Captain Sharif Riad, from Egypt, was a gregarious friend, laid-back in a Middle Eastern sort of way. He was very curious about Canada and the world. We would talk often about Egypt, its people and history. Sharif would finish his time in Sarajevo in two months.

Captain Yassir Adwan, my young Jordanian friend, was a character—logical, funny, with a lust for life. He was missing his wife and sons dearly. We would share many laughs together, but he too would leave the mission in a couple of months and go home to his family.

There would be comings and goings on the team; some members would leave, and others would join. These fellows were all good soldiers, yet with faults and frailties that, in the hell of Sarajevo, would endear them to me.

### OUTSIDE THE COMPOUND

My first move outside the compound was with Jean Bruyere and Ronnie Denyft, our deputy team leader and our link with the Serb liaison officer in Sarajevo. Ronnie was a veteran of the UN efforts in the Balkans. This was his third tour. He had seen a lot, probably enough to last him several lifetimes. He was our voice of reason, especially when a decision had to be made.

Our trip on this day was to visit the Belgians injured in the mortar attack that had taken place on my first ride over Mount Igman on the way into Sarajevo. We put on our helmets and vests and then hopped into a soft-skinned Toyota Land Cruiser. Our first stop was at a French battalion in Skenderija, right between the warring factions. This area had been the site of many shelling incidents and an all-out attack by the French to dislodge the Serbs. The French lived in a maze of hallways and storefronts that had once been a state-of-the-art underground shopping mall. The mall had been ransacked and was pockmarked with impacts. It was a very damp and unpleasant place. Our mission? We were hunting for booze. Jean had heard that their small battalion shop had managed to get some liquor in. A lot of busy talk produced two bottles of cognac. Happy, we went on our way, weaving through the back streets to avoid snipers.

The sights inside the city of Sarajevo were beyond what I would have imagined. Everywhere people huddled in the lee of buildings, out of sight of the Serb gunners. They scurried across streets. *Pazi Snajper* (Caution: Snipers) signs were everywhere—as if anyone needed to be told.

Looking around, I was impressed with the local ingenuity. This used to be a prosperous, thriving, bustling city. Now every remaining piece of arable ground was a garden. Once again I noticed how the hills were stepped to make growing space. It was amazing where food was growing: window ledges were lined with tins labelled "Donation from usa," their original contents used up and now put to use as planters for whatever would grow in them.

Our destination was Sector Sarajevo HQ, where one of the several UN military hospitals was located deep in the basement. UN soldiers carried a list of these hospitals with them at all times. The list included the hospital's location and what was available there. Some hospitals had a nurse and a couple of medics. This hospital had six surgeons and advanced life-support systems. It was a busy place that treated all injuries, and on this day four patients were in the intensive care unit. The three Belgian soldiers were fine; they had holes in them, none life-threatening. But the fourth patient, a Ukrainian soldier, was clinging to life. He had massive head injuries and was wired to every life-support system available. He died twice while I was there. A flurry of caregivers, and he was brought back to life. In this crazy place, his fate was not a result of war but one of the products of war—the black market. His fellow soldiers had beaten him to a pulp. The beating had something to do with holding out on some illegal sales. Now he'd probably pay with his life.

At the end of this busy day, I made my way back to my accommodation stumbling in the dark. I was shielding my flashlight while seeking out the route, trying not to draw attention to myself and my light. Luckily I had my helmet on, because try as I might I could never remember the low balcony on the way to the apartment entrance, and *bang*, I cracked my melon on the damn thing. Cursing under my breath, I made my way up the stairs. The two dogs, one on the first floor and the other on the second, barked out their warnings, which in the quiet of the night made them sound like the hounds from hell. Whispered threats to "Be quiet, go lie down" were hissed at the dogs from behind the door. I could imagine the dogs skulking away, their duty done.

I could smell the wood smoke from the tiny wood stoves, now in use since the Serbs had turned off the city's gas supply. The smell seemed so out of place in an apartment building. I could imagine people inside the flats huddled around a candle, waiting for their meagre meal, listening to small radios with weak batteries, hoping to hear some good news. These scenes were being played out all over the city.

Finally, at the top of the stairs, my door loomed out of the darkness. That goddamn European lock. Try as I might, I never did master the turns of the key that would get me in on the first try; it was usually by chance that I'd crack the code that would let me into the flat. Late at night, when the shelling and shooting would slow down or let up, an eerie silence would descend on the city. It would not happen often, and when it did it was very unnerving.

## MY ROOM AT THE TOP OF THE STAIRS

My room was usually dark, quiet and devoid of friendly family smells. It had a very small bed and a desk. The skylight window, though, was special; with it open, I could stand with just my head protruding—not a wise thing to be doing in this city—and get a rooftop view of the city. Being on the top floor, my room offered absolutely no protection from the bombs, bullets and projectiles that flew through the air of Sarajevo. All that separated me from the lethal sky was clay roofing tiles and an inch of ceiling plaster.

I had two candles to light my room, one on the desk at the head of my bed and the other on a shelf across the room. They created a calm ambience in my drab surroundings. Sitting on the edge of the bed, I would feel myself unwinding. I could sense my breathing, feel my tense muscles relaxing; my mind would wander from where I was to where I came from. I would often imagine Janice driving home through the rush-hour traffic in Edmonton. Were her thoughts with me, as mine were with her? Maybe they would meet somewhere in the ether of space.

When I lay down in bed, I could look up through the skylight and watch the streaks from tracer bullets and the flashes from the explosions. Most nights the shelling and machine gun fire would pick up after dark, as if the soldiers liked to see the fireworks of their work in the dark. The machine guns and the 20, 30 and 40 mm cannons that fired tracers would really rock and roll at night. Stitching the night sky they had a morbid beauty, yet on impact they could cut a person in two. Tracer usually is loaded in ammunition belts after every fourth bullet. The theory is that the tracer allows the machine gunner to observe where his bullets are going. I used to watch ten tracer bullets streaking across the night sky and think, *There go fifty little death machines.* Because what goes up must come down, and in the city they usually came down on someone.

The artillery impacts were like someone taking a flash photo in the dark. You would see the flash and light, travelling faster than sound, that would alert you to the boom that followed like lightning and thunder. I could tell when things got close; the bullets would make a sharp *crack* as they flew over the roof of the house, breaking the sound barrier as they flew past my ear. The louder the crack, the closer the bullet, and that usually meant: *Do something.*

The shelling and shooting and noise were so intense that I slept with ear plugs, trying to drown out the noise and the craziness around me. It didn't work. I'd wrap the pillow around my head like a giant pair of earmuffs. I remember often sliding onto the floor of my room when the cracks got too close. Oddly enough, though, I always slept on my bed and not under it.

The thrill and terror of the nightly fireworks would wear thin as the gunners got bored. The firing would reach a crescendo and then slowly die down to the odd sporadic burst. It would be time for the warring factions to snooze, drink and maybe sneak out of the trenches to loot or maybe slit the odd throat.

Eventually my body would take control and say, "It's time to rest," and just shut down. I would sleep solidly, being disturbed only by the really close impacts.

In the morning I would be awakened by the warring factions exchanging fire at the crack of dawn. The beginning of another day in Sarajevo. My mind would drift to what most males would be struggling with at this time of the morning: *Christ, I've got to piss ... Boy, am I hungry.*

# 3 | **Early Days in the City**

I STARTED TO RELAX a bit a few days after arriving in Sarajevo. Jean Bruyere had done some math and concluded that based on the population of Sarajevo (approximately 200,000 then) divided by five thousand impacts per day (a really bad day), you had a one in forty chance of getting hit. Then he factored in the area of Sarajevo and so on. His conclusion was that the probability of getting hit or shelled was remote; add in a bit of luck, and the odds were in our favour. Now, I've never been very lucky; Christ, I was in Sarajevo—that was proof of my lack of luck! Jean could keep his math-generated sense of security; I would just maintain my sense of paranoia.

The weather was still clear, hot and humid. The situation, "calm but tense." I was in the upper container making my first call home to Janice. A great call—to hear a voice from the outside world was a real treat. I finished the call, then stepped outside to chat with some soldiers from the Rapid Reaction Force who normally were working up on Mount Igman.

What happened next is difficult to describe. There was a slight "whoosh," a millisecond of warning, then loud explosions, a wall of pressure, shrapnel flying in all directions. We were blown into the air like the leaves being cut from the trees around us. The concussion and pressure on our bodies was amazing. We were ten to twenty metres from two 120 mm and one 155 mm impacts. In soldier-speak, that's big fucking bombs. All went black, yet I could hear people screaming: "Run! Run!" Then nothing. Next thing I knew my eyes were open; I was hurt but my adrenalin was pumping. Quickly I got up. It was quiet and my ears were numb, and my neck and head were killing me. I saw a French soldier still lying there and thought, *Get up, man!* I grabbed him; his eyes were blank with shock. I yelled, "Come on!" I got him to his feet and shoved him ahead of me, towards the safety of the bunker.

It all seemed to run in slow motion. I just wanted to get in the fucking bunker and never come out. "Swish! *Boom!*" Another incoming, bigger and closer. Pushing the soldier towards the doorway of the bunker seemed to take an eternity. Finally we stumbled into the bunker. A Danish medic grabbed us and administered first aid to the French soldier, who was bleeding and in shock. There was another wounded soldier there, and when the all-clear was given, we found a dead civilian just outside the compound.

I've done a lot of heart-pumping things in my life, but at that moment in the bunker my heart was ready to explode. I could taste the adrenalin, and I felt intoxicated by the rush of such a close call. My neck and ear were wounded. I was into my medical kit for drugs to ease the pain in my neck as soon as the all-clear was given. But I was on the biggest rush I had ever experienced; I had beaten death.

The aftermath of the shelling was interesting. We stayed in the bunker for some time. Everyone was nervous, smokers puffing away, people talking quietly in small groups, fearing that if you spoke loudly they'd hear you and you'd be shelled again. I couldn't hear much, just felt the numbness in my ears and a loud ringing.

We were on State Orange, which meant: "No movement outside without helmet and armoured vests." Kind of odd, and after the fact, like putting your seatbelt on after you'd had an accident. Regardless, everyone was tense. The whole headquarters compound was very vulnerable. I now knew that the whole city was vulnerable.

Now I was really paranoid, and would be for a few weeks. The thin-walled containers we worked in offered no protection, and we knew this, yet it took a conscious effort to leave one and venture out. I was always on the lookout for places to take cover, thinking: *If some-*

*thing comes in now, I'll dive under that vehicle or duck into that doorway.* My eyes were always scanning for danger and for places to hide when it arrived. I was so focused on "flight" mode that I became irritable, and I often went out of my way to criticize anyone who mentioned movement outside of my perceived area of safety—that is, inside the UN compound. I did not realize it then, but I was on the express train to crashing and burning as a result of my never-ending paranoia that every gun in Bosnia was trained on me. I should have realized that if something did come in, I wouldn't have time to take cover. The shit just arrives, no warning.

And eventually my fears were realized. About two weeks after being wounded, my brain went on autopilot and rebooted into survival mode because it could not cope with the stress I was putting on it. This change was not a conscious act on my part; it just happened, and thank God it did. I shifted into low gear, and a sense of calm came over me. I no longer obsessed about my fear of the unknown. I knew what I had to do to be safe and to do my job. My primitive brain was in charge, and the flight, fight or freeze response to situations simplified my decision-making. I started to assess risk more realistically and worked with the idea that anything bad that could happen would happen to someone else, not to me, and that made my life more bearable. Once I was back in Canada, my battle would be to get my brain out of the survival mode that worked so well in wartime but was out of place at home.

### INSHALLAH

My paranoia about every Serb gunner around Sarajevo having his sights on me came and went. In fact, it was not so much paranoia as an overwhelming feeling of vulnerability. I *never* felt safe. Moving about the city was the most difficult task. We never went anywhere alone; we always had two soldiers in a vehicle. Yet I never avoided it, even though some of the trips were pointless.

Captain Sharif Riad, the Egyptian member of our team, who had a month left before he would be on his way home, had both an inquisitive mind and a belief that "Allah will protect," or "*Inshallah—*

God willing." One day I went with my friend Sharif (he called me "my friend Fred") to have some communications gear repaired. Little did I know that he had no idea how to get to where we were going. I sat in the passenger seat, wearing an armoured vest and helmet, looking like a turtle trying to pull its head in. Sharif was in shirtsleeves, not wearing a vest or helmet: *Inshallah*. ("Is it my time to go? Then let it be so.")

Ronnie Denyft had a theory that you shouldn't drive too fast when being sniped at. Because if you were hit (especially if you were the driver), you could lose control of the vehicle and die in the ensuing crash. The theory was being put to the test, because Sharif was driving at the Mideast speed of "all out."

Our first stop was the UN maintenance compound, which was in an abandoned Sarajevo Transit garage. This stop had nothing to do with our communications repair mission. Sharif wanted to visit some Egyptian buddies who were responsible for the security of the repair shop. Now this garage was in a very vulnerable place in the Sarajevo suburbs. I noticed very little—in fact, no—work going on as Sharif chatted in the afternoon sun. I didn't like the vulnerability of where we were, yet Sharif seemed oblivious to it all. Later he told me that everyone had left because the shops had been targeted by mortar fire just before we arrived. Finally we moved on to seek out the communications repair shop, which Sharif said was in a French battalion's camp in the old Yugoslav army's Tito Barracks.

We were weaving through the streets of Sarajevo when I began to notice that we were very close to "Sniper Alley." I sensed that my Egyptian friend had no idea where he was going. This made me very nervous, because another Jean Bruyere saying kept rolling through my mind: "If you're lost in Sarajevo, you'll probably end up dead." Sharif and I eventually tucked in behind a French vehicle in hopes that the driver was going where we wanted to go. Thank Christ, he was. The main gate of this French battalion was one to two hundred metres from Sniper Alley. The French soldiers were pretty cranked up when we arrived. The gate sentries, very nervous, were wearing every bit of body armour and protection they had. Snipers had been shooting at them for the past several days, and it was not a good place to be.

French soldiers are very particular about identification. Everywhere I went in Sarajevo, wherever French troops manned checkpoints I was given the third degree. Regardless of the big white UN Land Cruiser, my Canadian uniform, badges, flags—you name it—the French would scrutinize my ID. Well trained, or anal, or just being French—who could tell?

Our entry into their camp would become a two-hour ordeal. From the time we arrived at the French battalion's gate until the time we left, they took our UN ID card and we were given another ID card specific to the French camp. During our visit I would meet and be scrutinized by everyone, from the private soldier who escorted us around to the commanding officer. Sadly, my mastery of the Acadian French language of my ancestors did little to aid in our epic search for the radio repair guys. After all the bullshit and wandering around, we finally found out that the UN communication technicians we sought were not there.

Almost a full day to achieve nothing except to learn two things: first, I would never go anywhere with Sharif again; second, I would never enter a French battalion camp again.

Our trip back would go down as memorable—quite fucking memorable better describes it. My friend Sharif had no idea where he was or how to get back to our digs. As we left, I was unaware of our predicament and Sharif was not going to admit he was lost. I was still new to the city and had yet to develop that Sarajevo "Spidy Sense" of something being just not right.

I looked up from my tortoise-like body armour to see that we were driving down an empty four-lane boulevard. My first thought was, *What a nice, quiet drive. No traffic.* But then, *I know that building. It's the fucking Holiday Inn, and I'm on the wrong side of it!* We're in the middle of Sniper Alley, doing forty kilometres an hour in an unarmoured vehicle.

I couldn't help myself: "You bastard, do you know where the fuck we are?"

"No." Bullet number one hit the vehicle.

Having never been shot at before, I wasn't quite sure what had happened until bullet number two hit us. Then it all became crystal fucking clear. At that point, Sharif's stoic "God willing" demeanour finally cracked and I noticed we were accelerating faster and faster towards the most dangerous part of Sniper Alley. We were heading to the big Red Cross building tucked in the lee of a large apartment block; it was our safe area and our immediate goal. Now we were travelling Grand Prix fast. I hunched down, hoping we were moving faster than the sniper could track. We ignored the Denyft theory of using lower speeds in sniper areas; we were like a gazelle being chased by the biggest goddamn lion in Africa. We drove like hell.

We crashed through the invisible safety barrier with me yelling, "Slow the fuck down! Before you kill us both!" Sharif's knuckles were white, his shirt was soaked with sweat and he mumbled something that sounded like a prayer. In an effort to preserve whatever diplomatic ties Canada still has with Egypt, I will not put down on paper what I said to my esteemed colleague. Suffice to say I did some ranting, there was a mention of camels and jockeys, a plethora of variations on the word fuck and a solemn promise that when he was around me never to say *Inshallah*.

## UNMO SURVIVAL TECHNIQUES

It seemed that there were as many theories of survival as there were UN team members in Sarajevo. One of my good friends, Rustem, had an air about him that exuded confidence and professionalism: all that Red Army corruption propaganda we had been fed during the Cold War was not evident in him. I thoroughly enjoyed working with Rustem. He taught me a lot about human nature and about how to survive in a war zone.

Rustem, of course, had his own theories. One that I never really grasped or became fond of was his opinion of why snipers shoot at you. My theory is quite simple: a sniper shoots to kill, and when he misses it is because he's a bad shot. Rustem's theory, however, was rooted in our daily routine. He lived in the flat below mine, and like a kid going to school I often waited for him so that we could walk to work together. Our route was a safe one, well thought out and safe from harm except for one twenty-five-metre stretch. At a certain point along the route we had to cross a street marked with those signs you found only in Sarajevo: *Pazi Snajper*. Like many streets in Sarajevo, this one ran at right angles to the front line. Straight and wide, it was a canyon down which bullets could fly towards unsuspecting targets. If you went to the end of any one of these streets, closest to the front line you could cross it easily using the wall of sea containers placed there as an anti-sniper screen. In retrospect, I wonder why we did not walk the couple of blocks to the sniper screen and then make our way to work. Had we become lazy, apathetic, cocky, stupid? Where had we left our brains?

On this particular day, Rustem and I were making our way down the hill to the park towards the sniper zone. We strolled and gabbed as if we were two fellows in downtown Toronto, on our way to work. "Good sleep?" "Yes, great, a quiet night." Niceties, totally out of touch with where we were and the dangers of day-to-day life in Sarajevo. Arriving at the edge of sniper canyon, we didn't even hesitate long enough to check the signs. No, not the street lights or stop signs of a normal world. We failed to take notice of the absence of people, the quiet, the lack of vehicles, all the subtle signs announcing that "all is not right where you are right now." A momentary lapse.

Bold as brass, Rustem and I stepped confidently into the street. *Crack!* The sound of a bullet breaking the sound barrier as it passed within inches of us. The asphalt of the street was nicked several yards down the road from us. We both realized we were being shot at. I wanted to do the honourable thing and *run*, but Rustem grabbed my arm and said (I'll never forget how calm his voice was): "Fred, don't run. They will know you are afraid, and shoot again."

Every ounce of energy my body possessed was now transferred to my legs, and I was ready to explode and fly to the other side of the street. Rustem's grip on my arm was firm, my head turned, and the son of a bitch was looking at me with that big gold-toothed grin, smiling.

We kept moving, me probably looking like I'd shit my pants, the safety of the far side of the street only a few paces away.

*Crack!* The second bullet passed behind us, and Rustem said: "He is playing, he does not want to kill us."

One, two, three and we were safe. Again I could taste the adrenalin coursing through my body, and a sense of euphoria took over. I looked at Rustem. He said, "If you would have run, he would have had to shoot you to stop you. You walk, he plays, he's happy."

"Fuck him," I said. "I don't like being some fucking Serb's plaything."

"Easy, Fred, easy. Come, let's go and have coffee and bread."

I never found out if Rustem's theory was based on experience or if was he just screwing with my head. I've decided that it was experience he gained in some of the other wars he'd been to. As for me, when in doubt, run like a deer. If I get shot it will be while running, not strolling.

# 4 | **Mama's Flat**

FTER I'D SPENT two weeks in the dangerous rooftop apartment, the lease had finished and the owner was not willing to renew it. Some of the fellows on my team opted to move into a new house in the old part of the city. The new place housed Ronnie, Rustem, Yassir, Jean, and the newly arrived Palo and Max. They would have a generator, and that aspect was tempting, because now they would enjoy the luxuries that electricity afforded.

I decided not to take up the offer; the new house would require a long drive through the city to work, and I was not keen on that. Where I was living it was a ten-minute walk, and I always felt less vulnerable when walking. An opportunity arose for me to move downstairs and live with a Bosnian family, the Mehmebegovics. I would be living with Mama, her sons Goran and Zoran, and my Norwegian roommate, Einar Johnson.

The Mehmebegovic family had been introduced to me one night in the beam of my flashlight during one of our numerous water patrols. I met Mama, Goran and their dog, Collie, in the darkened foyer of their apartment. They were friendly to me, a stranger, and grateful to the point of embarrassing me. I moved in with them on the fourth of August. Little did I know that they would end up being as close to family as I'd ever know.

The Mehmebegovics were a re-engineered family of the war. Before the summer of 1992, they were, by Bosnian standards, a typical, hard-working, middle-class family. Mama, the matriarch, was a tiny woman with long hair and hands that showed her age. She was sixty-fiveish, but the toll of the war made her look ninety. Her tiny frame looked as if it had been compressed, but oh, did she have a beautiful smile. Her eyes were dark, soft and gentle. To me she symbolized the war that killed the old and slaughtered the young. When she should have been enjoying her "golden years," she and thousands of her generation were scrambling to survive like they had in the last war, World War II.

Mama spoke no English but understood a lot more than she let on. The flat where she lived was actually Goran's; her flat nearby had been destroyed by a direct hit from a 120 mm mortar bomb, a piece of which now sat on a shelf in the living room. To Mama it was a reminder of good luck; she had been away when the bomb landed.

Her husband had died twenty-five years earlier, at a fairly young age, of a heart attack. He had been an officer in the Yugoslav navy, and they had lived on the Adriatic coast. Mama was of Serbian descent, he had been Bosnian. Theirs was just one of thousands of inter-ethnic marriages that, in this war, would cause so much suffering. Regardless of how journalists and politicians tried to sell this as a civil war, it was in fact an ethnic one. So here was Mama in Sarajevo, surrounded by Serbs, living with her sons who claimed to be neither Serb nor Muslim, who were defending the city solely because Mama was there and it was their home. My times with Mama at the kitchen table, chatting in my broken Bosnian, allowed me to look at this war in a way few people could. To me, and I believe to everyone who met her, Mama was a symbol of strength and of the will to resist, which were qualities that all Bosnians clung to.

I should clarify my use of the word *Bosnian*. In the country known as Bosnia-Herzegovina there lived Bosnian Muslims, Orthodox Serbs, and Croatian Catholics. When the war began, the Serbs started to call Bosnians of the Muslim faith Muslims in an attempt to create an image of the Serbs standing up and battling the Islamic hordes that were poised to spread their extremist faith throughout Europe. What the Serbs attempted to do was label the Bosnians as Muslim mujahedeen and hope that the prejudices in Europe and the West would aid their cause: an ethnically pure greater Serbia. So I promised myself I would never call a Bosnian of the Muslim faith a Muslim. I did not and would not buy into the Serb bullshit. If I had, then why not call the Serbs "Orthodoxists" and Croatians "Catholics"? Eventually the politically correct term coined for Bosnians, regardless of ethnic origin or faith, was Bosniacs. But Bosnian Muslims like to be called Bosnians, so that is what I call them.

## MAMA'S KITCHEN

My first night living with Mama's family was a noisy one. There seemed to be a lot of "outgoing" (firing by the Bosnians from inside the city out at the Serbs), and it sounded like all the weapons were in the backyard. One of the problems I had early on was determining what was outgoing and what was incoming. So, wrapped in my ignorance, I dove to the floor with every *boom*, *bang*, *whoosh* and *crack*. I felt rather embarrassed, lying on the floor in my underwear, looking for my helmet in the dark; it must not have been a pretty sight.

The next morning I was up early and attempted to leave the apartment without disturbing anyone. It was not to be. Mama was up, as was Goran, settled in the kitchen in a blue cloud of cigarette smoke with a *filjan* (small Bosnian/Turkish cup) of coffee between his thumb and forefinger. "Fred, coffee, come sit." I could not refuse. The kitchen was small and spotless, as was the whole apartment. Cupboards lined one wall, above an electric stove. An unused refrigerator was used as a pantry, since the electricity had been shut off long ago.

A large window made up the end wall, and amazingly there was still glass in it, quite a rarity in this windowless city. It looked out onto three large trees, green, peaceful and not hacked down for firewood, yet. Along the other kitchen wall was a day bed where Mama would sleep in the cold months, her feet pointed at the wood stove tucked in the corner. The stove, Goran told me, had been a novelty item he had installed in memory of Mama's younger days, when she had lived in the country. He couldn't have known then that the little stove would be a lifesaver during the war years.

The kitchen table was the centre, the gathering place for all that transpired in the apartment. It was round, about four feet in diameter. On that first morning, I sat at the table shy and embarrassed, feeling totally out of place. This family had so little and yet they were so hospitable, offering me coffee and bread.

I watched as Goran performed the coffee-making ritual. The coffee was ground, from beans that Mama had roasted in the oven, into powder in a brass hand-grinder. Goran put three teaspoons of the "black gold" (the beans were expensive and hard to come by) into a beat-up Turkish coffee pot, added four spoons of sugar, and finally poured water to about a half inch from the top. Then, onto the stove the brew went. Goran slowly stirred the coffee with a small spoon, totally absorbed in the brewing.

Bosnians called it Bosnian coffee, but having served in Cyprus, with its Turkish population, I had known it as Turkish coffee. This type of coffee was a holdover from the days when the Ottoman Turks ruled Bosnia. Strong and gritty, it was a coffee to be sipped from a thimble-sized *filjan* that held about two ounces of the black brew. It tasted fantastic. Sometimes we would have it with hot milk, if we could find some. It was always scalding hot, and very comforting.

Those first few mornings we sat in silence, me sipping my coffee, Mama and Goran enveloped in the cloud of Drina cigarette smoke, trying to clear the cobwebs of sleep. Mama's face told it all; stress, fear and anger had etched lines around her soft eyes. Sadness weighed heavily on her.

Goran was six-foot-plus, big-boned and strong, with the prominent features of his Bosnian ancestors. But he always looked tired. His three and a half years as a front-line soldier showed. He had lost about thirty kilograms since the war began. His face was gaunt and his arms were thin. Goran was also drained mentally. I often watched him sit and stare, his face vacant, lost in thought. Yet each day he would go to his brigade's position, somewhere in the Bosnian defensive ring around the city, to do his part to protect Mama and his city.

I enjoyed these morning coffees and the stunted conversations we had. It reminded me of a Maritime kitchen, where everyone gathered around the table and it became the centre of family life. I picked up 99 per cent of my Bosnian around that kitchen table. Many mornings, Mama began quizzing me on my vocabulary and we would discuss the weather (in Bosnian) in a typically Canadian fashion: "Nice day, looks like rain." I tried teaching her English, but I think she played dumb; she had little interest in learning another language.

I felt safe and at peace around the table with my friends. I actually enjoyed my morning ritual—getting up, dressing quickly, then heading for the toilet with my plastic pail that held about two cups of water, half of which I used to flush the toilet. I would use the rest of the water to brush my teeth, wash and shave. Shaving day to day was not something I cared much for or adhered to, but brushing my teeth was a must. Then, gathering up my kit, my "fighting and dying gear," I'd make my way to the kitchen.

I could tell if Goran was home by the pile of blankets on the couch. "Fred, good sleep, yes, *dobro, dobro*—good, good." Then the familiar sound of the seven o'clock news, a musical introduction, whose tune still sticks in my head. It was Radio Sarajevo, up and broadcasting as it did throughout the war. Goran and Mama always listened intently to the small, battery-powered radio perched on top of the large and useless boom box, now silenced by the lack of electricity. I watched their expressions for changes that would mean something significant had been said. I never interrupted; I knew the news was vital to them. Once it was over, I'd ask what had been said. Early on, it would be about deaths and injuries, how the stalled peace talks were going and how the future looked grim in the face of another winter of war. There was very little propaganda, just the facts; that's what the people wanted. After three years of war, they were wise to the bullshit.

After a couple of *filjans* of coffee and a slice of Bosnian army bread, compliments of Goran, I'd lace up my boots, put on my armoured vest, strap on my helmet and walk to work. I kept my boots in my room instead of in the entrance vestibule because after one particularly muddy day out and about in Sarajevo, I'd left my boots by the front door. Next morning I awoke to find them dry, cleaned and polished, compliments of Mama. I told her it was not necessary; she smiled and pretended not to understand. It was her way of thanking me for being there. But it made me feel uncomfortable.

On the short walk, I had to cross a couple of streets posted with *Pazi Snajper* signs. I did my trip at a brisk walk, pulling my head into my vest like a turtle. It is amazing how many vulnerable parts of your body aren't covered by body armour.

## LIVING LIGHT IN MY ROOM

My room in Mama's flat had belonged to Goran's daughter, Anna, before she flew to Bergen, Norway, with her mom and brother as refugees at the beginning of the war. There were a few reminders that this used to be a girl's room. A poster on the wall depicted two people embracing on a hill overlooking San Francisco, and the caption read, "California Dreaming." A few stuffed animals on a shelf and several pictures of teen magazine heartthrobs were taped to the wall, and against another wall was an upright piano that she had used for her daily practice.

The room was spotless—the result of Mama's nervous energy spent on constant cleaning. And by Sarajevo standards it was safe—it had thick walls in a tightly packed neighbourhood, with nothing of military or ethnic value nearby, which by this time in the war meant absolutely nothing. Now, everything was a target.

I am still amazed at how I would unwind after a day on the streets of Sarajevo. The place and the people I lived with gave me a real sense of security. Back in my room at Mama's, I'd sit on the edge of the bed and deflate. I could feel the stresses and pressures of the day ease their way out of my mind and body. Sitting there staring at the wall, no thoughts, hands on my knees, palms up as if meditating. I was only conscious of the fact that I had made it through another day.

Regardless of the kind of day I had, the feeling would be the same: total relief. As I sat there I would slowly become aware of my surroundings. The sound of the leaves rustling outside my window, music from a nearby flat, the buzz of people, voices, laughs, yells and curses, all intertwined. I knew I could survive my time here, maybe because I had learned to cope with my fears. Although I had many fears, I worked hard to not let them rule me. But there were times early on, alone in my room on the top floor, vulnerable and gripped with fear of the unknown, when I was driven to tears. Lying on the floor as bullets cracked overhead and shells hit nearby, knowing that I was alone, I felt naked, vulnerable to the whims of whoever was blasting away. I had no gun to shoot back with, nowhere to run, no one to talk to.

I often thought I would be ashamed to admit my fear. But there was nothing to be ashamed of, especially for the uninitiated.

I lived out of a rucksack and a small carry-all. Two uniforms, two pairs of boots, three sets of underwear, three pairs of socks, jacket, sweater and my fighting and dying gear. Several books, none of them challenging or deep, just entertainment. My attention span since arriving was short. My Walkman, with a pair of small speakers and a dozen tapes, drowned out the noise of war outside; my small shortwave radio was permanently tuned to the BBC World Service. I brought a small photo album that held a mix of family pictures, which brought on memories and emotions from home. I enjoyed showing off the photos of my family, yet looking at them made me envious of where they were, and I always felt guilty for having volunteered to leave them for a year. Janice, who supported my crazy endeavours, was always on my mind, giving up so much so that I could go off and risk my life and our future—for what?

There was no heat or electricity in my room. For light, I used a candle and my mini-flashlight. It is amazing how much light a candle offers. I soon find out that writing or reading by candle is very hard on the eyes. I could only manage about a half hour before my eyes started bugging out. (It provided an honest excuse for keeping my letters short.) When I read in bed, I placed the candle on the headboard so that the light hit the page, being ever so careful not to shade the pages with my head.

I discovered, based on careful research, that if you knock the candle onto the bed, your head or the pillow, the candle goes out in about 99.9999 per cent of the cases. And though the wax made a hell of a mess, no serious conflagrations were started. I slept in my army-issue sleeping bag for a year. Thankfully the bag had a removable, washable cotton liner. If not for that feature, it would have been an awfully ripe nest to sleep in. My life when I wasn't working was simple, almost monastic; outside, in my day-to-day job, things were stressful and confusing enough to counteract my silent, orderly nights.

## AWAKENING

I lay in my bed warm, comfortable and secure. It wasn't a real bed but a sofa, the back folding down to become part of the bed. The valley formed between the back and the seat held me in its grip. Janice wonders now why I sleep on my back; it's from six months of sleeping on that fold-down sofa.

My sleeping bag was warm, snug and reassuring in my unheated room. I'd worked a twenty-four-hour shift and had gone to bed at 0700; it was now about 1400. I lay there taking in the sounds around me. The leaves were still on the huge poplar outside my window. The rhythmic rustling of the breeze was soothing; it was a familiar sound from home. I heard voices outside; some young, some old. They were out enjoying the sun and a relatively quiet day. Mothers felt that the streets in this part of town were safe, so they let their kids out. They were playing soccer in the small courtyard nearby; their voices were loud and got louder as the ball neared a net. A stereo pounded out music somewhere nearby; I could hear the steady thump of some popular Euro-tune. Dogs, with their keen hearing, barked at unheard noises. Voices shouted *"Ti''sina*—shut up!" They didn't.

The lack of fuel for automobiles made it all so quiet, so different—like a time before machines. I lay there, savouring the burst of normalcy in this crazy city. All the sounds were human and personal. I didn't spend many mornings like this, but when I did I savoured them and soaked up all the comfort and peace of mind they offered.

# FIRST BODY

**FROM A DISTANCE THE** smell was sweet yet unfamiliar. It grew
more intense as I moved closer to the source. Curiosity, or perhaps a
morbid sense of what war produces, drew me on. Deep in a rarely used
portion of my brain, I sensed what the source of the putrid smell was.
I stopped dead in my tracks when I walked into an invisible wall of
stench. Saliva gagged into my mouth, nausea welled up in my throat.
The taste of bile mixed with saliva as the uncontrollable reflex of
vomiting racked my body.

The arm was lying where it had landed after the explosion, about
twenty feet from the body it had once been attached to. It looked as
if it had been ripped out of the shoulder socket. It could have come
off a mannequin, had this not been Sarajevo, where limbs without
bodies and bodies without limbs were common sights. Knowing now
that the stench came from a human, from someone like me, I gagged
and retched even more. My gut was empty. I gulped air in through my
mouth, not daring to breathe through my nose. There was nothing
left to puke, and I managed to get control of my dry heaves.

His body lay face down on its left side; where the right arm had
been was a brown, dry mess, now covered with flies. They were everywhere, all looking for a place to lay their eggs. The earth below the
wound was dark with the blood that had drained out of him and into
the soil. The blinders that came from the shock of seeing something
that my mind could not immediately process had me focusing on the

73

shoulder where his arm had once been. Looking at the body, I wondered if death had come quickly. Or had he lain there in shock and died of blood loss? I gave a dry, open-mouth retch again. The fucking July heat was suffocating. I shook my head and thought of what I had gotten myself into. To think I had volunteered for this.

This was my first body, and it was not as I had imagined it would be. I had hoped it would have been in one of the makeshift morgues that dotted the city. Somewhere that was not as graphic as this, maybe covered with a sheet—a bit of dignity, if there is any dignity in dying in war. Who was he? A father, a brother, a husband? *Do they know he is gone?* Dead, lying out here in the sun, with me gawking at his remains. I thought of his mother. *He has a mom, we all have a mom, she will be wrapped in grief at the loss of her son until the day she dies.* The saliva kept filling my mouth. At least the nausea was gone. I just kept spitting as if I were trying to get the taste of decay out of my mouth.

One of my buddies slapped me on the back and knocked me out of my trance. "I wonder if he could use a hand." Then a nervous laugh. But the old standby—using black humour to ease the awkwardness—had lost its effect. They no longer knew how to react. They had all seen too much of the refuse of war; I think they all pictured themselves lying there in that poor bastard's place. In time I would be like them, numbed by the horrors of war, too fucked up to care or think like a normal human being. We didn't linger. We had confirmed another dead body, no ID on him. For UN statistical purposes, we would report his location to our HQ. Maybe the word would make it to whoever gave a shit, and someone would recover him. More likely, though, the dogs would pull him apart and scatter him to the four winds.

We retraced our steps to our vehicle in silence, as if we were respecting the fact that we were in the presence of the dead. "Roll the fucking windows down. We'll stink for days." I felt a physical relief as we pulled away with the fresh air blowing through the windows. No one talked; everyone seemed lost in thoughts of their own mortality. I turned my face towards the window and filled my lungs to cleanse them as we made our way through the Sarajevo suburb of Dobrinja. With its bombed-out buildings, the place looked like the face of the moon.

People scurried about, as if moving with a sense of purpose would defy the sniper's aim or the impact of another shell.

My brain raced to find a place to store the image of the body, its smell and taste. The dead had one thing in common: regardless of how they died, there was always the smell, that putrid smell. I was full of memories of the stench of the dead. It would find a place in my memory, but as my experiences of the horrors of war grew, the image of that first body would dim to become just another bad memory. None of the images ever went away; they became enmeshed with each other, and I would only be able to remember some of this and a little of that.

# 5 | **The Heart of the Family**

GORAN SAT on the foot of the daybed, cigarette between his fingers, his thick head of black hair ruffled and sleep still fogging his mind. He stared intently at the small pot of coffee perched on the hot spot of the tiny wood stove. Bubbling like a tar pit, the coffee slowly frothed to the rim of the pot. The whole process was ritualistic, almost a black art. You could see the anticipation in the brewer's face and it was all done on a tiny wood stove—the nostalgia item. At the critical moment, just before the pot overflowed, Goran the master coffee brewer snapped it from the stove, averting disaster. The froth subsided; Goran filled the pot to the top with cold water and placed it back on the stove for the final critical boil.

"Fred," he said without taking his eyes off the brew, "first time never fill to top." In seconds the froth rose again and crested at the rim.

It was done. Small stainless steel saucers with a *filjan* in the centre were readied for use. A gentle dipping stir, a delicate pour and Mama handed me a steaming cup of Bosnian coffee. She then took a small metal pitcher from the back of the stove, where condensed milk (now rare in the city) had been warming.

For some reason Bosnian coffee is sipped, not drunk, at near scalding; they use hot milk so as not to cool off the coffee. My first drink of Bosnian coffee had scalded the roof of my mouth. This ain't your Tim Hortons double-double. I quickly learned "the sip," almost inhaling the coffee. I also learned not to drain my *filjan*, because the bottom is where the coffee sludge sits.

Goran taught me the subtle way of holding the *filjan* between my thumb and my index finger, remaining fingers extended, "like a man," as he said. Over a few ounces of coffee you could see there were thoughts of what life used to be like. The kids and wives, now living miles away as refugees, would have been bustling around the kitchen, getting ready for school and work as they would in any home in North America. That time was gone, but everyone prayed it would come back someday. The normal life.

## AROUND MAMA'S TABLE

I often tried to discover what Mama and Goran's thoughts were during the many hours we spent around that cozy kitchen table. Our conversations were hampered by our inability to speak each other's language, but not as much as one would think. A Serbo-Croat dictionary, the only one we had, was always close at hand, and my dear friend Miro Lysina was often there. Miro had moved into the flat above Mama's with a family who would come to rely on him to the point of abusing his kind heart and good nature. His language skills and his sensitive, inquisitive nature made for some very thought-provoking conversations.

There were long pauses as we'd gather our thoughts and try to organize them so we'd get our point across. I often think about the time and care we took in choosing our words so that we'd be understood the first time. If we weren't, no big deal; we'd try again another way. (The world might be a much better place if we reflected on our words before we put them out for public consumption. If nothing else, our pauses between words would make us look wise.)

I often used my hands and facial expressions to make a point. Some nights it was like a game of charades, with a big explosion of understanding and relief all around when a point was made. Mama and Goran thought my antics were entertaining and comical, but in the end we did communicate.

The candles provided a strange, intimate atmosphere, casting shadows on the walls and a yellow glow on our faces as we all leaned into the small circle of light. The silence did not make us feel uncomfortable like it does back home, where we feel bound to fill any void with words. At times the silence inside was broken by a shot or impact outside; I would try to catch Mama's or Goran's expression. It was not the startled response you would expect, but a flash of anger, the way someone would react to a barking dog. They knew that someone might be dying as a result of that annoying noise.

## THE WOODEN SHOES

Mama's wood stove sat in the corner of the kitchen, on the right of the doorway. Goran often told me that it had been one of the keys to their survival during the past three years. The stove was a miniature version of the one my grandmother had when I was a kid: white, with a small oven and a cooking surface of about eighteen by twenty-four inches. The firebox was very small, and not airtight like those of modern wood stoves; it burned wood like the furnaces of hell. But what it did do was provide heat, warmth and a surface to cook on.

Mama used her now-useless electric stove as a breadbox. Like her refrigerator, this modern convenience had not seen electricity for some time. All over the city, people had died during the winters because they had no heat to warm themselves or no place to cook their meagre food. But there it sat, Mama's wood stove, white and spotless, scrubbed to gleaming by Mama as if it were made of gold. Goran promised that if the war ever ended, he would keep the stove forever as a reminder of their survival.

Finding fuel for the wood stove was a constant problem. The city had been deprived of any and all combustible fuel. The wood from the park benches, hand rails, fences, trees, shrubberies—all long gone. Whatever could be burned was burned. One evening, sitting in the kitchen lit by the IKEA candles Janice had sent me, I watched as Mama knelt before the stove. She carefully poked and prodded the coals, enticing a few embers to life. Then from under the stove she produced a pair of worn wooden clogs. Delicately turning the toe of the shoe so that it would fit into the firebox, she slid both shoes in.

The next day, Miro, Rustem and I made up a bullshit excuse to get some wood from Pale, about thirty kilometres east of Sarajevo. It was no easy task to get there. What normally was a fifteen-minute drive in peacetime would take us the whole day—if all went well. These forays into the "dark side" were never comfortable or easy.

But amazingly, this time all went well. We made it to Pale with little harassment at the various checkpoints and drove straight to the market, which was teeming with goods. I was always amazed that although Pale was so near Sarajevo, you would swear there was no war in Bosnia. The farms and homes we passed on the way there were untouched, and life went on. People there seemed oblivious to the slaughter going on just a few kilometres away. It reminded me of the German civilians who lived in the towns near the Nazi concentration camps; they too appeared to be oblivious to the "final solution."

We loaded up our vehicle with vegetables, meat and other groceries, leaving room for the wood we hoped to gather. On our way back, we eyed the farms that looked as if no one was home. From time to time we'd stop at a farm and liberate a few sticks of wood. The tricky part would be getting back into the city with this "Truck of Plenty." Bullshit would be our best asset. Miro and Rustem could turn on their Slavic charm and bully through the checkpoints. It was a definite asset to have a command of the local language, and they used it with amazing skill.

In the end, the mission was a great and surprising success. We got the wood and supplies through the checkpoints at the cost of some UN diesel fuel, cigarettes and some small Canadian maple leaf pins I always carried with me.

The wood was received as if it were gold. We divided it among all the families in the apartment block. We knew they would ration it in hopes of a ceasefire, and maybe a return of the gas heating, before another murderous winter arrived.

## AN OLD WORLD TRADITION

The little wood stove was the heart of the family. Mama often sat on the end of the daybed warming her arthritic hands, sore from the dampness and cold, and obviously in pain. When Goran arrived home from the trenches cold, wet, hungry and tired, she gladly relinquished her seat to him.

We would sit quietly as Mama busied herself with supper. Our eyes were transfixed, mesmerized by the glow from inside the stove, visible through the gaps in the jury-rigged door. It was as if we were in a trance—a long, comfortable silence.

At Mama's the meals were never rushed; we ate and paused, talked and drank, and then dug into our food with renewed hunger. As fall went, winter came and daylight shortened, meals inevitably were eaten by candlelight. Three candles carefully positioned by Mama would illuminate the kitchen. Mama rarely joined us in these meals. I guess it was Old World tradition; she would set the meal, move out of the way and let us eat. Einar and I sometimes tried to bring her to sit at the table, but she always resisted. Goran used to explain, "This is Mama." Yes, this was Mama, the matriarch taking care of her sons, both natural and adopted.

In the fall, when the siege let up and food became more accessible, our main meal would take place around four o'clock. I don't know if the four o'clock suppertime was normal for Bosnians or just convenient for all our comings and goings, but for me the timing was perfect because by then I was always starving. My morning meal of bread and *kava* (coffee) at seven was all that kept me going until late afternoon. And the anticipation of Mama's supper was always worth it. You'd think we were setting up for a four-course meal, but we weren't. The meal was always simple, but it was hot, well prepared and usually plentiful. The surroundings and the company added to my enjoyment.

These simple meals were treated like feasts. We would sit and gab, drinking cognac or brandy and maybe eating roasted peppers, and then Mama, beaming with pride, would present her meal. Usually it was accompanied by *oohs* and *aahs* and exclamations of "Mama, this is fantastic!" We were always amazed at what she produced with so little.

Early on in my stay, our meal consisted of roasted peppers (*paprika*) done right on the stovetop, potatoes (*krompir*) and, with luck, a chicken (*piletina*). If there was no meat (*meso*), then a soup would hold centre stage. There would be a loaf (*hleb*) of Bosnian army bread, which Goran picked up on his way out of the front line. His pay as a soldier was one loaf of bread and two packets of cigarettes per day. The cigarettes were horrible (I'm not a smoker) but the bread was a treat, with its thick crust and heavy texture. It was never cut, but broken and pulled apart. It was used to dip in and absorb soup or meat juices, then as a napkin to clean the lips before being put in the mouth. Goran often said, "Fred, the only utensil you need for a Bosnian meal is a spoon for the soup."

Maybe Mama's simple food, and making do with little, reminded me of my childhood. I was brought up poor; my father was a labourer and my mother a mom. The warmth of the wood stove, the smells, Goran's jovial presence, and the tot of cognac before the meal—that was an event! We talked and laughed about our day, about the war, about our hopes and dreams.

You're probably wondering where we got cognac in Sarajevo. Well, let's not forget Einar, my fellow UNMO. He had his sources in the "Nordic Mafia." The Danes and the Norwegians covered two areas of the city that had particular perks. The Danes guarded the UN Commanders HQ and therefore had the ability to get in and out of the city. With this came the logical idea: you're in Kiseljak with a vehicle, so why not stock up? The Norwegians ran the Movement Control at the Sarajevo airport (when it was open), so they had easy access to aircraft coming into the city. You figure it out. It worked for us; in fact, I don't think there was a meal where we didn't have either cognac or beer.

### MAMA'S SONS AND THEIR WAR

Goran's comings and goings were always a great strain on Mama. Would her number one son return? It was easy to gauge her feelings about the fears this war had brought to her life. I could not get much from Goran or Zoran about this, and I never pried into what they did or what went on in their piece of the war.

Goran had a schedule for his timings to go to the front. In broken English he would tell me, "Goran go ten o'clock come back two o'clock *sutra* (tomorrow), then free one day." He was always excited about his "free" days; they usually meant twenty-four hours out of the front lines to relax at home with Mama, take Collie for a walk, or maybe chance a walk into the centre of the city for a coffee with friends. Coffee bars thrived in the city throughout the war, serving those who could afford the prices and had the nerve to make the trip.

Zoran came and went, rarely staying overnight at the apartment. Like Goran he was very gracious and devoted to his mother and brother. And like many Bosnians he was thin and looked malnourished. His eyes were dark and his jet black hair was long and unkempt. When he smiled, which he did often, there were gaps where his teeth used to be. His love of his mother and his city was his reason for staying behind when his wife and two children had left for Heidelberg, Germany, as refugees early in the war. Like his brother, he missed his family, but his need to protect his mother outweighed his loneliness. I do not think that either Zoran or Goran could have looked themselves in the mirror if they had left their mother alone in Sarajevo.

Before the war, Zoran had been the road manager for the Yugoslavian national basketball team. He had travelled all over the world, but now his world was the maze of buildings that made up the front line in the city. He was a paramilitary policeman whose job it was to clear buildings and root out Serb snipers who had managed to hide in the abandoned buildings that surrounded the city. He told me that the job was tedious, involving days of observation followed by a quick raid, which often meant arriving at a sniping position that had just been vacated. It was frustrating work, but he realized that any good sniper always had plans for a quick escape.

I enjoyed the suppers when Zoran dropped by and shared his experiences with us. But he would usually steer the conversation towards what life in Canada was like. I often wondered what it would have been like to have met Zoran and Goran in their pre-war lives. I doubt that I would have recognized them, because the war had such a profound effect on them both physically and mentally.

The strain was hard for them to hide, and there were times when I would see a physical change in Goran or Zoran. I would check the incident/impact reports at work and try to put two and two together, and at times, a night or day of heavy shelling or activity would match their moods. I wish I could have talked with them more about their feelings, but language and respect for their space limited it.

However, like most soldiers, Goran sometimes did talk about the humorous side of this war. That is, if war can have a humorous side; maybe I mean the absurd side. He recounted an incident that took place in Dobrinja, near the airport, a place of intense house-to-house fighting throughout the war. It was just coming on dusk. He and his buddies were observing from their trenches when, lo and behold, a Serb soldier climbed out of his trench and began to stagger towards their trench. They held their fire, curious about his intentions. He took a lazy, almost leisurely, stroll right over to their position. They cautiously helped him into the trench. Once disarmed, he was sat down and offered a cigarette; he was pissed to the gills.

He absolutely refused to believe that he was now in Bosnian hands. So they tucked him away in a dugout where, like a good drunk, he went to sleep. Everyone was anticipating his awakening, accompanied by a hangover and the realization that he was now a prisoner of war. Well, he did awake, and the Serb would not believe that he was in Bosnian hands until he was allowed to look back at his trenches. There were his buddies, waving at him (waving goodbye, no doubt) and probably thinking, *Budala*—idiot!

Goran said this had happened about a year and a half earlier. He had since seen the fellow several times on work details; no doubt he's now living a life of sobriety.

## COLLIE

Collie, the family dog, looked just like Lassie. In the absence of children and loved ones, she had become the family baby or, as Goran called her, his "lady." I'm not a fan of dogs. Having been mauled a couple of times as a kid, I harbour a severe mistrust of the beasts. Not with Collie, though; she was a real sweetheart, easy and gentle and loved by all who met her.

Collie was great company for Mama when her boys were away. She was a fixture in the kitchen on the floor by the wood stove—a reminder of sanity in war. Mama would faithfully take Collie out for walks and some air (never straying more than fifty metres from the house) and a roll in the grass. That dog could sense Goran coming up the lane and would bark, anxiously awaiting his arrival.

The explosions agitated Collie and all the dogs in the surrounding area. There would be a bang, and a round of barks, yelps and howls would follow it. The animals sensed the danger. When things quieted down in the city, Goran and I would walk to the park, an old Muslim graveyard, in the centre of the city. Goran called it Collie Park, since Collie was the grand dame of the park and all its K9 patrons.

There were hundreds of "pets," especially dogs, in Sarajevo. It was hard to imagine keeping a pet when all the necessities of life were so hard to come by. I suppose it was a desire to cling to what was once normal. People kept their pets until the last—some lucky ones were able to keep them until the war ended, and having a pet made sense again.

# 6 | The Bosnians Were Hurting

WHAT WAS GOING ON in Bosnia in the summer of '95 was that the Bosnians were hurting. Certain areas had been designated as UN Protected Areas (UNPAS). Designation was not a good sign. There was a cartoon in the press: this old fellow is sitting on his doorstep, and another fellow passes by, pushing a wheelbarrow piled high with all his worldly possessions. The fellow on the step says, "Where are you going?" The wheelbarrow fellow replies, "Quick, you should leave. We've just been declared a UN Protected Area!"

The UNPAS of Zepa and Srebrenica had fallen to the Serbs, and CNN's images of women and children being herded off as refugees filled the TV screens. I cannot imagine the agony and helplessness that women must have felt as their daughters, sons, husbands and fathers were hauled off by drunken Serb soldiers.

No. They were not soldiers. I'm a soldier, and I would never do that. These guys were just fucking animalistic cowards. Every time I met a Serb at a checkpoint, I could not help but think, how many people did you rape? How many did you shoot in the back?

What was missed, and what would not come to light for some time, was the fate of the Bosnian men and boys from Zepa and especially Srebrenica. Their mass graves would be found by satellite imagery and eventually by war crimes investigators. In the end, a conservative estimate of five thousand men and boys dead or missing and presumed dead would be bantered around in the Western press.

The image of Serbian General Ratko Mladic grinning into the video camera saying, "You'll be safe. No one will hurt you," still burns my mind when I think of him, just another fat fucking war criminal of the first degree. A lying prick.

As you can see, it was not difficult to pick sides. When it came down to morals, the Serbs had none. I've argued this with people in and out of the military, and the fact I point out is, "I've never stood at a *Serb* mass grave." Bosnian mass graves abound, usually full of old men, women and children, and if the cut-throat Serbs were lucky, they would have thrown in a few young men to top it off.

The UNPAS of Sarajevo, Goražde and Bihać were surrounded, and it was only a matter of time before they fell as the others had. It was siege warfare, plain and simple. Everyone in the UNPAS counted time hourly, daily, monthly, yearly. It had been three years of *rat* (war) for them. The Serbs were making gains all over Bosnia, and the outside world seemed powerless to stop them.

No, I'm wrong. They didn't care to do anything. I often wondered what it would take to light a fire under the asses of world leaders. The Serbs were the bullies, the bad guys laughing in our faces, doing as they pleased. It was frustrating and heartbreaking to talk to the Bosnians. They believed—and this belief was based on their experience—that the UN Protection Force was useless: we were like eunuchs in a whorehouse. I always tried to portray myself as "Fred from Canada and can I help?" I didn't try to legitimize myself just because I wore the UN badge. I tried to keep my word and never promised anything. A broken promise, regardless of the reason, was lost credibility.

The Bosnian situation was bleak on all fronts. These people had no resources or combat power to go on the offensive. It was strictly a defensive war in the summer of '95, and it was all crumbling after three and a half years of fighting. I could see it in Goran's eyes, the way his shoulders slumped. He was exhausted, and Mama was slowly dying back at the apartment. It was difficult to gauge their commitment; they were so angry at their political masters, who were failing them. Goran would say, "We are holding, risking our lives to give them the time to give us a peaceful way out of the war. But when will it come?" There were only broken promises of ceasefires, truces, peace plans, hopes and dreams. The Bosnian people were all used up. They were losing.

## JOURNALISTS AT MARKET

In Sarajevo I learned many things I didn't want to know. I was amazed at how much blood there is in the human body, for example. I inadvertently ended up downtown after a mortar bomb landed in the street in front of the indoor market on Mula Mustafa Bašeskija Street, in downtown Sarajevo, killing thirty-seven and wounding Christ knows how many. When I stumbled onto the scene, the wounded were all gone and most of the shredded were dead. (Shrapnel shreds the fragile human body.) What was left of the shredded people was blood, everywhere, running in the street and splattered on the walls like a cheap abstract painting. There was no smell; the dead were fresh. Shovels were brought out and the remains scooped into plastic tarps, rolled up and carted off, perhaps to be identified later by a piece of clothing or a ring on the finger of a severed hand. At least there'd be something to bury.

I had been in this spot a hundred times. It was a crowded place about fifty metres from the open-air market, where a year ago the same thing had happened, killing sixty-seven. People had felt safe here; the streets were narrow, the buildings high, the chances of a bomb falling here were slim, or so they thought. This was not a front-line trench, but to Serb gunners I guess it was a worthwhile target. This was an ethnic war, so it didn't matter whether civilians or soldiers were hit.

I have no idea what outrage this bombing caused in the rest of the world, or how the media portrayed it. I had no access to outside news. The media wolves had come and gone; they had captured the anguish of rescuers dragging the wounded, dead and dying to cars to be rushed to Kosevo Hospital. But the grisly aftermath—the litter of human body parts—was ignored. There is nothing sensational about a clean-up.

The Bosnian war had become someone else's war. It usually made the news well after the latest gossip about the O.J. Simpson trial. The images on CNN were dwindling; viewers had become bored with the images of dead and dying Bosnians.

I know I am being hard on journalists. They have a deadline and a waiting public to feed. Their editors demand a constant flow of information for their readers, so I suppose reporters and photographers can't get too caught up and humanize every tragedy. But I avoided them like a dose of crabs. I felt there were a lot of Pulitzer wannabes in Sarajevo all looking for "war porn" (to quote Peter Maas, author of *Love Thy Neighbour*). I don't mean to preach, and probably I'm not being fair to the people who captured the images that pressured the politicians to get off their fucking fat Western asses and stop this war. But I didn't want to be near them.

### SURVIVING WITH DIGNITY

By 1995 the siege of Sarajevo was in its third summer and the people were just barely surviving. Sarajevo did not smell as bad as I imagined it would. You would expect the stench of garbage and human waste to be overpowering in the heat of summer, but people recycled almost everything and wasted nothing. Not a crumb or peeling was thrown away; therefore very little garbage. No stench of rotting meat, because there was no meat.

There were dumpster-type garbage bins and small piles of garbage placed at the ends of streets, in empty lots or demolished buildings. The dumpster bins were often burning, black acrid smoke rising from the plastics in the garbage. The piles of garbage seemed more like a compost heap that never got bigger. A pile of garbage on the street near my accommodations always remained the same size, but I know it must have held garbage from about fifty households.

It was the sense of dignity that I kept noticing in the people of Sarajevo. Skenderija, once a modern, high-end underground shopping mall in the centre of the city, was now occupied by a French battalion right in the middle of no man's land. Some stores were still open and offering several items for sale. One such shop had a few toiletries and was staffed by a strikingly attractive woman. She wore makeup, her hair was done, she dressed well and had an aura of pride. Yet when I saw her close up, I noticed the telltale signs of war. She was thin, and her makeup could not hide the dark area under her eyes or the lines that stress had etched on her face.

The UN dump, out by the Sarajevo airport, showed a different face: it was a snapshot of affluence in a dying city. Dozens of trucks, laden with half-eaten food from UN kitchens, disgorged their contents daily at the UN dump.

Some families lived in, on and around that dump. There was almost no need for the UN drivers to unload their trucks; the youngest and fittest of the scavengers would wait below and catch the treasures as they were thrown off. I watched guiltily one day as we waited in a lineup of vehicles to get access to the airport. The salvaging process was organized and methodical, and well practised over the past three years. This all went on under the watchful eyes of the Serbs manning a nearby checkpoint. These Serbs seemed like decent people. They could easily have targeted the unfortunates at the dump, but they either felt sorry for them or thought it was enjoyable to watch the Bosnians rummaging like rats to survive.

### UNMO ROUTINE

Our tasks at work fell into two categories: survival and spying. On the survival side, we manned our operations centre 24/7 and carried out tasks such as water patrol and quest for food, firewood, vehicle fuel and luxuries, including booze and colas. On the official (spying) side, we conducted liaison patrols to the warring factions, patrolling from Sarajevo to Pale. We maintained contact with Sector Sarajevo UNMOs and, when freedom of movement permitted, with other sectors in Bosnia.

Our team's routine varied. It always began with morning UNMO brief, followed by taskings for the day. If we were lucky to not have a patrol to do, we could spend the day tucked away in the "upper container," our hangout/hiding place in the compound. Even with our diverse ethnic backgrounds, we all agreed that out of sight was out of mind.

Some of the fellows, such as the Spanish, Bangladeshis and Russians, had what we called "mafias," which consisted of men who worked in the UN compound but, unlike UNMOs, lived there, too.

They therefore had accommodation inside the wire. Compatriots would disappear into someone's room and relax, play cards, shoot the shit, drink, whatever. They were out of sight, so no one bothered them. It must have been nice to go and gab in your own language, because the working language of the UN is English. We could sense the men's need to have contacts with home, the comfort of hearing a familiar language and participating in familiar customs.

Most of the soldiers came from countries that rely heavily on family connections, and the need to be part of a surrogate family was important to them. The Canadians, on the other hand, were not as tight. I think the Canadians on UN staff avoided the Canadian UNMOS unless they needed us for something. That suited me just fine; I preferred the company of my teammates. They were a much more interesting lot, and there was so much to learn from them. Talking about Canadian problems and concerns seemed so petty in a place like Sarajevo.

We had access to water in the UN compound, so to keep everyone in our block of flats supplied with water we would undertake daily water patrols, which were always a chore. We had several five-gallon jerry cans which we would fill from the tap behind the kitchen in the UN compound. We'd load the jerry cans into our vehicle and then make our way back to our flats. We often thought how ludicrous it would be to get our asses shot off while delivering water. Arriving at the block, wearing our helmets and armoured vests, our work began: lugging the fifty-pound containers up five flights of stairs. We'd begin topping up the water containers in the apartments from the top floor down.

Everyone in the apartment building was so appreciative—especially old Tameo, who lived alone, was about eighty years old, had a feeble leg and was probably a bit senile. I remember the first time I brought Tameo water. He came to his door in his undershorts and a grubby T-shirt, can in hand, announcing how great I was and how thankful he was. The compliments were all in Bosnian, so I understood nothing, but I sensed his tone and saw his tears. His apartment was large, but he lived in the kitchen and one small room. Tameo had no big containers to fill, so instead he brought me dozens of pots, pans, bottles and jugs. I filled every one of them while he guided me from place to place, pointing with his cane, crying and thanking me. When I was finished, he wanted to know my name. I told him, "Fred." He repeated it and said "Canada" while pointing to the Canadian flag on my shoulder.

Tameo never forgot my name. Every day I could see him looking out of his window. When he saw me he'd call, "Fred, Fred, Canada!" and would point to his wrist to ask me the time. I would tell him with finger gestures, and then he would thank me profusely. Holed up in his apartment, water, food and time were what his life now revolved around. He was old and alone, and in what should have been his golden years, his world had gone mad. Tameo died alone in his apartment on November 19, 1995.

## PHONING HOME

One thing we Canadians had going for us was the telephone links with Canada. The UN had a satellite telephone system called VSAT that allowed calls in the former Yugoslavia. In addition, Canada had its own link with home through another system. So, on a good day, I could use the two systems and talk directly to home for free. It was excellent. About 75 per cent of my calls made it through. The lines were clear and loud, and the only thing to get used to was the two- or three-second voice delay. It always amazed me, and the people I called, that I could phone them from Sarajevo. I would time my calls so that I would be able to catch Janice at home at about eleven in the evening, Edmonton time (in Sarajevo it would be six in the morning).

I wish I could have thanked the Canadian Army Signallers. Once they heard that a soldier was calling from Sarajevo, they'd link the call right through. I surprised a few people with my calls, especially my dad. He was seventy-four and in awe of modern technology— especially a clear call from Bosnia. The first time I called him, he was incredulous. He asked, four or five times: "You're calling me from Sarajevo?" He worried about me and where I was. He saw the reports on the daily news, and he knew Bosnia was being ground down.

# 7 | Night Drive and Other Excursions

**M**Y FIRST NIGHT DRIVE in a pitch-dark Sarajevo was with Rustem, the Russian member of our team. Rustem often joined us at Mama's table. He lived for awhile in a flat upstairs but eventually moved to our UNMO house in Baščaršija. Rustem spoke perfect English and had had quite a career. He had served in several of the former Soviet Union's wars of expansion and retention in Afghanistan, Mozambique and, oddly enough, Cambodia. I enjoyed working with him; he provided insight into a system that I had been trained to fight. Now we were buddies serving on a mission that was trying to bring peace to a piece of the former Soviet sphere of influence.

I used to cross my fingers like the cross-hairs on a sniper's rifle scope and say: "Rustem, five years ago I'd be looking at you like this." He'd laugh and agree. He was a Muslim, born in Uzbekistan. Like most Bosnian Muslims, he didn't practise his religion; it was like me being Catholic. We had great talks about our families (he had a wife and two boys, ten and twelve years old), our homes and the ways of life in our countries. Things weren't so good in the former USSR; his family was in St. Petersburg. He would have loved to immigrate to Canada so that his boys could get a good education and have a future.

On this particular night-time excursion, we were travelling to Sector Sarajevo HQ in an armoured Land Cruiser. We were weaving our way through streets so dark that even though there were about a quarter of a million people around us, we couldn't see another soul. The few vehicles on the streets, mostly taxis, had their lights out. We kept ours out too because they would have drawn attention to our white UN vehicle and made it just another target. As we crept along the streets, our eyes adjusted to the darkness. All we could see were shadows moving about, people living like rats and cockroaches, trying to get the necessities for survival.

Since all of the water collection points were prime targets for snipers, most people waiting to fill up their jugs felt safer standing in line in the dark. We came across one such sight at the Bulevar Meše Selimovića bridge, where hundreds of people waited. They looked terrified. I'm sure they hoped we wouldn't turn our lights on to avoid hitting them. Sometimes UN people new to the city, or just fucking stupid, would light the crowd with their headlights. Panic would ensue, precious water would be spilled and containers would be lost; but worst, Serb gunners would sometimes punish everyone in the crowd with a few well-placed mortar bombs.

The city, a surreal enough place by day, became even stranger by night. I saw children out playing, mothers watching, safe under the blanket of darkness. The kids would be kept inside during the day, moms not wanting their children to join the more than ten thousand killed or wounded in Sarajevo so far. For the adults, a few coffee bars were open, usually tucked away in the back streets, out of sight of Serb gunners and snipers. By the light of the eerie glow of candles and the smouldering ends of their cigarettes, they were trying to socialize.

Our ride that night seemed to take hours. I was so wrapped up in what I saw, or couldn't see. It seemed that the darkness made sounds louder, and as a result people always talked in whispers. We saw dim light coming from the homes lucky enough to have candles, but people were smart to keep the glow well back in the bowels of the house, out of the sight of Serb gunners.

Eventually I grew accustomed to getting around the city in darkness and silence. In fact, now I think of darkness as a friend and not as something to fear.

## FEAR AND UNMO SUPERSTITIONS

Even the routine of a typical workday in Sarajevo was punctuated by periods of intense fear, almost to the point of paranoia. I tried to rationalize that fear comes from real threats and paranoia from perceived threats, and that perceived threats can be reasoned away with logic. In a perfect world, and to someone with a clear mind, it all makes sense. But the fear I experienced in Bosnia, especially in Sarajevo, was like nothing I had experienced before. It was as a result of the ever-present threat of danger to life and limb that came with living in the middle of a war. I observed it all around me. I could see it in everyone's eyes, speech, movements, superstitious habits, even their smoking habits.

The fear was stimulating, especially after a close call. You can get quite the buzz from cheating death. All your senses become crystal clear, everything becomes focused; you are aware of everything. I had never experienced these feelings before. In Sarajevo, just walking to work was an "in tune" experience—hugging the walls, looking at doors, roofs, windows, hearing the minute details of life around me. Sensing how quiet it was. Where were the people? Were they moving faster than usual? Were there kids out? Were there soldiers around? The speed of a passing car. Was the weather clear? Overcast? Rainy? Was it a crappy day for snipers? What time of the day was it? What day of the week? What had been said about Bosnia on the morning BBC News World Service? What was the mood of Mama and Goran? The list was endless. All so subtle, these things that fine-tuned your fear.

On my first walk in the city with Goran, I felt naked wearing only my running shoes, blue jeans and sweatshirt. I had begun to feel safer in a vehicle, but I knew this was a false sense of security, because unarmoured vehicles offered as much protection as my sweatshirt and blue jeans did. Even wearing a helmet didn't make me feel safe. *Boom!* Something would go off and I would instinctively cover my helmeted head with my hands. No matter how often I told myself "Don't do that!", when I heard *boom* up would go my hands to protect the old melon—guaranteeing that my hands would get mangled. Go figure.

Little superstitions grew quickly. One taboo in our team was that we must never say the words "calm," or "quiet," by themselves. For some uncanny reason, when we did, *boom!* Something would happen. So with our huge human brains (which have long lost the instincts to survive, in my view) we would say "Calm . . . but tense." As though we had to appease some ever-present ogre who listened to our words, waiting for a slip of the tongue, ready to punish us with a *boom!* We laughed about our quirks, but I could see in my teammates' eyes that they were as serious about them as I was.

Our two major rules were: one, never run; and two, never yell, unless someone's life is at risk. We never ran to our vehicle if we had forgotten something in it. We never yelled, "Hey Bob, bring me the radio from my car"—yelling meant danger. We were no different from the wildebeests on the African plains: we were always ready to take flight, to run and hide to save our lives. Sarajevo was a very dangerous place. We were the prey; the predators surrounded us, and we never knew when or where they'd strike. I was always planning my escape; good exercise for the mind, but when I had to run and hide it never quite worked out the way I had planned it.

One scenario I could never get a workable plan for was being on the toilet or in the shower in the UN compound during a strike. I often wondered if my modesty would be the death of me. Not likely; I'd have run to hell and back, buck naked, to save my ass if I had to. Pretty traumatic stuff, eh? But this is what went through my mind when I had time to dwell on the endless possibilities of my fate in Sarajevo.

In some perverse way I miss the fear and the heightened sense of awareness it gave me. I don't miss the total exhaustion that followed it. After a day out and about in the city, once I was safe, wherever that might be, and the elation of having beaten death or injury had subsided, I would arrive home exhausted. By bedtime I would sleep like a dead man.

## A TRIP OUT

The pressures of living and moving about in the city had been steadily building, and I needed a break. We were entitled to two days off per month, and for us this included two crossing days (to get in and out of Sarajevo if all went well) and two travel days to get to (most times) Zagreb. So I had six days coming to me after about forty days of work. Excited, anxious, nervous and brimming with a whole new bag of fears, I looked forward to my first trip out of Sarajevo and into Zagreb, maybe Budapest. All I wanted was food and some peace and quiet.

The trip would not be easy, because we would retrace the Mount Igman route. The situation on this overland route had not changed since my memorable inbound trip; it was still very dangerous and unpredictable. UNMOs did not have to travel out in the formed convoys that snaked over Igman daily. Because we had two armoured Toyota Land Cruisers in our team, the UN command in Sarajevo (the French) gave us permission to free-run out of, but not back into, the city. (Why only the one-way trip? We never found out.)

Ten UNMOs in two cars were to leave the Sector Sarajevo HQ at 2330. We gathered in the operations room of the HQ for a briefing on our expedition. There were a lot of motherhood statements, because no one could predict how the trip would go. My Canadian friend, Major Mark Douglas, would lead us. His driver, a Polish major, was on his way home after six months in Sarajevo; he had been over the route a dozen or more times. There were two Dutchmen and an African UNMO with him. Our car was made up of a Frenchman and three Africans. We needed a driver for our car; the Frenchman of course was not interested, and the Africans were notoriously bad drivers. So, in the interests of safety, I volunteered. Better to have one's life in one's own hands, I reasoned.

At around midnight we mounted up and, before leaving, removed the fuses for all the lights in and on our vehicles. We would use the cover of darkness to hide our movement. Then we were off. I had no idea where I was going. The Polish driver, who knew the route well, drove like a bat out of hell into the blackness of the city. I vowed to stay close behind him.

The trip through Dobrinja, then across the airport to Donji Kotorac and through Butmir, was interrupted by the dozens of checkpoints but was still fast. We crossed from Bosnian Sarajevo to the French-controlled UN airport to and through Serb-held lines around the city. All went amazingly well—ID cards at the ready, no room for contraband in our vehicles, and the *Vojni Promatra*'*c* (military observer) markings on our UN vehicles meant that we posed no threat and were not a source of weapons. Everyone knew that UNMOS were unarmed.

I often lost sight of our "Polish Mario Andretti," but I knew Mark would be on his case to slow down so that we could catch up to him. Once we were into the village of Glavogodina, the road narrowed to one lane. There we met a civilian convoy sneaking into the city. A lot of gun waving, and we were forced onto a small side road until the convoy went by. Ever fearful of mines, we stayed in our vehicles with the doors open to get some air (windows don't go down in armoured vehicles). We were waved on, much to our relief, because we had to be at the French checkpoint at the base of Igman by 0430. At this time they would man the mortars, which covered the UN movement on the mountain.

We arrived with a few minutes to spare. The French were nervous and agitated. They weren't aware that there was a civilian convoy on the mountain and that there had been the potential for a firefight.

They waved us off at two-hundred-metre intervals, and I immediately lost "Mr. Mario" in the dust of the road. My French co-driver and passengers were oblivious to their surroundings and looked at me like I was some kind of expert on Mount Igman. I figured I'd make no turns and just keep going uphill, a simple plan that worked.

We passed the vehicles and troops of the Rapid Reaction Force that had just moved onto Igman to protect UN troops. It was good to see them. Then, there in the darkness on the side of the road, I saw Mr. Mario, stopped; his car had broken down. He had failed to check his fuel, and when the right fuel tank went dry, he had switched to his left one. Lo and behold, it wouldn't draw, even though it was full. So he was effectively out of fuel. Nobody carried spare fuel, because it was always stolen. Great, here we were on the side of Mount Igman, no fuel, and the sun not far over the horizon. A plan: our car would go back down to see if we could scab some fuel off the Rapid Reaction Force guys.

Off we went, and as luck would have it, the last Bosnian check-point wouldn't let us through because we didn't have papers authorizing our return. *Fuck!* "You guys wouldn't have a bit of fuel we could borrow?" *Yeah, sure.* "Piss off or we'll shoot you," was my loose translation of the Bosnian response. Well, what to do, other than creep back up the hill and hope for a kind passer-by? *Hold on. What's that, a French UN reconnaissance car tucked into the tree-line? Away you go, Frenchie, get us some fuel, there's a long wait.* I can imagine the hesitancy of the soldiers. Here in the dark, a French naval officer trying to bum a jerry can of fuel for a UN vehicle? I guess the common language was the key, because he returned lugging a full can of gas. *Great! Let's get out of here.* We returned to our Polish friend, who was amazed that we had fuel. We all knew that being stuck on the side of Mount Igman was not a good thing. The Africans, however, were hard to read. They were almost giddy—out of fear? Or were they just oblivious to our situation?

Thank Christ, we were chugging uphill again. *Just get us to the top and out of direct harm's way*, I kept thinking. I was glad to be moving; our position on Igman was not a good one, and I would not have been keen on being there when the sun came up. The rest of the trip to Malo Polje was uneventful, and it was great to be up and over the mountain.

We paused for only a few minutes to stretch and breathe in the cool, crisp mountain air. Everything seemed greener. Maybe the grey cloud that constantly hung over my head in the city had moved off and allowed me to appreciate my surroundings. I could have spent my entire time off right there, breathing the fresh air and soaking up the sun.

We had a couple of more hours' drive to the Malaysian battalion, where we could park our armoured Land Cruiser and switch to a passenger van for the drive to Split, Croatia, on the Adriatic coast. The mood was good; the drive downhill, through mountain meadows and pastures, was like travelling in Bavaria. Then I began to notice that the car made an odd noise whenever we went into a right-hand curve. I assumed it was the nature of these unwieldy four-ton Toyotas.

Wrong! On a hairpin curve, with a steep drop on the left and a cliff on the right, something under the Toyota snapped and I lost control. *Bang, crash!* First thought: *We've hit a mine!* The Frenchman screamed at me to pull over. I tried to keep the car on the goddamn road. The Africans held on for dear life, eyes bugging out of their heads.

I realized what the problem was when the wheel passed us and bounded off down the road and into the valley below. Brakes and axle dragging, we ground to a halt, safe and sound on the uphill side of the road. The Frenchman was still babbling while I was trying to pry my hands off the steering wheel. The Africans laughed and slapped me on the back, congratulating me on my stellar driving skills (shit-house luck). Worst of all, we could see the other car off in the distance, oblivious to our harrowing predicament. We hoped they'd soon realize we weren't behind them anymore and turn around. But not until a couple of hours later, when we didn't show up at the Malaysian battalion, did they come looking. It was going to be a very long day.

Finally, the car was fixed. Well, not finally. The military police that we'd left the van's keys with "misplaced" them. We destroyed the ignition on the van's steering wheel, got it started, drove another six hours and, after driving for a total of twenty-four hours, arrived in Split. Tired, sore, head fucked—but hey, we were out of Sarajevo and in the land of the living.

We checked in to a hotel that catered to UN soldiers looking for a place to rest. This was also a place where the UNHCR put up refugees until they could be moved to longer-term accommodation. Most of the UN soldiers at the run-down hotel were from contingents that could not afford a leave centre or didn't have the funds to send their troops home on leave. For Mark and me, it was a place to stay for the night so that we could catch the UN shuttle flight to Zagreb in the morning. We were tired and dirty, and amazed at how peaceful it was. We sat on our tiny balcony overlooking the Adriatic, sipping cold beer, absorbed in our thoughts. Then I had a long, luxurious shower, stretched out with the balcony door open and the sound of the waves lapping at the shore, and drifted off to sleep. I woke up early, cold and still tired, with a cool breeze blowing through the open door. I'd had a terrible sleep; the bed was too soft and things were too quiet. I guess I had become accustomed to the boom and bangs of Sarajevo.

Our trip to Zagreb went without a hitch, and we were soon in the Canadian UNMO apartment that we shared whenever we made it into Zagreb. We all paid $50 (US) a month, which guaranteed a bed in a four-bedroom apartment that was within walking distance of UN headquarters. There was always "room at the inn" because there were never more than two or three Canadians in Zagreb at any one time. We donned our civvies and headed to the UNMO HQ to check in and see if there was any mail or messages. On our way back to the apartment, we had supper at one of the local bars that made pizzas as large as a garbage-can cover. After our feast, I sat there nursing a beer and feeling guilty that a war still raged only fifty kilometres away. It was my first encounter with the guilt that still haunts me today.

The next day, Mark and I hopped on the train to Budapest. Somehow we failed to get off the train in the city and ended up in a small town, miles from Budapest. The comfort of the European train and its rhythmic motion must have lulled us into a kind of dumbness. In no time at all, we became a source of entertainment for the conductor and the station master, who had quite a laugh at our expense. I can imagine what they said to each other: "Make sure you put them on the next train to Budapest, and tell them it's the *big* city at the *end* of the line. It's called Budapest." Finally, well after midnight, we got into Budapest, checked into the first fleabag hotel we could find and slept the sleep of the dead. The next day it was nice to wander the peaceful city streets, relax in the cafes, watch the people and soak up the sun. But our time off was too short; the guilt I was feeling grew.

### RETURNING FROM BUDAPEST

As if the journey hadn't been stressful enough, a certain amount of additional stress was created by the thought of returning to Sarajevo. The make-up of the group going back in was not the same as the one going out. Some fellows on the out trip would be transferring to another team site outside Bosnia, and better still, some were finishing their tour of duty. Others just had a knack of coming up with ways to scam a few extra days off. Travelling back to Sarajevo on this trip, it was me, two Dutch fellows, a Portuguese and an Irishman. The two Dutchmen were from one of the Sarajevo teams; the Portuguese and Irish fellows had just been posted in and were making their first trip into the city.

We met at the UN gate at the Zagreb airport. The Dutchmen and I were travelling light, but the Irishman and Portuguese had all of their kit. We went through "Maybe Airlines," which like all things UN was slow, bureaucratic and run by a bunch of rear-echelon motherfuckers (REMFS) who just loved jerking soldiers around. I was dismayed and my spirits were down when they announced that the flight would actually leave. I'd been hoping for a delay so that I would have another day to relax in the peace of Zagreb. No luck this day. We were in the air and arrived in Split within an hour.

We lugged our baggage to the airport parking lot, where four outgoing UNMOS gladly handed over the van which would get us to the Mal Bat (Malaysian battalion) at their camp in Konjic, where we would load into the armoured Land Cruiser for the trip over Mount Igman and into Sarajevo.

I could feel my stomach in a knot, and the pain in my neck was building. That particular ache is my personal stress indicator. It is slow and progressive, but a clear sign to me that all is not well. I did not want to go back to Sarajevo. I could only imagine what it had been like for the World War I and II soldiers who would come out of the line for a couple of weeks only to return to the same hellhole. To live with that ever-present sense of impending doom that came with their battles. Well, Sarajevo was my battle, and my first several weeks there had been terrifying. It wasn't the terror and fear of what I had actually experienced, but the ever-present fear of the unknown that stalked the brain and brought on the pain in the neck. The fellows in the French Foreign Legion call the fear "the worm"; it will work its way into every inch of your mind and body if given a chance.

I was privately embarrassed about my fear. I know the other men felt it too, but like me they hid it and worked hard at keeping it at bay. The Portuguese and Irish fellows were probably anxious, but I knew they were not experiencing fear. That would come in due course, once they were in the city. As I write these words and revisit that trip, I feel the ache in my neck as if I were once again on Mount Igman waiting to descend into the city.

The initial leg of our journey took us along the Dalmatian coast from Split, Croatia, to Metkovic, where we turned east towards Mostar. The seaside road, overlooking the blue Adriatic Sea, villas and small tourist hotels, acted like a tonic. The scene was so serene, such a far cry from what was going on inland. Here, the only evidence of war was the lack of tourists. The hotels, once filled to capacity, were now empty. The Germans, Scandinavians and East Europeans now went elsewhere. They did not want to sacrifice their meagre holidays to the whims of war.

The tunes on my Walkman soothed me and the view of the calm blue sea put the ache to rest, for now. All this changed when we turned east and headed into Bosnia from Croatia. The signs of war became visible once again and my ache gradually began to grow.

From high on a hillside road we saw the historic city of Mostar, which nestled in a river valley below. The town had been a pawn in a three-way tug-of-war between Serb, Bosnian and Croat forces. It had been pummeled into an uneasy submission, a stand-off between, oddly enough, the Bosnians and Croats. "Do you want to go into the city and have a look around?" the Dutch driver asked. "Why?" I said. "It's just a small version of Sarajevo. Let's keep on going so we don't get stuck somewhere in the dark." I'd always had a keen sense that as UNMOS we were unarmed, and we advertised the fact by putting *Vojni Promatra'c* all over our vehicles, thus proclaiming our vulnerability to all.

We rolled on through the desolate countryside. The bridges across the ravines along our route had been destroyed to prevent enemy movement, so we crept around the ravines' edges on roads cut by the UN engineers. It was all quite precarious, especially when you met a huge UNHCR vehicle creeping towards you. The roads were wide enough, but just. I looked out my window, and all I saw was air. At the real hairy spots you could see the evidence of the unfortunates who had eased too far over: broken wrecks strewn about on the valley floor. Probably just as many UN soldiers had been killed by the roads in Bosnia as by weapons. It's as if the whole country was out to get you, one way or another.

Our trip was tedious, finally ending the second stage back at the Mal Bat in Konjic. Here we would spend the night. In the morning we would transfer ourselves and our kit to the armoured Land Cruiser, leaving the van for the outgoing UNMOS to pick up in a few days. The Mal Bat base was small but functional; about three hundred soldiers here patrolled the local hills and manned several checkpoints and observation posts in the surrounding countryside. They had plenty of vehicles, all with very low mileage. The troops here didn't do much; they basically survived (especially in winter). I base this remark on reports from the UNMO team in nearby Konjic and the mint condition of and low mileage on all their vehicles. Regardless, they were very hospitable, offering us bunks in a transient tent and a supper meal of curry and rice. I was starved, and devoured a couple of plates of food offered by the smiling cook. After the food, all we wanted was to sleep, so it was an early night for all of us. I was beat and drifted off quickly, only to be awakened by Muslim prayers at 2300, blaring over the PA system. Most Malaysians are Muslim, so my sleep would continue to be interrupted regularly by the call to prayer.

Now my mind and imagination started wandering. The worm was at work. I had a fitful sleep full of imagined horrors. Morning did not come soon enough; tea and bread for breakfast, and farewell and thanks to our hosts.

The final leg of our epic was the most dangerous and difficult, to the top of Mount Igman and a descent into Sarajevo. My neck was really aching now. We made our way up to the old Olympic ski-jumping facility. It was now occupied by part of the French contingent; they maintained the road and escorted the convoys down into Hrasnica, a town on the outskirts of Sarajevo. A tense sense of urgency usually surrounded the French whenever they were in charge, but up here, coupled with the knowledge that they would make another run into the city, the tension was very high. I could sense that these troops would sooner be anywhere but here. We were guided in by a French sergeant who eyed us with a look of annoyance, like a French waiter showing you to your table.

Once we were tucked in among the other UN, UNHCR and media vehicles, we dismounted and had a long-awaited piss. There would, hopefully, be no stops on the way into the city. I walked away from the buzz of the crowd and looked for a place on the mountainside to fix my gaze. The air smelled of Alpine forest, fresh and cool. My view avoided the scars of war, and I could feel the ache easing.

My mind wandered to Jasper, Alberta, and camping weekends with my family. Janice and I, and sometimes Erin, would head for the mountain park every chance we had, to rest and wander the trails around the park. Back then I never thought I'd have to rely on those memories to ease my mind, yet thankfully I could. I was always amazed at the size of the trees in these mountains—spruce, fir and pine, tall and straight, their aroma like a soothing medicine. *"Let's go! Mount up!"* I was ripped up from the tranquillity of my memories, and the ache in my neck returned.

From experience, I knew we'd mount up and sit there, bundled up in armoured vests and helmets, and wait while the Frenchmen sorted out some new disaster. While we waited we left the doors open. It was hot and the five of us were pretty cramped. Amazingly, this time we were off in about ten minutes, creeping along like a big white caterpillar, all stop and go and painfully slow. We fell silent. The Irishman and Portuguese sensed our nervousness—they feared the unknown; we, the known.

I found my mind wandering ahead of me and into the city below. I knew nothing had changed. If anything, the shelling had intensified. I had a feeling that the Serbs wanted to finish the city off and take what they felt was rightfully theirs. I loathed them and the terror they brought on the city and its people, which would in a short time include me.

Before the war, the Mount Igman route was just a track. At one time passable only by woodcutters and hunters, now it was a lifeline to the outside world for the besieged city. The French maintained and improved the road as best they could, but the road had its limits, as did the Frenchmen. It was a narrow passage, steep and full of hairpin curves, and its lower end was within easy range of both Serb and Bosnian guns. From the summit of Igman down to the safety of my accommodation, I would feel the worm grow. I wished I could have been anywhere else but in Bosnia.

Our trip down was painless, albeit slow, with a lot of stops for traffic coming up and the French engineers carrying out maintenance on the road. It was nice to be able to get out of the cramped vehicle at these halts to stretch my legs and smell fresh forest air and enjoy the sun. It was like being a world away from the city below.

The lower reaches of Mount Igman were strewn with the wreckage of war. The side hills were covered with burnt, wrecked vehicles. The rusted hulks were an indication of the length of the war; they went back almost three years. The burnt, blackened ones were recent victims of the run into the city. A lot of people lost their lives on this part of the mountain, most as a result of vehicle rollovers while trying to negotiate the precarious, no-room-for-error switchbacks. Once a vehicle rolled on Mount Igman, there was no doubt that people would die.

The Serbs knew that one well-placed shot could get a convoy to panic like a flock of sheep sniffing a wolf. Once the panic hit, there was nothing stopping the race down the mountain, and vehicle rollovers were inevitable. But there was no race or panic on this trip; just a slow, laborious creep down to the city below. The worm was having a free run at my fears. I just wanted to get down across the airport and into the city of Sarajevo.

All my fears and anxiety were for naught. Our trip down Mount Igman into Hrasnica went without incident. The route through Hrasnica had not changed, nor had the human debris of war. Being in a normal vehicle with windows, I had a clear view of these people, who lived on the fringe in this war-torn country. They all pleaded for "paquets." None were given; our passage through this Serb area had to be quick. We had nothing to offer except sympathy. We, however, knew where our next meal was coming from, unlike these poor buggers, who had no idea when or if they would eat again. We zipped through Hrasnica and then into the Serbian area around the airport called Stup.

## THE WORM OF FEAR

Where is this story leading? Well, right to this spot, a French army checkpoint on the Bosnian side of the airport in Dobrinja. It's at this crossing point that our part of the convoy was stopped. This left us sitting broadside in between the two warring armies. It was unusual to be stopped at this checkpoint, especially when all the vehicles weren't UN. As we sat there exposed—hot, tired, hungry and just wanting to end this fucking trip—I felt the worm boring deeper. My every fibre vibrated with fear, anxiety and anger. "Why the fuck aren't we moving?"

The Portuguese and Irish fellows looked at me as if to say, "What's with you? Relax, be patient." They had no idea how dangerous this place was. The Dutchmen stared ahead, their gaze transfixed on the vehicle in front of them, as if willing it to move.

My head snapped from left to right, searching the gaping holes that once were windows in the surrounding buildings. *Snipers—where the fuck are they?* As if seeing them would ease my panic. I felt as if I were going to explode. I wanted to open the door and get out, move away from the vehicles that seemed such easy targets to me. The fear was like a poison, and I could feel its effects. My breathing quickened, my mouth was dry. I felt hot, my palms were sweaty as I clenched and unclenched my fists in anger. "Come on, you fucking frog bastards, let us through!"

The Dutch fellows stared ahead, and the Portuguese and Irishmen just wanted me to "shut up and calm down." I was making them nervous. The urge to fight, flee or freeze was eating away at me. The longer we sat, the more the urge to flee took over. "Come on, you useless bastards, let us through!"

There was, in hindsight, no need for me to get so worked up, but hindsight is 20/20. At that point the worm, which had been working its way into me over the past forty-eight hours, struck a nerve. It triggered my fears of both the known and the unknown. And it won. *I'm getting out of this fucking vehicle, and I'm walking to the safety of the Bosnian side. I can't take it.*

But then the vehicle lunged forward. We were moving. I eased my grip on the door handle. I felt ashamed. I had come within a hair of succumbing to the worm and I now felt weak, embarrassed. I just stared out the window; I couldn't look the others in the eye.

Had they too come close to snapping? Had they been taunted by fear? I was looking, fishing for support or justification for my actions. I had been weak. Had they noticed my weakness for what it was? Did they even realize what had gone through me? It didn't matter. In the end, my fear and anxiety were mine; it was my inner battle, and I had almost lost. It was just luck that we had begun to move.

I was exhausted. I wanted to be alone, lie down, close my eyes and mentally be away from this place. Nothing had changed, Sarajevo was still dying. There was no hope; no one outside cared, and I could sense that people were giving up. If I had to be here I was glad to be with my UNMO team; but most important, I was looking forward to being with Mama, Goran and Zoran. I tapped into their strength and courage not to run.

However, although I was overjoyed whenever I could get out of Sarajevo, always upon returning I would be weighed down with a load of self-imposed guilt for abandoning Mama, Goran and Zoran in the besieged city. There always was a distinct feeling of "us and them," because they knew we *could* leave, and we always had the secure feeling that if the UN mission ever fell apart we *would* leave. I tried not to make a big deal out of leaving Sarajevo, but I relished the thought of peace and quiet and all the amenities of Zagreb.

Mama and Goran must have been strong not to show resentment. I don't think I could have held it back. But three years of war and deprivation had numbed so many of their feelings that jealousy was just another one. We'd always bring stuff back from our excursions, gifts of food and drink or souvenirs of our travels. To me it seemed that these gifts were intended more to ease our guilt than to show gratitude for their care and friendship. Mama and Goran always accepted these things graciously for what they were, gifts. They, living on the fringe of humanity, taught me lessons in dignity and civility that I will never forget.

But before you could bring back those gifts, you had to make some tricky travel arrangements. If all went well, you could go from war-torn Sarajevo to "normalcy" in hours. Later, when the UN flights were reopened in and out of Sarajevo airport, and if you managed to get a seat out, you could be in Zagreb in less than ninety minutes. And within an hour, you could be showered (hot water!) and shaved, have clean clothes on and be sitting in a warm, well-lit restaurant, eating and drinking whatever you wanted. True to the precedent established in my first trip out, I never quite managed that ideal transition; mine always took longer. I'd usually end up sitting on the edge of my bed, stunned in my new surroundings, slow to move, not quite sure of where I was. I was letting the tensions bleed off, trying to shelve the guilt. "It's not my fuckin' war" never worked for me.

# 8 | The Dead and the Living

YOU COULD not avoid death in Sarajevo. The city was like a giant terminal ward in a hospital called Bosnia.

The day was clear. The Dayton peace talks were under way, and the ceasefire around Sarajevo was holding. Rustem and I were returning from a trip to Pale on a liaison visit. On the edge of Sarajevo, we stopped to take some pictures at the old military citadel that overlooked the city. From the road below the citadel you could look out over the whole city. We felt safe because we considered the situation "calm but tense." The Kovaci graveyard was right below us. It was huge—it had grown tremendously since the war had begun.

A woman sat beside a fresh grave, one of dozens that dotted the hillside. She rocked back and forth, praying and sobbing, wiping her eyes, looking skyward. Feeling guilty, I turned my eyes away only to find another woman and her child standing beside yet another fresh grave. She was a young woman, wrapped in anguish. Her child clutched at her dress, afraid and confused.

I saw scene after scene of people enduring their personal tragedies in this field of the dead. The sight of this graveyard, its grieving families and the city sprawled out below us, with its dozens of graveyards, thousands of dead and tens of thousands agonizing over their losses, was heart-wrenching. I was drawn back to the woman who was rocking and crying, lost in her pain. I turned to Rustem.

"Let's get the fuck out of here."

"Yes, Fred, let's go." He too turned away from the scene. As we drove into Sarajevo I was struck by the thought that I'd never heard crying in our graveyards back home.

## BRANCHO

I first met Brancho one afternoon when I arrived home to find Zoran, Goran and Mama with this large, tough-looking man. He was menacing and bristling with guns, a symbol of his position in his new life spawned by war. Brancho was a major in the Bosnian special police in Sarajevo.

When Zoran introduced me, Brancho looked me over and was intrigued by the fact that I was Canadian. *He was interested in me.* Brancho ran the police unit, which ferreted out Serb infiltrators and snipers who got into the city through the Bosnian front lines. He offered few details about his job and his unit. The "former system" paranoia about secrecy still had a grip—especially among the police.

I could see by Zoran and Mama's actions and politeness towards him that Brancho wielded power. Goran, on the other hand, could not have cared less about Brancho's station in life. Goran was a soldier, a front-line one, and he had no time for the prima donna antics of the police. I found out later that for two hundred Deutschmarks, Brancho could get you a passport in less than forty-eight hours, compared with the two or three months it normally took.

I never felt comfortable when Brancho visited; he was a dangerous person, especially if he wasn't on your side. Months later, Goran would tell me that the deference to Brancho had a purpose. Zoran, who was a policeman, wanted to get off the force once the peace accord was signed. He also needed a visa to travel to Germany to visit his wife and kids, who had been refugees there for the past three years. It all worked out in the end. But it was like dancing with a bear: the bear always leads.

Brancho, I was told later, had moved to Canada, somewhere in Ontario, and was earning a living as a truck driver. Probably he entered with false documents, which he had easy access to. Makes you wonder about our system and how deeply they look into people's backgrounds. My memories of Brancho are of his guns. If those guns could talk . . .

## MADAME CHEMSA

Madame Chemsa lived in the flat above me and was quite the woman. She was seventy-five, and before retiring she had been a professor in one of the universities in Sarajevo. I'm pretty sure her faculty was philosophy; she was a very worldly and well-read woman.

We hit it off immediately. A real treat for me was that she spoke English. Her words were always correct, well chosen and genuine; she had an intense need to learn. She had a son and daughter who lived in Canada, in *Torr-ont-oo*, as she pronounced it. She had a lot of questions about Canada, especially Quebec, including the now-familiar question: "Why do they want to separate?"

Madame Chemsa was respected by everyone who knew her. She had a way of making everyone feel comfortable. Like others her age, she was saddened and angry about the war, which had engulfed her home. Her family had been Partisans in World War II, fighting the Nazis and their supporters. Her father and one of her brothers were killed by the Nazis. She showed me a picture of them, taken somewhere in the mountains of Bosnia during the war. Pointing to her father and brother as if it were yesterday, pausing lost in her thoughts, I could see that even after fifty years she had never gotten over the loss.

Madame Chemsa lived alone in her flat above Mama's. A friend, Madame Turkiyana, who lived nearby would visit daily, and sometimes when the city was active with the sounds of war she would spend the night. Every day, in the early evening, Mama would comb her hair and head upstairs to join them for a visit. Over coffee and cigarettes, the three of them would talk and laugh. Mama told me jokingly that they were Tudjman, Milosevic and Izetbegovic, blatantly mocking the seemingly pointless peace negotiations in Switzerland between the presidents of Croatia, Serbia and Bosnia-Herzegovina. I would have loved to eavesdrop on these matriarchs, who with their more than two hundred years of combined wisdom and insight could in all likelihood have brought an end to the war. Having fought the Nazis in World War II, they were caught up in another terrible war at a time when they should have been enjoying the final years of their lives in peace and tranquillity. Many, like our neighbour Tameo, would die alone in terror or lapse into a state of trauma that would follow them to their graves. The old were robbed of their past, and the young of their future. I hope Madame Chemsa is enjoying the peace. She was one of the lucky ones who survived yet another war.

### TRIP TO KISELJAK

Kiseljak is about twenty kilometres from Sarajevo. At that time the town was known as the black market centre of Bosnia. Kiseljak was fat with shops and black marketers; you could get anything there for a price. ("Need a UN vehicle? You can get it here, with a new paint job if you want.") The trip to Kiseljak had its own peculiarities, situated as it was at the end of a series of four checkpoints known as the Sierras.

They were numbered from 1 to 4—Sierra 1 being near Kiseljak, Sierra 4 in Sarajevo. We had formed a strange relationship with the Serbs who manned Sierra 4. I think the initial contact was made by Miro, our Czech, in an attempt to get to Kiseljak. To be able to get through the Sierras was a big deal: it meant food and goodies. So it was in our best interest to foster this relationship with the guards at the Sierras.

The Serbs who we got to know were a strange bunch. These guys ruled their world. They were special police, not soldiers, and wore purple, almost black, fatigues to denote their police status. They were a mixed bag of characters, and I never knew who was in charge at any given time. All were quite menacing in their own way, always brandishing guns and usually pissed to some extent.

One fellow stood out: a young, short corporal who seemed to be the mouthpiece whenever we were there. The other one who seemed to equally dominate the conversations was a woman. For the life of me, I can't remember her name, but based on her size and attitude it should have been Ilsa, She-Wolf of the ss. This was a hard woman, almost six feet tall and weighing about two hundred pounds; always overly made up and doused in perfume. Ilsa wore all the bells and whistles of her trade, including a big, chrome-plated, 9 mm pistol, a definite symbol of her status. The corporal and the She-Wolf spoke some English, which made for interesting conversations.

The other fellows who came and went from the checkpoints were your average thuggish checkpoint guards. With a Canadian present, the conversation seemed to gravitate towards—what else?—hockey. You'd swear they had Wayne Gretzky in their midst. They knew all there was to know about "The Great One," and the guards figured that I, being Canadian, must know him personally. I am not a fan of the sport. The old "bullshit baffles the brains" tactic worked well in this situation, and the language barrier worked in my favour. My lack of hockey knowledge was attributed to something being lost in translation. These talks were usually held inside the guards' bunker, where the wood stove roared and the slivovitz flowed. Now that crap is strong, especially in the early morning on an empty stomach. To the Serbs, drinking at this time in the morning was hospitality, but to me it was murder.

We picked up a lot of information and local intelligence during these bullshit sessions. As much as this crew looked incompetent, they weren't. Their task of manning this vital checkpoint was not taken lightly by their superiors. They were switched on and probably gathered as much information from us as we did from them. When we were outside, the Serbs were always looking beyond us at their enemy, totally aware of the situation and always in charge. The whole place was mined and easily defended, if necessary. Eventually the Sierras would be open and movement would be unrestricted. But until then, Sierra 4 would be a hard place to get through.

On one occasion, our familiarity with and knowledge of the Sierras, especially number 4, helped prevent a high-level confrontation. Miro, Max, Palo and I were heading to Kiseljak in an attempt to get Miro and me on a helicopter to Split for a few days off. The Sarajevo airport was still closed, and it was worth trying for the helicopter ride in Kiseljak instead of the 24- to 36-hour drive over Mount Igman. So we loaded up and thought we'd try our luck through the Sierras.

We made our way through the Bosnian checkpoint in Dobrinja, then through the two French ones near the airport. Arriving at Sierra 4, we noticed several UN vehicles escorting a high-level Dutch military official. It was the standard four-car escort, which was waved to a halt by the Serbian corporal and his crew. Normally a group of this size was cleared through various channels well in advance, so the Serbs' reaction was that this was an unannounced crossing. It was about to be handled badly.

Initially we paid little attention, expecting that the convoy, once the Serb escort arrived, would be waved through. But when we saw the Serbs' Kalashnikovs come off their shoulders, we knew things were not right. Immediately I thought, *At least we're in an armoured car.* The situation quickly escalated. The Dutch security troops got out of their vehicles, and a standoff—or worse—was about to begin. The Dutch were in a bad spot; the French troops were over a kilometre away and could not help. From out of the ruined buildings came Serb soldiers who had remained hidden until now.

This was not good. The Serb corporal squared off with a tall lanky Dutch officer, and he was not happy about being told: "We are UN. We have the right to pass." *Jesus Christ, asshole, do you know where you are? The UN has shit-all in this part of the world; you are going to get your ass shot off!*

It was time to see how much our friendship with these fellows was worth. Miro headed for the corporal while the rest of us mingled and chatted up the Serbs we knew. "*Dobar dan. Kako ste?*—Good day. How's it going? Cigarette?" Separating and distracting them allowed Miro to deal with the boss. Thankfully the Dutch officer kept his mouth shut. He knew he had lost, and now just wanted to get his high-priced passenger out of the danger he had put him in. Miro was slick, he knew the language and how to make the corporal feel that he was the boss (and he was) and that these guys were assholes (and they were). Miro said that they were *budala* (idiots) and that he would report them to the big UN guy in Sarajevo. "By the way, we're hoping to go to Kiseljak. What could we bring you back? Cigarettes, cognac?"

I was shocked and amused to hear the corporal say, "Disposable diapers and baby powder. We cannot get either here, and I need them for my baby girl."

"*Nema problema*—no problem," Miro said. "Now, let these guys through and I'll make sure the shit lands on his head," pointing to the tall, embarrassed and, by now, very nervous Dutch officer.

A few more words were fired at the Dutchman by the Serbian corporal, and then it was over. We all laughed; the tension was relieved, like having a good crap. Max (a Dutch UNMO) had a chat in his native tongue with the Dutch officer and told him to mount up. Moments later the Serb escort car arrived, and we were shepherded across the bridge over the Zeljeznica River and onto the road to Kiseljak.

Close call, not for us, but for them. Max said that the Dutch escort leader "thought" that this would be the shortest route to Kiseljak. *Stupid bastard, that's how you die in Sarajevo. You assume, you get lost and you disappear.*

The ride to Kiseljak was uneventful and quick. To our surprise, when we arrived at the UN compound the Dutch convoy was there. We were approached by an elderly and, judging by Max's reaction, very senior Dutch officer. He thanked us for our handling of the situation at Sierra 4. He could not believe that the choice of route for his departure was taken for granted and that they were travelling without a translator. The Dutch officer shook our hands, thanked us again and was led away by the now-sheepish Dutch escort leader. Max said that the elderly fellow was the commander of the Dutch army, General (insert long Dutch name!). We were impressed. Now—where the hell were we going to find Pampers?

**THE BOY**

In Kiseljak I volunteered to stay with the vehicles, a necessary safeguard everywhere in Bosnia. It was a warm, sunny and very peaceful day as I sat on the curb, such a contrast to Sarajevo. Out of the corner of my eye, I saw a young boy about ten years old sitting on an embankment and staring out over the pastures that butt up against the town. His hair was short and had the hallmarks of a homemade haircut: patchy and thin in places, like the ones my dad gave us when we were kids. His clothes were ragged and threadbare, and he was desperately thin.

The young fellow had the look of so many of the kids I had seen since coming to Bosnia—dark, deep-set eyes, protruding cheekbones and toothpick-skinny arms. All the features of hunger and the strain of war on the young. I thought of my son Ben when he was that age. He, too, was thin and dishevelled but he never wanted for anything. I dug into my pockets and found a little Canadian flag pin. I always carried them, to reward helpful kids or to break the ice in a tense situation at a checkpoint. I also found a few "bonbons," as the Sarajevo kids called the candy we gave them. I approached him and greeted him: "*Dobar dan.*"

There was no response, no sign of recognition. As I moved around to face him, he was startled by my presence. There was fear in his big, dark eyes. He tilted his head as I spoke a few words to him in Bosnian, then he touched his ears and I realized he was deaf.

I stood there looking at him. He had the look of a cornered cat—tense, ready to spring and flee. I put out my hand and offered the candy. He just stared at me, untrusting, and then he saw the red and white flag pin and his eyes locked onto it. I motioned for him to take the candy and the pin. Hesitating, he cautiously took them from my hand. He nodded his thanks, and I smiled and walked back to the vehicles.

Any kid in his state would have devoured the candy, but he was looking at that little pin as if it were the gift of life. As I watched, he took the fastener off the back and pinned it on his grubby T-shirt. Once he had it pinned on he looked at it, admiring the splash of colour he now possessed. Then he put the candy in his mouth and, like a man savouring a cool drink, put his head back, faced the sun and relished his good fortune. I realized I was looking at someone experienced far beyond his years. As I drove away, I left him basking in the midday sun.

## HAPPY BIRTHDAY, ANNA

Goran's daughter, Anna, would be celebrating her seventeenth birthday in Bergen, Norway, where she, her mother and her brother had lived since 1992. They were lucky; they had left as church-sponsored refugees. Goran was very proud of his children. They had been achievers prior to the war. His son, like any thirteen-year-old European, was into soccer and had quickly risen in the youth leagues in Norway. And Anna was well on her way to becoming an accomplished pianist. During one of our periods of electricity, usually unannounced and these days lasting only three or four hours, Goran showed me a video. It was of Anna performing on a television talent show. She was good and had showmanship.

I could see that Goran and Mama missed their family terribly. Tears came to their eyes as they talked of the time when they would see Goran's wife and children again.

Even though Anna was thousands of miles away, we would celebrate her birthday. The day of the feast had been planned for some time now. We had been hoarding food and booze for a couple of weeks in anticipation of the celebration. In this crazy city, the birthday would be a small touch of what it would be like to be normal. There would be guests from all over the block of flats: Madame Chemsa, Madame Turkiyana and some dear friends of Goran—his best friend and maid of honour from his wedding. The kitchen would be crowded, but we would all fit around the table. The day began with Mama busily preparing food dishes before I got up for work. I left for work with thoughts of food and friendship warming my soul.

Luckily my day was nondescript—a bit of this and that, nothing to shock or cloud the mind. The smell of cooking greeted Einar, Miro and me as we climbed the stairs leading to the flat. We were salivating like Pavlov's dogs. The meal and celebration started early to take advantage of the daylight, but nevertheless we would go through several candles before the night ended. The atmosphere was almost like Christmas: the kitchen snug and warm, mouth-watering smells, Mama proudly tending to the oven and the bubbling pots. Goran moved about setting the table, trying to squeeze in yet another place setting. I hurried off to wash and change; we would wear nothing military to overshadow the festivities. There were drinks laid out—cognac, for all except Mama, who did not drink; for her, a Coke sat beside her multi-purpose aluminum mug. There were appetizers of prosciutto, cheese and veggies. As people began arriving, they exchanged hugs and kisses. Goran was ever so formal in his introductions and played the part of a gracious and honoured host.

"*Sjediti*—come sit." We worked around the table into our places, some of us with our backs to the wall, locked in for the duration of the meal. Everybody was talking, going through the checklist of "How is so and so, where is he, how is his family?" and so on. Goran calmed us down and offered a welcoming toast, "*Zivjeli*—cheers." We gulped our *slijivovica* (homemade plum brandy) down; our glasses were refilled and were never left empty. We snacked on cheese and vegetables, teasing our stomachs for what was to come. The meal began with *pasulj*, a bean soup that was soaked up with great pieces of Bosnian army *hljeb* (bread) and *kajmak*. *Kajmak* is similar to cream cheese; it's made from boiling whole milk, skimming the froth from the top and whipping it into a butter-like consistency. Zoran was the *kajmak* expert; he'd found this batch downtown, at probably a hefty black market price. A dollop of *kajmak* in the *pasulj* and some on the *hljeb*—aaahh, what a taste.

Nothing was rushed. We talked, told jokes and laughed even when we didn't get the joke. There were roasted green and red peppers. We picked them up by the stem, wrapped our lips around them and pulled the seed pod out to discard it. Beer, wine and cognac flowed, compliments of the various mafias. There was more than enough for all, and by night's end maybe a bit too much for some.

*Burek* was Mama's specialty. It is an ethnic dish found throughout the former Yugoslavia. I've eaten it in dozens of eateries, but Mama's was by far the best, as everyone agreed. *Burek* is a light pastry like a Danish or a croissant, filled with spiced ground beef or pork. Mama knew that we loved it, and she had made dozens for the supper. You'd take one, spread it with yogurt or *kajmak* and eat it like a doughnut, no utensils required. I could only manage two or three; others had four or five. I always warned invited diners at Mama's about how good the *burek* was and not to get carried away by eating too many, because there was a main dish to follow.

Tonight the main dish was a joint of *svinjetina* (pork) on a bed of sour cabbage, baked slowly for four to five hours so that the pork literally fell from the bone. You should have heard the *oohs* and *aahs* as Mama placed the well-used, blackened roasting pan in the centre of the table. No one moved until compliments were made to the cook. Mama, as usual, was shy and embarrassed. She was smiling, not from the compliments, but with the sheer joy of having friends around her table. Then Goran, breaking us from our reverie, said: "Eat!"

A sumptuous meal of *pasulj, kajmak, hljeb, burek, svinjetina* and plenty of drinks made us a happy lot. By now the daylight had gone, and candles illuminated the joyous scene. Scenes like this were a flashback to pre-war Sarajevo: close-knit families enjoying life and what it offered.

We were full to bursting. The table was not cleared, just in case someone wanted just a little more. Everyone eased back, cigarettes and drinks in hand and the compliments flowing, reminiscing about the past and the good times. It was a cleansing of the sorrows and deprivations the war had brought.

But the feast was not done; this was a birthday, and you can't have a birthday without a cake. Don't ask me where the hell Goran got this *kola"c*, but there it was, a huge, hazelnut, fully iced, seventeen-candles-blazing-away "Happy Birthday Anna" cake. We couldn't believe it, yet I knew that if anyone could find a cake in Sarajevo, Goran could.

The cake was the *pièce de résistance* to top off an amazing meal, the kind I had not had since leaving Canada. And to accompany the cake, *Bosanska kava*, strong and hot coffee. Then we all joined in for a birthday tradition found around the world: we sang "Happy Birthday" to Anna. We sang it loud—really loud—as if to mock the Serb gunners on the hills around the city. Outside it was cold and dark, and thankfully quiet. Nothing marred this perfect evening. Late into the night we sat and drank and dipped back into the food, laughing. All that was missing was the birthday girl, Anna.

We all jumped when the phone rang. Oddly enough, the phone system was one of the few public services that could be relied on throughout the war. We wondered who it could be, because everyone Goran knew was here. Goran answered. Initially he was shocked, then his eyes brightened and a big grin lit up his face. Anna was calling to wish her dad and grandmother all the best on her birthday. There was not a dry eye in the place as Goran and Mama huddled around the phone, sharing their love over the miles in the face of this miserable war.

### THE VACANT LOT

In the zoo that was Sarajevo, silence was cherished as well as feared. We knew it would end in some terrifying way for someone. Usually the end came with a crash, boom or bang caused by a weapon of war. No comfort or relaxation, just the knowledge that *they* were still out there, poking holes in our silence.

When I was out walking at night, I could see faint glows from inside other homes. Everyone was careful not to expose that warm glow to the eyes of the Serb gunners and snipers. By the end of the third year of the war, people were very careful with everything else as well, as if to say, "I've come this far. I want to be here when it's over."

But some were unlucky despite their precautions. One morning, Goran and I visited the ruins of an apartment where a family had lived. They had been killed the evening before, probably while sitting in the kitchen—Mom, Dad, two or three kids, blasted beyond recognition by a direct hit to the flat. I saw their flat blown open to the world, a gaping hole where the wall used to be, and belongings strewn about. They had survived so long in this hell, but they had lost out to the madness. Looking at their rooms, I felt as if I was invading their privacy. Goran turned to me: "Fred, this is normal."

But, though Sarajevo was a dangerous place in the summer of 1995, there were places in the city where people felt safe. One such spot was a vacant lot next to a house shared by five members of our UNMO team. The house, which was owned by a retired university professor, was tucked away on a small narrow street in Starigrad, near the old part of the city. One of the perks of living there was that they had a generator, which provided lights, hot water and television. So I visited often.

The vacant lot was at right angles to the front lines and afforded protection from observation and snipers. During the daylight hours, the lot was a beehive of activity. It was dusty and its edges were strewn with debris and rubble, but the rest of it was clear, making it the perfect place to pursue the great European pastime, or should I say religion, of football (soccer).

From first light to last, there was always someone kicking a ball around the vacant lot. The piles of debris became bleachers for the people intent on watching the games. And many cheered, as though they were watching the World Cup.

For me it was the eight-to-ten-year-olds, who had the most energy and least skills, that provided the best entertainment. In a cloud of dust, with yelps and yells, an unknown number of street urchins would be chasing the ball all over the lot. No rules, limited skills, but energy and enthusiasm beyond belief.

I figured if it wasn't safe their moms would not let them be there; moms ruled. In fact, I used the "kid barometer" to gauge the level of tension in the city: the greater the number of kids out playing and the younger they were, the lower the perceived danger level.

The moms of the kids in the vacant lot were never far away. They would stand and chat on the street or watch from windows—proof that the unimaginable fear of losing a child was sometimes overcome by the urge to let kids be kids in a city that had seen hundreds of children die.

One sunny afternoon I leaned out the window of the house and just listened to the kids in the lot. It was peaceful, sunny and warm—a very quiet day. Then BOOM—*fuck, fuck, fuck*—an impact, close, very close. I hit the floor. The sound I will never forget was of the children screaming. Their screams lasted a few seconds, then silence.

I could tell by the silence that no one was injured. If someone had been hit, the yelling would have changed from cries of fear to screams of pain and agony. I grabbed my first-aid kit and ran to the lot, purposely slowing down and tentatively making my way around the last building, hoping the lot would be empty. Thankfully, it was. I hated being the first on the scene; you never knew what you would find. I scanned the roofline, and I could see dust rising from the impact a block away. Some other poor bastard had taken that one. It was amazing how the day had changed from fun to fear and then silence. That's all it took; a brush with death, and everything changed.

I wandered back to the house, wondering if the Serbs knew of this place and were trying to target it and its young people. Probably not. The shell was just one of those random acts of terrorism where they fired the gun and didn't give a shit where it landed, like shooting fish in a barrel.

As I stood on the street, the kids slowly returned to the vacant lot. They looked like baby gophers, popping out of their hiding places. First it was the moms who poked their heads out to see whether it was safe, their hands holding on to their kids', not quite ready to let go.

Within minutes the sounds of the game grew louder. Again there were yelps and yells; it was as if nothing had happened. But for the moms, the mood had changed. There was fear on their faces as they cast their eyes skyward, trying in vain to see the death that could come without notice. What a way to live, to raise your children. Living in fear of loss beyond belief, but overpowered by the need to live life like a normal human being. I sat on the doorstep of our rented house and was amazed by the mothers' courage. The sun was again warm on my face, and the sounds of the children playing happily in the vacant lot filled my ears.

# THE FINGER

**IT WAS EARLY, JUST** after sunrise, and the city was quiet. Normally when I walked to work I kept my head up, alert to dangers, pausing, stepping into doorways, scanning the roofs and streets for snipers. Then I spotted the finger. It was lying there on the sidewalk as I stepped out of a doorway. I stopped and stared at it, then looked around to see if someone was playing a practical joke on me. *No, Fred. This is Sarajevo. This is no joke.*

I knelt and took out my pen, and used it to roll the finger over. It was pristine, white, well manicured and had been severed at the knuckle. I looked around and sniffed the air for any hint of the putrid smell of a decaying body from whence the finger might have come. But the air was clear; just the acrid smell of burnt-out buildings scented the morning air. I looked at the ground; there was no blood trail, just a dusty, dirty street that I had travelled dozens of times.

I thought, *You've been standing here too long. Get moving. Someone could have you in their sights right now. Go! It's harder to hit a moving target. What about the finger? Leave it; let someone else deal with it. Pick it up and mail it to President Clinton. Tell him it's a gift from Sarajevo and to stuff it up his ass.*

I dug around in my pockets and found a piece of paper. I looked around, then knelt down and placed the paper beside the finger. I used my pen to roll it onto the paper. I took the paper, rolled up the finger in it and tucked it away in my pocket. It seemed like the natural thing to do—to show it some respect, because it was part of a human. I ducked back into the doorway, scanned the roofs along the street and moved off to work.

Arriving at the UN compound I worked from, I looked around and found a small overgrown area not covered with gravel. Using the heel of my boot I kicked a small hole in the turf, big enough for the finger. I looked around to make sure no one was watching, then took the small package out of my pocket, knelt down and placed it in to the hole. *Fuck.* The paper I had wrapped the finger in was the list of UN medical facilities located inside the city: *I need that list!*

I picked up the finger and rolled it out of the paper, checking to see if the paper was okay. *Good, no blood, nothing gruesome.* I looked at the finger in its grave; hopefully whoever had lost it would feel no aches or pain in the stump. As I knelt there, an image of my grandfather, rubbing the stump where his right forearm used to be, came to mind. He used to tell people that his stump ached because the hospital had not buried his arm after it had been crushed in a mining accident and then amputated.

I stood up and used my boot to scrape some dirt over the finger. I stepped on the earth to compact it, folded the precious paper and placed it in my pocket. I wondered if that missing finger was the only pain the owner felt in this war.

# 9 | Goražde

GORAŽDE WAS ONE of the UN-proclaimed protected areas on the "Dark Side" (the Serb part of Bosnia). During the summer of 1995 two other large Bosnian UNPAS fell to the Serbs. Srebrenica and Zepa were surrounded, pummelled and then attacked. The fall of Srebrenica was widely covered by the world media: the separation of the women and children from the men ("men" included any boys over the age of thirteen) for movement as refugees was reminiscent of the selections at railheads in Auschwitz during World War II. The women were terrorized, abused, raped and murdered, and several thousand of the men were never seen again. When the Dayton Peace Accord was signed in 1995, the question arose: where were the men of Srebrenica and Zepa? Later, their remains were discovered in mass graves. Finally their fate was known to the world and to their families.

But Goražde held out and was isolated for three and a half years. More than fifty thousand people were crammed into a small town surrounded by hills dominated by Serb gunners. An eight-man UNMO team was the sole UN presence there in November 1995. There were convoys each week out of Sarajevo, manned by the Russian contingent. The Russians did amazing work pushing their convoys into Goražde. They protected and negotiated the crossing of United Nations High Commission for Refugees (UNHCR) trucks loaded with supplies through more than 120 kilometres of Serb-held territory. The convoys were not always successful and were often looted well before arriving at their destination, but without this weekly convoy Goražde's fate would have been the same as that of Srebrenica.

I made my first trip to Goražde to establish physical contact with our team. They had not been out for over two months, and our sole communication had been the odd distorted radio message or an infrequent satellite link-up. It was time to go in and see how they were doing.

Ronnie Denyft, our deputy team leader, did a lot of preparation to allow our passage to Goražde. A vet of Bosnia, Ronnie was firm and persistent with the reluctant Serbs, who eventually (after two weeks) gave in to our demands. Two cars and four UNMOs would be allowed in. Winter had come to the mountains, and this guaranteed that a Norwegian UNMO and I would be driving. Winter driving skills were rare in our team, as it was made up of men who came from countries with no or minimal winters. I also wanted to see Goražde and the land between it and Sarajevo.

It was a snowy, wet day in Sarajevo when we set off. Our vehicles were loaded with supplies for the team, and each of us carried our own emergency kits in case we were waylaid or taken hostage. The Serbs did not like UN personnel, and they liked them even less when they were wandering about Serbian territory. Mama and Goran were quite concerned about my trip to the Serb side, especially about the long drive through what they considered the home of the Devil.

Most of our checkpoint crossings were the same ones we used to get to Mount Igman, and usually these crossings went well. Once we were clear of the suburbs of Sarajevo, we turned southeast towards Serb territory. Things slowed considerably at each checkpoint. Our official papers helped, but the decision to let us move on or not was always at the whim of the soldier at the checkpoint. We were always threatened and had guns waved in our faces. Then we were searched and had our UN ID cards taken to be "checked." It was all standard Serb macho bullshit. You'd have some pimply-faced seventeen-year-old with an AK47 and his belly full of liquid courage (slivo) playing the big man. They were toadies acting the part of the big tough in an attempt to impress their bosses and maybe move up the food chain. Some jerk would actually be in charge, but he would delay his participation to let everyone know who the real boss was today. Then the toadies would back off and hand over our papers to him. He would look totally uninterested, as if to say, "Why are you wasting my valuable time?" These guys pissed us all off because, first, they were not soldiers, just local thugs, and second, they were only in charge of the few metres of road we had to pass over.

Our approach was to be firm and professional, always pushing the fact that they were dealing with real soldiers. Not being armed made us less of a threat but more of a target for robbery. If we'd had guns, then it would have been: "Our guns are bigger than yours"—in other words, "Our dicks are bigger than yours." The power struggles at this level were not rocket science; it was simple pack mentality. The alcohol level at these checkpoints was another factor you had to deal with. If the guards were pissed, then most of the reasoning and logic went out the window. We then adopted the "Buddy, would you like a drink?" tactic. I became a jovial Canuck traveller, and the others played their parts too, with me offering cigarettes and Canadian flag pins and all of us sharing a drink. And all the time we thought about how much we detested these guys.

Whatever method we used, our mission was to get through to the team in Goražde. Our tactics worked. We were not delayed more than a half hour at each checkpoint, except at one, where the Serbs had pulled over a French convoy. This checkpoint controlled the intersection, which sent you to Pale or to the interior of the Dark Side and then on to Serbia and Belgrade. So this was normally a tight-assed place. The convoy with its French escort was made up of high-ranking UN officers and officials wanting to go to Pale for Christ knows what. The Serbs were ultra-uptight, suspicious and belligerent. Thankfully, Rustem went forward and pleaded our case. The guards were used to the Russians and their weekly convoys to Goražde, and Rustem fared well in the local language. I think the Serbs thought we were small fish, and besides they were having much more fun jerking the French around. So we were waved through, much to the disgust of the brass in the convoy. A few well-placed words in a non-confrontational manner got us a lot further than the "We're the UN; we have freedom of movement" ploy.

## ON THE NOT-SO-OPEN ROAD

The hundred kilometres or so to Goražde now lay open to us. It was snowing and the roads were not clear; it was going to be a white-knuckle driving day. The countryside reminded me of Canada—hills and dense forests, small farms and no signs of war. It felt good to let my eyes wander at a distance. In Sarajevo there were no vistas; everything was in your face. But there were no threats here. We were far from the front lines, and we relaxed.

Our Toyotas made short work of the distance, and the four-wheel drive made the snowy conditions easy going. Rogatica, a small industrial town, was our only stop before Goražde and its front-line checkpoints. Most of the town's industries had fallen into disrepair due to sanctions and the departure of the male work force to the army. A half-hour pause to have our papers checked by the "warlord of the day," and we were out of there.

The hills came up on both sides of the road, which wound through the valleys and gorges so typical of the mountainous areas of Bosnia. Signs of war and ethnic cleansing began to show as we moved closer to our destination. Vacant, burnt-out, destroyed vehicles and farm machinery—all signs of lost lives—so typical of this country. The snow seemed grey. The sun, now hidden by clouds trapped in the hills and mountains, gave the place an atmosphere of utter despair. From a military standpoint, Goražde was much worse than Sarajevo. It was smaller, and therefore the shooting range to targets (people) was much shorter. In military terms, we'd call it a "good killing ground"—it was a piece of ground where the full weight of all your weapons could come to bear on the enemy.

Our last Serb checkpoint was about five kilometres out of town, where the road crossed over a dam. It was a surprisingly quick crossing. I guess they felt we were no threat. They already held the upper hand, and if they wanted to take us out they'd have us in their sights whenever they wanted.

The short distance from the checkpoint to the outskirts of town was littered with evidence of very heavy and desperate fighting. Vehicles of all kinds had been used to barricade the road. They were either riddled with bullet holes or torn apart by explosions. The homes on either side had been smashed to rubble by house-to-house fighting. The clouds were low in the valley—a godsend, because the low cloud limited the visibility of the Serb gunners and snipers.

The defenders' checkpoint was located at a barricade constructed from a large truck and some buses. The roadblock showed all the signs of very heavy fighting. We were greeted by a ragtag group of men, without uniforms, lightly armed and all looking the worse for wear. Their faces were gaunt, thin from malnutrition and the stress and strain of war. They smiled gap-toothed grins, glad to see anyone from the outside world. Rustem let them know why we were here and gave them the news of the peace talks. Since the talks had begun, the Serbs hadn't fired a single round into the town. The Bosnians said it was unnerving, this silence, after years of constant shelling, sniping and attacks. "It looks good for peace," we told them. But we knew we could not predict the fate of Goražde in the talks taking place thousands of miles away, in Dayton, Ohio.

Now that we were inside the enclave, we felt safe to use our radios to contact the Goražde team. We had maintained radio silence during the trip; everyone was very suspicious of an UNMO with a radio mike in his hand, especially the Serbs. To them we were spies always relaying info, not to the UN but to the Bosnians. Not likely! Our radio communications system was the shits—no range and very unreliable. As for the Bosnians, we gave our information up the UN chain of command—what they did with it, we could not care less. The Goražde team was glad to hear that we had made it and dispatched a car to guide us into their team site.

While we waited at the checkpoint, I couldn't help but notice again how shabby and beat everyone looked. They looked at us with pleading eyes. The besieged people of Goražde had so little contact with the outside world that when someone did come, they were overwhelmed by the need to tell their story and ask for help. They felt that no one cared, they were forsaken. I knew this was true.

Our escort arrived—a Norwegian, who was really glad to see us. He'd worked with a fellow in our team, and together they had a great gab in their mother tongue. He told us that his team leader was not in town, that he and another fellow had managed to make their way out for some R and R. We moved off at the request of the Bosnian checkpoint guards, who said, "You make too much of a target, go away, fuck off. . ." We understood, and left.

### INTO THE TOWN

My first images of Goražde are still prominent in my dreams. I should say, in my nightmares. With the low, grey clouds and the dirt and soot coming from thousands of wood fires, the town could have been straight out of a Dickens novel. As we moved into town, all eyes turned and looked at us. These looks were not like the ambivalent glances of the Sarajevo locals. You could see and sense the anger and disgust with the UN. Goražde had been pummeled; nothing had escaped destruction. These were abandoned people, pawns in some gigantic chess game, and they knew it. Almost on cue, their shoulders would droop, their heads would bow as if to say, "We are defeated."

Everyone in Goražde was worried about the coming winter and the lack of wood for cooking and heating. The town had not had gas in years, so everyone was burning wood, when they could get it. The lower reaches of the hills around the city were bare. I was told that at night the men would sneak out under the cover of darkness to harvest firewood. The limit of their cutting and their willingness to risk their lives was evident in the tree line. Where once a thick forest had stood, there was nothing below the tree line. The sharp contrast between the tree line and the barren clearcut marked the "no go" line of risk taking. What made it so disheartening was that the hills above the "no go" line were tree-covered—tons of fuel wood right there, but was it worth dying for?

Windows were covered with the familiar UNHCR plastic. Their glass had long ago been blasted out. Most houses and even the apartments had a single stovepipe sticking straight out of a window. I saw little smoke coming from these soot-blackened stove pipes. Everyone looked hungry and cold; only the lucky ones would have wood to burn and maybe food to eat. I felt very guilty, almost responsible for their misery because I wore the UN badge, because I came from a well-to-do country. It was I who should be bowing my head in shame.

We made our way to the centre of town; the UNMO team was

accommodated in what was once Goražde's main bank. Here, strangely, there was the clutter of woodpiles everywhere, and smoke hung low in the streets—not the sweet smell of burning dry wood but the acrid smoke of green wood. And another strange sight: a coffee bar across the street, crowded with men sipping Turkish coffee. *Nothing else to do, might as well sip coffee and talk.* This is a scene I saw often in the most desperate of places.

### MR. UNHCR

A very friendly English-speaking Bosnian soldier guarded the UNMO house. The UNMOS weren't sure why he was there: to guard them, or to report on their comings and goings? More than likely the latter; no one cared to protect the UN, because the UN of course protected no one. The team was in good spirits and keen to hear what was going on in the outside world. Their accommodations were comfortable but cold; they only heated the operations room and the kitchen. We were given a briefing on the local situation, which we already knew was desperate.

Then we ate soup and bread, made by one of the team members in the woodstove. The soup was thin but tasty and hot; the bread was fresh and heavy. We talked of who was still in the mission area (Bosnia) and who had been lucky enough to have gone home. Whenever the talk went to "So and so is finished and gone home," there was usually a silent pause—we all envied that person and wished it was us. After lunch we unloaded some supplies for the team and asked if a Canadian named Brian Sadler, who was working for the UNHCR, was in town. He was.

Brian was a retired air force navigator in his late forties who had landed a job with UNHCR. I can't remember when or where I first met him, but we bumped into each other from time to time. He had volunteered to work in Goražde as the UNHCR representative. No one else would take the job. Brian was a dynamo, a real doer. He was the type of person Goražde needed.

Word was sent to Brian that we were in town and had some items he needed as well as some mail for him. In no time he was at the UNMO house with a big shit-eating grin and bubbling with enthusiasm. After the initial introductions and handshakes, he was keen to show us the town and brief us on its prospects. As we walked he talked of the shortages, the despair and the grim outlook for the coming winter.

He knew everyone and they knew him, especially the children. Everywhere we went, we were surrounded by shy, half-starved kids. They were different from the Sarajevo kids, who were hustlers; here, there was no one to hustle. Wearing tattered, grubby clothes, they would stand at a distance and stare and grin. They all showed the signs of malnutrition, the gaunt hollow-eyed face and toothpick-like limbs. Yet Brian was enthusiastic: things were changing, albeit slowly. His warehouse and distribution centre were quite efficient, and when the convoys came there were more supplies getting through. He felt that peace was on the horizon.

Brian showed us the improvised water-powered generators on the river. Dozens of these ingenious craft were tethered in the river, which bisects the town. They were quite simple, made from the rear ends (differentials) and alternators of destroyed cars, of which there were many. Attached to where the wheels should be were two paddle wheels, and the drive shaft was connected to the alternator. This whole unit was attached to a makeshift raft tethered in the river. The current of the river would turn the paddle wheels, which rotated the alternator and produced electricity. From these contraptions, a spider web of wires ran up the riverbank to the houses and buildings along the shore. Unfortunately, the power supply was weak and could only be generated over short distances. So only the houses close to the river benefited from these ingenious yet simple water-powered generators.

Brian wanted us to visit a refugee centre in an old school. It was a four-storey apartment block set in a sports field, and it looked grim. I had now seen enough of these people to realize that their situation was the shits, so I was reluctant to go to the centre. I felt we were acting like tourists and should respect whatever dignity they had left. Regardless of my feelings, I felt I had to bear witness to what was going on in Goražde. I did not want to back up my arguments about how the world fucked up with the words, "I heard such and such." No, I wanted to say: "I saw this!"

When we arrived at the refugee centre, the stairwell was dark, wet and icy. In places it reeked of urine and human waste. It was colder inside than out. Some kids scurried about, fewer than I had expected. Brian told us that most were in school, and sure enough, the UNMOS had set up a couple of classrooms and were teaching these kids. It was more like a multi-age daycare, designed to give the moms some space and time to prepare their meagre rations. There were a few old books but no paper, some pencils and not much else. However, the kids smiled and sang us a rousing song, clapping and singing their lungs out.

We visited a few families that Brian was concerned about. In one room we saw around twenty people. I have no idea how many families this constituted, but it was crowded. The floor was covered with rugs. In the corner, with its stove pipe sticking out the plastic-covered window, was a tin woodstove. These homemade rigs devoured wood at a furious pace but at least provided a cooking surface and some heat. The ceilings in these rooms were at least twelve feet high. That's where all the heat was, yet there was no choice for these people but to live on rugs on the floor—any furniture that was made of wood had been burnt long ago. One of the women was pregnant, and Brian was worried because she was not well. We noted that she might require evacuation, which we could help arrange on our end in Sarajevo.

It was a sad place, a ghetto reminiscent of Warsaw during World War II. I guess some people in the surrounding hills had learned a lot from the handiwork of the Nazis. We met a few more people and tried to give them some hope. "Peace is coming," we said. All they did was smile weakly and nod. They had heard it all before. We made our way down the stairway, trying not to slip on the ice. The light of day and the fresh cold air were a relief—physically and mentally.

We had a long drive ahead of us and plenty of assholes to deal with, so we bade Brian and the UNMOS goodbye. Rustem said, "It's ending; keep heart. It will be over soon." UNMOS—forever the optimists. We mounted up and made our way out of town, back to a better life in Sarajevo.

Left to right: Larry, me in uniform, Marie and Neddy at Marie's first communion, Pointe St. Charles, Montreal, 1967.

Janice and me on our wedding day, Verdun United Church, Montreal, 1972.

Dad and Mom visiting us for
Christmas in Winnipeg, 1987.

Erin and Ben pose with me before I leave
for my second tour of Cyprus, 1986.

*facing, top:* The UN-controlled checkpoint in the Sarajevo suburb of Dobrinja, 1995.

*facing, bottom:* "Welcome to Sarajevo": the Sarajevan suburb of Stup, 1995.

*above:* The UNMO command post in Sarajevo, 1995. Left to right: Rustem Zarbeeve (Russia), João Lionel (Brazil), me and Ronnie Denyft (Belgium).

*above:* Mama roasting coffee beans in her kitchen, with her wood-burning stove behind her.

*facing, top:* I'm standing (right) with Yassir Adwan (left) and Sharif Riad (centre), who unwittingly drove our vehicle down Sniper Alley. This picture was taken before our wild ride, I think, because my hands aren't around Sharif's throat.

*facing, bottom:* The remains of a Serbian soldier, Sanica Valley, 1996. *photo: Glenn Sylvester*

*above:* Read and heed: Sarajevo, 1996.

*facing, top:* Einar, me and Miro toasting Mama, who had prepared a feast from food we had scrounged on a trip to Pale. *photo: Goran Mehmebegovic*

*facing, bottom:* The aftermath of the rear tire falling off our UNMO vehicle as we raced down the backside of Mount Igman: *some* of us are laughing.

*facing, top:* Taking a break on Mount Igman before making a dash on the exposed portion of the only route into Sarajevo, August 1995.

*facing, bottom:* The Kovaci graveyard in Sarajevo, 1995.

*this page, top:* Dinner around the kitchen table. Left to right: Goran, Madame Turkiyana, me, Zoran, a neighbour, Mama and Madame Chemsa, 1995. The only available light was provided by the camera flash. *photo: Einar Johnson*

*this page, bottom:* Hungry kids looking for handouts on the Goražde bridge. Few trees remain on the hills in the background; they have been cut for firewood.

*facing, left:* A 1996 ambush in Bosnia's Sanica Valley destroyed this Serbian vehicle and killed its three passengers, who were trying to escape. A spine and pelvis are in the foreground. *photo: Glenn Sylvester*

*facing, right:* Dad and I check out the hardware at the CFB Gagetown open house, 1998: "Think we should buy this to snowplough the driveway?"

*above:* Two of the good men of 2 RCR during the Bosnian SFOR Mission, 1999: Major Bill Pond, OC, G Company (left), and Bob Girouard, CSM, G Company. Bob was killed by a suicide bomber in Afghanistan in 2006.

# 10 | Let the Bombing Begin

W̲E HAD been given the choice of either vacating our current accommodations and moving together into one house or moving into a UN bunker for safety: the long-awaited NATO air strikes were about to be launched against the Serbs. The talking was over, and the ultimatums had come and gone; the strikes that should have happened at the onset of the war were finally going to happen.

Air strikes had been used before in an attempt to stop the Serbs. They had proved to be too little, too late. One of the recent Serb tactics was to take UN personnel hostage if air strikes were threatened and to detain the personnel in facilities that the planes were likely to bomb. This tactic worked, and the strikes were as feeble as the world opinion on the Bosnian situation. However, we felt it would be different this time.

There had been a lot of scrambling to ensure that the UN was correct in its estimate of the origin of the 120 mm mortar bomb that started it all. UNMO reports (all of them) said "origin unknown." However, NATO said it was the Serbs, and I agree with them. That was why we were sitting here waiting to get shelled, because the Serbs had been blamed and were getting their asses whacked real hard. Even if the Serb retaliation was symbolic, it was really rough on the nerves to just sit and wait. Supposedly there were talks going on as to what the UN wanted, which was the removal of all heavy weapons within twenty kilometres of Sarajevo. Strangely, the Bosnians had already complied, and the Bosnian Muslim army had put its heavy weapons into lockup until further notice. I was hoping for some kind of ceasefire.

The UN had wisely moved all its personnel out of the Serb-controlled areas, thereby negating the Serbs' ability to take hostages. The other factor was that world opinion, especially American, had been galvanized by the scene of the Market II shelling incident in downtown Sarajevo. There, thirty-seven people had died and scores were injured by one mortar bomb. This tragic event seemed to be the trigger for action after so many years of inaction. Diplomatic efforts ebbed and flowed, ultimatums were issued and deadlines were at hand. The UN wanted all Serb heavy weapons moved out of range of the city. The Serbs, with their pig-headed "nobody pushes us around" attitude, basically said "Piss off" to the negotiators and decided to call their bluff and see if the world had the balls to take them on. In their standoff the negotiators blinked, so the largest NATO response to a crisis since its founding was put into motion.

The UN, in its infinite wisdom, wanted all UN personnel inside one compound. This, to us UNMOs, did not make sense because it meant that if the Serbs wished to retaliate, they would have to target only one location. We also enjoyed our independence and our ability to blend in with the locals, making us a very small, insignificant target in the city. So we struck a deal with our UN bosses that we would all move under one roof at our house in the old city until the air strikes were over.

I did not feel right about leaving Mama and Goran. I felt as if I were deserting them. I knew they would be safe, and I would have been, too. But Ronnie, our deputy team leader, insisted that he was responsible to account for our whereabouts at all times and that it would be easier if we were all under one roof. As I left, I told Mama that I would return as soon as I could. I felt she was more concerned about my safety than her own.

It was amazing how many UN personnel were aware of the impending air strikes and took advantage of that knowledge to go on leave or have business that took them out of the city. No one really made any attempt to disguise his or her exit. Either I was really stupid or I had too much pride to run. My biggest gripe was that I did not want to move, because I enjoyed living with Mama and her boys.

## HELL RAINS DOWN

On August 30, at 0200, NATO struck and hell rained down on the Serbs, finally. The multinational brigade on Mount Igman began the air strikes and artillery fire.

We were used to the sound and impact of artillery and mortar shells, weighing anywhere from thirty to one hundred pounds. But we were not ready for the sound of fighter-bombers and thousand-pound bombs. In addition to carrying out the air strikes, the NATO Rapid Reaction Force had been cooling its heels on the backside of Mount Igman, waiting for the order to engage non-compliant Serb units, especially the artillery units. The plan and the firepower impressed the shit out of us. We hoped it would have the same effect on the Serbs.

The next day we moved out of our apartments and into a house in the old town. I ended up at our UNMO house, where I was given a sofa in the parlour. This house had once been lived in by a university professor. He had rented it to us for a reasonable price while he lived elsewhere with his daughter. The house was large, and in its day it had been quite comfortable. It was located on a small side street in the old part of town. The surrounding area showed the scars of the war: the car parked in front of the house had a bullet hole through the windshield on the side where the driver had been sitting. Judging by the amount of dried blood on the seat, he had died there too.

Life inside the UNMO house was relatively peaceful, mainly because four of our group were out of the city on leave or wandering about the countryside on liaison visits. Miro was staying elsewhere and Jean lived with a family across the yard from us, which left me, Rustem and Palo in the house. Conveniently, our team leader and his right-hand man were out of the city.

Everyone was on State Red—all UN personnel had to remain in their bunkers. Except for the UNMOs: we were on duty, in our flimsy container—only two of us, on minimum manning. We expected the

Serbs to retaliate by shelling a UN position. It was crappy to sit here unprotected, waiting for something to happen before we could run to shelter. We did not have a bunker with proper communication capability, so we remained in our container with nothing between us and the big bad world. Everyone else was snug inside a bunker, except for the commander and some of his personal staff.

I sat at the radios monitoring the UNMO reports, giving info to the UN commander's crew. I was scared—really scared—that I would die. What made it really difficult was that I was alone most of the time, with no one to talk to, just me and my worm of fear that slowly ate away at my nerves. *I don't want to die in this town. Hurry, December, so I can get out of here!* I had been in more life-threatening situations, but I felt that in those I had more control—I could drive, run, walk away from the danger or talk my way out of the situation. But during these air strikes I had no control. If the Serbs wanted to shell the compound, there was no one to stop them.

I was quite skilled with the team's laptop computer and the program we used to send our daily situation reports, and during my twelve-hour shifts I tried to relax at the laptop by playing endless games of solitaire. However, with the other computer I was still, as one of my friends called me, a Luddite. One day, as I sat alone in my flak vest, poking away at the keys in hopes of finding the games icon, lo and behold I happened on a document that fed our suspicions about the regional senior military observer (RSMO). I was intrigued but not shocked; I and my teammates often discussed the many less-than-covert visits he paid to the Pakistani embassy and his extended trips away on liaison visits. The consensus was that his position as RSMO in Sarajevo was a well-orchestrated move by the UN to have a senior officer at the UNPROFOR HQ who came from an Islamic country. The documents were a detailed log of his visits to and discussions with the Pakistani ambassador in Sarajevo.

Along with the many pages of notes was a series of detailed assessments on the "Islamic" aspect of the Bosnian government and army. The focus of the assessments was on rebuilding Bosnia when the war ended, with a strong slant on the place of religion in the government and the army. As I read the report, I realized there were forces at play in the Balkans under the guise of the UN that were a lot more intricate and subtle than any of us had imagined. It all made for a good read, and my twelve-hour shift passed quickly. The report was the final piece of the puzzle that I and my mates had been trying to piece together since before the NATO air strikes. We wondered how it came to be that the RSMO, Zilule and Yassir all ended up on leave and out of the city prior to and during the air strikes. Did they have inside knowledge from the Pakistani diplomatic world that the air strikes were coming? Did they take advantage of this knowledge and conveniently get out of town—leaving a Canadian, two Belgians, a Portuguese, a Czech and a Russian to man the team site during the largest NATO air strike to occur since the organization's founding?

### PAYBACK TIME

NATO spared no expense in convincing the Serbs that it was time to comply. I also felt that NATO was doing its best to make amends for the times when it should have gotten involved but didn't. I guess better late than never. Most of the raids took place at night, but there were some precision strikes during the day. That did not matter to us, because we felt good every time we heard an impact—it was payback time.

The mood of the city was upbeat. I was downtown one day and noticed more people out and about, enjoying the sense of security that the NATO planes seemed to offer. Everyone knew this was what should have been done years ago. Back in 1992–93, "Big Brother" USA was not interested; George Bush was fighting for a second term in office and wanted no part in the Bosnia conflict. When he lost the election and Bill Clinton took the presidential reins, a policy of looking inward and dealing with U.S. domestic problems took hold. So Bosnia languished in the hands of madmen because Big Brother felt that region was not a priority. A quarter of a million people would die before the collective consciousness of the world turned towards Bosnia.

One sunny day the sounds of heavy bombing came from the direction of Lukavica barracks, a large Serb strongpoint near the airport.

I made my way to the attic room, where the skylight looked out over the rooftops towards Lukavica. The explosions were deafening and black clouds rose over the area. In the sky above I counted six NATO aircraft circling, patiently waiting their turn to dump their destructive loads. It felt great knowing that the Serbs were on the receiving end as I watched an aircraft peel off and dive and release its bombs. I yelled, "Take that, you fucking bastards," not giving a thought as to who would suffer. I felt like a kid watching the schoolyard bully finally getting his due. Through my mind there flashed a kaleidoscope of faces, the faces of the innocent dead and wounded people I had dealt with over the past four months.

Being always in the city and living with the constant threat from the Serbs, I had lost most of my objectivity and impartiality. It was for me a simple fact that regardless of the propaganda, the Serbs were the oppressors and in almost all cases the Bosnians (Muslims) were the victims. So it felt good to watch the payback. I remember taking some pleasure from the rainy nights, when I imagined the Serbs in their trenches, wet and miserable. There was nothing intellectual about my views; it was good vs. evil, victim and victimizer. Fuck the politics of it all.

A few weeks later I had a chance to survey the bomb damage close-up. We were in Lukavica barracks for a liaison visit. The strikes had been precise and very effective. The whole landscape had changed; so had the attitude of the liaison officers. The bullish attitude was gone; they knew things were changing as we spoke. Everyone wanted to be helpful, reasonable and especially co-operative. Meetings that were once platforms for rhetoric and chest thumping were now following an agenda, and real decisions were being made. It was quite interesting, and it caught us all off guard. Could peace be somewhere on the horizon?

### A WALK WITH GORAN

Goran had been on leave for several days, waiting to be demobilized. Sarajevo was peaceful, free from shelling and sniping for a couple of weeks now. The Dayton talks were on and everyone felt that peace must come from this initiative: the ceasefire around the city was holding. There had been other ceasefires, about thirty-five in the past three years. Some had lasted hours, others weeks, but all had led to nothing but renewed war. We all hoped that the war was at an end.

It was with this feeling of confidence that Goran and I took to the streets for a walk through places that were once too dangerous to visit. We were simply looking for a coffee shop and a stroll in the streets. Goran was proud of his city, and he wanted to show me around and tell me of its lost beauty.

The day was cool but the sun felt warm. The streets were busy, and people moved with purpose and with a spring in their step, as if ready to sprint at the sound of an explosion or the crack of the sniper's bullet. *Let's make the best of the situation* seemed to be a Sarajevo trait. *You never know when you'll be scurrying like a rat into its hole.*

Goran and I strolled around with the attitude that it was over, that we wouldn't ever run again. We made our way down the hill from the apartment along the maze of paths made by people during the war. The paths avoided open spaces, which were vulnerable to sniper fire. We went by the small garden plots nestled between the apartments, long since harvested, hopefully for the last time. These small patches of food made the difference between life and death for a lot of people.

We came to a park on Tito Boulevard. In its day the boulevard had been a bustling street that ran through the centre of the downtown. The park had some of the oldest trees in the city, as well as several very old Muslim graves from the Ottoman Turk period. Kids were out buzzing around, playing football or just enjoying their freedom. Their mothers were slow to trust the ceasefire and watched the kids like hawks. At the old Muslim graveyard in the park the trees were stripped and splintered but the grass was lush and green, probably from the dozens of fresh graves. The old grave markers were tilted and half-buried from neglect over the years, but the new, neat rows marked the fresh graves of young men who had died defending their country. There were not many, because the graveyard had ceased to be used as one many years ago. These new graves had been symbolically placed in a high-traffic area for all to see. In Sarajevo you did not need another fresh grave of a young person to remind you of sacrifice; you were surrounded by deprivation and death.

What always struck me about the military graves was the youth of those who were buried there, especially since I had a son and daughter who were the same age as these unfortunate souls. Goran always made a point of stopping to read their names. He'd point and draw my attention to this one and then that one. I would acknowledge this with a nod, we'd linger for a few moments and then move off slowly; it was as if he did not want to leave them alone. It was difficult for Goran; here a deep sadness showed in his eyes and in the way his shoulders sagged.

Our sombre mood was lifted by the sight of people bustling about. Goran wanted to show me where his part in the war had begun. He said it was his first action, the place where, by chance, he was drawn into three years of war. We walked down the street beside the presidency building to the small park behind it. On the way, Goran met a friend, which was not unusual—it seemed that Goran knew everyone. They were happy to see each other still alive. A twenty-minute conversation ensued, which I guessed was a brief recap of what each had been doing over the past year or two. It was accompanied by lots of laughter, broken by moments of silence when someone who had not made it was mentioned. It was a treat to watch these veterans talk to each other in a way that only men who have faced death can.

We moved off past city hall, to stand in the doorway of the old Press Club, which had been redeveloped prior to the '84 Olympics and had had a vibrant Western feel. It was a place for the young and trendy people to hang out and try to look and act like Americans.

It was much quieter now. A lot of fighting had taken place in this tiny area. The buildings and roads were pockmarked with the impacts of artillery, mortar and small-arms fire. There was no glass in the windows, the roofs were full of holes and the streets held the debris of war. The area was so open and vulnerable that it had eventually become a no man's land. Now, out of habit, people picked up their pace when they entered the killing zone. They still did not trust the peacefulness of the day.

Goran leaned against the wall and lit a cigarette. For several moments, he stood as if in a trance, looking at the small park. It lay nestled between the approaches to the bridges on what was the Bosnian side of the river. I call the area a park, but it was a small modern square, devoid of trees and greenery. The space was multi-level, made up of concrete steps, benches and planters. The centre of the square was lower than the surrounding ground. It was here, early in the war, in 1992, that a small group of Bosnian defenders prevented Serbian tanks from penetrating into the centre of the city to wreak havoc. Goran and I did not cross the street to the square but stayed in the shade of the doorway. He was lost in his memories of that day. Then he spoke: "Fred, in war there is a lot that happens that is pure luck. We were very lucky here on that summer day in '92."

He told me how on that day he had been drawn to the square by the sound of gunfire. Like all Bosnians early in the war, especially those in Sarajevo, he was lightly armed. The city dwellers normally had little or no use for weapons: they had the police and their army to protect them! Goran had his father's World War II 9 mm pistol. Yet with that pistol, he was automatically a member of one of the "People's Militias" set up to protect the city. So there he was, rushing to the sound of a struggle with his pistol and a handful of bullets.

He approached the area cautiously, hugging the walls of the presidency building, always mindful of the snipers, who had begun their deadly harvest of victims. Goran told me that he was terrified but felt he had to be there. Peeking around the corner, he saw several civilians crouched behind the concrete planters and benches. They called him forward, motioning for him to stay low and yelling "*Brzo, brzo—fast, fast.*" It was very hot. They were trapped under a broiling sun, with no shade or water, on what would become a very long day.

They knew the Serbs were on the other side of the river. The shots they had heard were coming from the other side of the bridge. The Bosnians were armed with one shotgun, Goran's pistol and a rocket-propelled grenade (RPG) launcher with three anti-tank rockets. Terrified, they could hear the roar of diesel engines and the squeaking and clanking of metal tracks. Tanks. The noise of tanks strikes fear into the hearts of all defenders, regardless of how well armed they are. But these fellows could not be considered armed at all. At this close range the shock effect of the sound of the approaching tanks had an unnerving effect. The fight, flight or freeze response became a personal battle. No one moved. They couldn't. Lying there, their mouths dry from the heat and fear, they wanted to run, but they couldn't risk being seen. They were pinned down.

*If we run, we die. If we stay, we die. Maybe they'll pass us by*, were Goran's thoughts. The tanks approached the bridge and turned onto it. Stupidly, the tankers had no infantry to support them. I guess they figured that no one would take them on. Goran said the tanks had no idea that he and his tiny band of defenders were cowering in the square.

The lead tank reached their side of the bridge; it was time for the defenders to do something. As Goran paused in the telling of his story, his eyes focused on the bridge as if he had been drawn back in time. He spoke as if he were talking to himself, pointing and gesturing to where he and his friends had been. The tanks were close, maybe fifty metres away, and moved cautiously, although still unaware of this small band. The fellow with the RPG crept forward to the edge of the perimeter wall and peered around the corner. I could sense Goran's fear and excitement as he pointed to the position. The man took aim, and *bang*! the anti-tank grenade took off. The fellow had no idea where to aim, he just fired at the tank.

Luck, as Goran put it, was with them. The grenade missed the tank, overshot the back of it. But it struck the external auxiliary fuel tanks, which the tankers had foolishly left on the tank. *Boom!* Up they went, spewing flames and fuel all over the place—it was very dramatic and impressive, to defender and attacker alike.

The lead tank ground to a halt, the crew bailed out and ran for the cover of the rear tank. Goran and his friends let off a few more shots from their meagre weapons. It was a convincing show. Here was a flaming Serbian tank blocking the bridge and bullets flying at the retreating troops.

Luck and bluff worked their magic. The Serbs withdrew, feeling there must have been a formidable force defending the bridge. A force that must have had an anti-tank capability, as demonstrated by the destruction of one of their tanks. The tank hissed, popped and smoked. Goran said that he and his friends sat there in awe of what had just happened. A few minutes before, they were sure they were going to die right there in the square. Then one lucky shot changed it all. Goran stayed there until dark; then he and his fellow heroes crept off to find water and food and to revel in their good luck.

We moved across the street and sat where Goran and his friends had cowered. I could scarcely imagine how they must have felt as I looked across the street to where the tank had been. Goran was quiet, lost in the reverie of the scene of his first battle in a war that would last another three years. Then he turned, and we walked in silence to Tito Boulevard, where Goran put his arm around my shoulder. With a big smile, he said, "Fred, coffee?" It was good to be alive.

## A CASUALTY OF WAR

The good nature that made Goran such a popular fellow in Sarajevo was a factor in the great number of visitors to the flat at 8 Rizaha Stetica. Some would visit for minutes, others for hours. Most were soldiers who had come to car pool to the trenches they occupied around the city. Goran, always the gentleman and gracious host, would introduce me as his "friend from Canada." Quite the way to fight a war—live at home, then go to work and do your shift in the trenches. It made sense: no need for barracks, and it spread the troops all over the city.

It was during one of these visits that I met a veteran and a casualty of the war. His wounds were not of the body but of the mind. He had seen and done enough, and finally cracked. Goran later told me, "Fred, this is a very brave man, very brave." He was short and thin, his face looked tired and strained. His eyes told it all. He'd blink over and over again, and his eyes would dart about the room, never staying on one thing for more than a few seconds. He held a cigarette between his nicotine-stained thumb and forefinger. When he drew on it, he sucked hard and long. He needed his smoke. His name, oddly, was Riley (I never found out the origin of his Irish name), and he had been an architect before the war. Like so many others, and not by his own choice, he had either been caught up in the war or captured by it.

Our introductions were formal, as was Goran's habit. I shook Riley's bony hand and tried to look him in the eyes. His grasp was so weak that I could feel his bones were void of muscle. Our eyes met and I could sense anger and fear, yet I could also see that this was not the same man I would have met three years ago. It was as if he were ashamed of what the war had done to him.

I could tell that Goran had a high regard for Riley, because his visit was conducted in the parlour and not in the kitchen. I sensed that this regard was not for what the man had done prior to the war. I doubt they would have moved in the same circles then. His respect seemed to come from Riley's war deeds and the friendship that only brother warriors can express.

We sat in the comfort of the parlour on a voluminous sofa and in an atmosphere of closeness that encouraged talking. They smoked; it was the same nervous chain smoking that I had witnessed before in a totally different place: the veterans' hospital in Ste. Anne de Bellevue in Montreal, where my father-in-law had spent the last two years of his life. There, at any given time, you could find a hundred or more vets in the lobby smoking area. They smoked with an intensity that was hard to believe. Never having been a smoker, I figured it calmed their nerves. Whatever their reasons, it identified them as men who had seen too much and suffered things that were lost in the deepest reaches of their failing memories. Janice once told me that when she was a kid she would hear her father calling out in his war-ravaged dreams, "Give me a fag, mate." He was wounded twice during World War II and harboured its demons until he went to his grave.

I could picture Goran and Riley huddled in a trench, cupping a cigarette between them. Speaking in whispers of their hopes and dreams of when the war would end. Now they sat in the warmth of the well-lit parlour, leaning forward, elbows on their knees, cigarettes dangling between their nicotine-stained fingers, speaking in low tones. I watched Riley's hands. They trembled slightly, and I could see his neck and ear twitch on the right side of his face. His eyes were never still, as if he were afraid he would miss some unseen danger. He reminded me of a junkie trying to make a buy on the street. The sad thing was, Riley had overdosed on the horrors of war.

Out of the blue, Riley began speaking to me. He caught me staring at him, and in a mixture of Bosnian, English, German, Italian and French, he told me how the war had fucked him. Riley told me of his past, his success as an architect and of the buildings he had designed in Sarajevo. He had been *someone*, and I could tell that this had been very important to him.

And he told me that a lot of his friends were gone. Goran nodded in agreement, but did not add to the conversation. I think he felt that Riley's talking to me was therapy for both of them. Since the end of the war, Riley had spent most of his days and some nights at the Kosevo hospital psychiatric ward. The mood-altering drugs that would control his fears, depression and nightmares were in short supply. Riley felt safe there, not ashamed when he woke up screaming and sobbing; he would be surrounded by people suffering their own horrors. The drugs might be few and far between, but the Drina cigarettes were plentiful and sometimes alcohol helped to deaden the dreams and numb the consciousness.

Riley told me the war was so ironic at times. The ward at the Kosevo hospital, where the casualties of the mind went, was once run by Dr. Radovan Karadzic. He was now leader of the Bosnian Serbs who surrounded the city, the architect of the suffering being dumped on the Bosnians. Karadzic's gunners knew the hospital and targeted it with deadly accuracy throughout the war. Was this the payback for his dismissal from the hospital, resulting from a pre-war controversy about his credentials as a psychiatrist?

Riley held me in his distant gaze. I was compelled to listen. I said nothing; there was no need.

I could retell his stories of the horrors of his war. They were so clear and lucid, exactly what you'd expect to hear from a frontline soldier. They were of misery, fear and sorrow. Yet when I tried to put the words on paper, it didn't seem right, it felt all wrong. Imagine your worst fears, losing your child in a horrific way, having your friend's brain's splattered over you as you drink coffee in what you thought was relative safety. Think of what it would be like to have no control over your fate, to live in constant fear of the unseen, of an unknown killer lurking everywhere. No restful sleep, no quiet place for the mind to wander, no escape. This was Riley's life. I sat and listened to his ramblings and pieced together his war and its effect. There were long pauses when he would take a deep draw on his cigarette, almost smoking it in one breath. His eyes would grow still as if they were looking into his mind, searching for something, some thread of reason to tie it all together. When Riley spoke, Goran sat in silent agreement. Just a slight movement of the head and shoulders, as if nodding to say "Yes, it was like that."

Then Riley's war flashback ended abruptly, and he switched to talking about his painting. It was as if he had come out of a trance. "I paint for the peace it gives my mind," he said, catching me off guard with his change of subject. Goran had told me that Riley was a good artist and that he quelled the demons with his paintbrush. There were a couple of his works in Goran's flat, dark and sinister but with a beauty of their own. I could see that in each painting there was always a small point of light or a small bright spot. Maybe it was an indication that his spirit had not been broken, that there was light somewhere in the future—because now there was a future.

We talked about Canada and the peace Canadians enjoy and take for granted, about family and the importance of a life well lived. Out came the photos of Janice, Ben and Erin, of me as a proud husband and father. "Would you like me to paint them?" Riley asked. He offered to sketch Erin and Ben. I politely refused, but realized I was wrong as soon as the words left my mouth. I was offending both him and Goran, who shot me a sideways glance. I quickly recovered. "Yes, I'd be delighted. You pick the photo; I'd be honoured to have your work." I had not realized that the offer was his "thank you" for listening to him. I could see it in his eyes, which had now stopped their darting and seemed relaxed.

The mood changed. We relaxed and laughed at some little thing; I think we laughed just because it felt good. We drank brandy and washed it down with *filjans* of strong coffee supplied by Mama, who had joined us now that the serious talk was over. The evening was good for all of us, acting like a group session or an AA meeting. We vented the pressures of our minds and souls.

Riley's beautiful pastel sketches of Ben and Erin now hang in my living room. Whenever I look at them, I think of Riley and wonder how he is doing. There are so many wounds a soldier carries—the worst are the ones you can't see. I am forever the optimist and hope his demons are at rest, or at least at bay.

## 11 | Flight Out

IN SEPTEMBER 1995, American diplomat Richard Holbrooke and his team were in Sarajevo carrying on shuttle diplomacy between Zagreb (Croats), Belgrade (Serbs)
and Sarajevo (Bosnians). In late August he had lost three members of
his negotiation team in a vehicle accident while coming into Sarajevo
over Mount Igman. As a result he was adamant that he would not
travel over Igman. It was too dangerous and time consuming. So he
demanded of Slobodan Milosevic, the Serbian president, that the airport be reopened to facilitate travel to and from various talks.

On September 17 Miro and I were at the newly opened Sarajevo
airport, trying to bum a ride out on one of the departing planes. The
day before we had tried to get out via Kiseljak on a helicopter bound
for Split, then on to Zagreb and a couple of days of freedom. The
plan had been doomed from the beginning. However, at that time
we didn't know that the Sarajevo airport was supposed to be opened
the following day, at Holbrooke's insistence. We could have kissed
Holbrooke's ass, because the airport was indeed reopened, and Miro
and I scrounged a seat on the plane through our buddy Einar. He
had connections in the Norwegian movement control section. These
guys called themselves "Maybe Airlines"—maybe the plane will come,
maybe it won't. But our contact promised there would be a plane. We
made our way through security; imagine, security at the Sarajevo airport! A couple of burly Danes checked our papers and ensured that
we each had a helmet and armoured vest to wear on the plane.

The bowels of the old airport had been looted; all that was left was concrete walls and some bare light bulbs. The French ran the airport, and I must admit that with what they had they did it well. Because the roof leaked terribly, the waiting room was a tent in a corner of the second floor. Unlike North America airport lounges, there were no chairs, no snack counter, no magazine store—but you could smoke until you exploded.

Our fellow travellers were few; the word had not gotten out that the airport was now open, so Miro and I were guaranteed a seat *if* the plane came in. There were a few French soldiers (all young and anxious to get out of Sarajevo) a couple of journalists (usually with questionable credentials that could be easily purchased in Zagreb) and some Danish, Russian and Egyptian soldiers. In all, there were about twenty of us.

*So where is the fucking plane? Has it been held up in Zagreb or Split? Did it break down or get shot down? Come on, where's the sound of that big bird?* Then a faint roar, and in came an Ilyushin, a huge Russian cargo plane contracted by the UN to haul whoever, wherever. We couldn't see it because we were locked up in the waiting room, but we could hear its deafening roar as it tried to come to a stop on the short Sarajevo runway.

Eventually we were summoned to the plane. The plywood door opened, and a French soldier with full body armour gestured to us to follow him. Out the door and down some metal stairs, in single file, we lined up behind a sandbagged wall. This would be a very quick turnaround. We watched the well-choreographed French air-movement guys unload six huge pallets from the cavernous belly of the plane in about three minutes. We got the thumbs-up and hustled our asses out onto the runway. I felt quite exposed because I knew that somewhere a Serb or Bosnian soldier had his sights on us. *Up the ramp and into the beast, sit down, seat belts on, if you want.* I took my armoured vest off and sat on it to protect my ass from ground fire.

So we were on the first UN plane to land here in months. We were ready, engines running, ramp up. *Let's GO!* Nothing. Waiting on the runway, exposed to the world in this huge white airplane that may as well have had "Shoot me" written all over it. *Christ, let's go!* Our Russian crew chief/loadmaster wouldn't tell us why the wait. He just shrugged and held ten fingers to tell us how many more minutes. This was not good. We didn't trust the Serbs or the Bosnians not to pop a few bullets into the plane to see what it would do. We were definitely not comfortable.

Miro pointed to the front of the aircraft, where a small passenger door opened. *Who's coming?* It must have been someone they didn't want the Serbs to see, because the plane was oriented so that the small door faced the Bosnian side of the airport.

*It must be someone important.* There was some movement through the door; some fellows in overcoats, suits and dark glasses were obviously providing security for someone. We got the critical eye. *No threat here.* A nod through the doorway, and our special guests arrived: Alija Izetbegovic and Mohammed Sacirbey, the president and foreign minister of Bosnia-Herzegovina. Bumming a ride out of Sarajevo.

I found out later, from Holbrooke's book *To End a War*, that the president of Bosnia and his staff were on their way to Zagreb to meet with the Croatian president Franjo Tudjman to discuss a ceasefire in and around Sarajevo. But at the time all the other passengers just looked at each other, sharing the same thought: *Now we'll get shot down for sure.*

The door closed, and within seconds we were taxiing down the runway, turning around and roaring back down it with the engines yelling, *Shoot me down if you don't want this war to end!* Every fibre of my body was willing the airplane to climb and put distance between me and the Serb gunners. The Ilyushin is a big and heavy plane, and very slow to climb. You could feel it lumbering through the air, taking its good old time. But fortunately, either the Serbs didn't notice the special passenger or they too wanted the war to end. I like to think the latter is more accurate.

So there we were, cruising over Bosnia with Alija and Mo (as the locals called them) on the plane. I had a chance to look at the seventy-plus-year-old president of Bosnia. He looked his years, and more. He was exhausted and was nodding off. To his followers, he was the symbol of the Bosnian resolve to have a place of their own, a country. In my mind, I wished him all the best; however, Miro elbowed me and said, "I will go and talk with him and tell him he is a (add Czech accent) fucking bastard!"

"Hold on, Miro!" I said. "That wouldn't be a good move. Keep your seat belt on and relax!"

"No!" Miro said, "He's one of the problems. Pig-fucking old bastard." (Probably wanted to say, "Pig-headed fucking old bastard.")

"Miro, relax, it will do you no good." I also thought that the young guys with the dark glasses and overcoats might have something to say about Miro's comments, something like "Bang, bang, you're dead!"

So Miro settled into his seat and glared at the president—who slept all the way to Zagreb, blissfully ignorant of the Czech dissenter in his midst. Who knows? I may have prevented an international incident and saved the president's life—or, more likely, Miro's!

Suffice to say, the whole flight (two hours), including the Sarajevo take-off, was a non-event. We landed in Zagreb safe and sound. The president and his staff were whisked away in a Mercedes limo, while Miro and I looked for his buddy with the little rear-engine Skoda, which would take us to Miro's place outside of Prague for a few days of R and R. Miro, true to his fiery nature, got the last dig in: he gave the president's car the finger as it raced off the airfield.

In his book, Holbrooke said that Izetbegovic was three hours late for the meeting and that President Tudjman was quite pissed off about the delay. So where did he think the president was flying in from, Disneyland?

### A SNOWY MORNING

I awoke early that morning in December 1995, my mind still foggy from a heavy sleep. My room was cold. It was always difficult to leave the warm cocoon of my sleeping bag. I slept naked, so the insulating value of the sleeping bag was not lost to T-shirt and underwear. But I paid dearly once I was out of the bag, dancing around the room, trying to pull on my underwear, socks and uniform. My dance over, I paused, still shivering, to look outside and survey the day's weather. Snow, wet and heavy, had piled up on everything; there was not a breath of wind to disturb it. Every branch of the tree outside my window had about six inches of snow neatly piled on it. It was so still and quiet; I could hear my own breathing and could imagine everyone else in Sarajevo in bed, avoiding the cold and snow. It was so peaceful!

Peed, brushed my teeth and quietly made my way to the kitchen. The little stove glowed with heat, the coffee simmered, Mama sat warming her hands and feet.

"Fred, good sleep?"

"*Dobro, dobro*—good, good," I replied.

"*Puno snijeg.*"

"Yes, lots of snow."

Being Canadian, I am expert in talking about the weather. Except that it was now in Bosnian. Mama found it quite amusing that I seemed so fixated on the weather. I learned a lot of my Bosnian while discussing the weather each morning with her. At least my first Bosnian words weren't swear words. (Goran taught me those later.) Mama poured me a *filjan* of steaming coffee and went on to tell me, with a mix of Bosnian, English, French, Italian and hand gestures, how today (hopefully) the plastic on the windows would be repaired and she would have glass windows again. Goran had found a "source" of glass, and finally it was possible to repair the windows destroyed by impacts and bullets. Mama was quite excited.

The morning ritual in the kitchen set the tone for what I hoped would be a quiet day. Once again it was comforting to sit there, sip my coffee and eat the day-old bread and gab with Mama and Goran about the weather and the hopes for the day to come. Our shyness and flimsy grasp of each other's language had disappeared, and our morning conversations had grown and developed a character of their own. We gravitated towards subjects we knew we could converse on. Each day brought a few more words or subjects that would move our knowledge of each other closer and closer.

During the fall our talks often turned to the Dayton peace talks and the faint hopes for a lasting peace. Sarajevo had been visited by countless emissaries of peace, but none of the ceasefires had lasted or come close to ending the war. These talks were different; there seemed to be a real will on the part of all concerned to end this awful war.

Time to go. I put on my boots, jacket, scarf and toque and left my helmet and armoured vest in my room. No need for it—there was a ceasefire and the peace talks were ongoing. *Must show the locals that we have faith in the ceasefire, right Fred?* It was eerily quiet outside. I made my way down the driveway, paused and stood very still and listened for some of the familiar and deadly sounds of the city. No booms, bangs or cracks from the weapons of war that usually terrorized the city. No cars, barking dogs or yelling. Just a dead silence, made greater by the thick blanket of new-fallen snow.

I made my way down to the street. No footprints of early risers in the snow. I stopped to survey the bomb damage on the buildings. There were deep scars in the walls, no glass in the windows; roofing tiles had been blown away by blasts from artillery and mortar shells. The only vehicle parked on the street was the Médecins Sans Frontières (MSF) vehicle, parked in front of the house where several of the doctors lived. The doctors and nurses of this organization are an amazing bunch; MSF is one of the few non-governmental organizations that actually helps people. Its vehicles, armoured and painted white, had large MSF letters on the side to ward off targeting by Serb gunners. Sort of a warning that "you may need us someday." The whiteness of the vehicle blended in with the snowy surroundings; maybe it would be a quiet day for them too.

The air was cool and fresh, as if the city had been cleansed of the smells of war. The blanket of wet snow dampened the usual smell of garbage from the pile at the end of the drive. The smoke and the smells of the cooking fires had yet to rise from the blackened chimneys that protruded from the windows of the houses. It seemed that everyone was snug in bed, hoping that someone else would get up and get the fire going.

I made my way along Rizaha Stetica Street, calf-deep in snow. I noticed that the names of a lot of streets in Sarajevo had changed.

One day the street name signs were blue, and then they were changed to green and looked new. I asked Goran what the change was all about. His answer should have amazed me, but I after a couple of months in Sarajevo not much did. He said that the city leaders had come up with the patriotic idea to rename all the streets to reflect the names of Bosnian heroes and other historical and cultural figures.

So here, in the midst of war and the epic struggle of a city and its people to survive, the municipal bozos came up with and implemented this harebrained idea. Risking life and limb, city workers were sent out to replace signs such as ours from whatever to Rizaha Stetica, the name of a painter who used to live on this street. Goran, with a grin on his face, said it would "boost morale." It was obvious that he too had a hard time believing such stupidity. I thought it was absurd—maybe it would have been a good idea in peacetime, but it was shitty timing in a city where the time and effort could have been much better spent.

The wet snow made for slow going, and in no time I realized I was overdressed. The weather was a lot milder than I thought, and my Canadian equipment, which was well designed, had me sweltering. I was, however, fortunate to have such good equipment. Most UN troops were poorly equipped for the Bosnian winters. The most ill-equipped were the contingents from the warmer countries—Egypt, Malaysia, Bangladesh, Pakistan and so on. They suffered dearly from the low temperatures, and for the most part they were ineffective once the cold weather hit.

The guard dogs that usually terrorized me from the yard at the corner were nowhere to be seen. As I rounded the corner, my view of the city widened. A fair amount of it lay spread out below me. It looked deserted, without a trace of movement or life. It seemed odd. What time of day was it? I checked my watch, thinking maybe it was a lot earlier than I thought. But it was seven o'clock. Where were the people? It seemed as if everyone was thinking the same thing: *Why get up? It will just be another day of struggle.* I was in no hurry, so I stopped walking and, out of habit, leaned against a building, making myself a smaller target.

I enjoyed the solitude and took some time to survey the place I had called home for the past four months. I looked out over the city, surveying a scene that was so familiar to me. This part of Sarajevo, like most of the city, was in a valley. Its lower slopes were covered with houses and apartment buildings. The buildings were a mix of new and old, some built over a hundred years ago, others gaudy additions for the '84 Winter Olympics. I could see telltale wisps of smoke start to rise from the stubby, soot-blackened chimneys. There used to be lush, tree-filled parks in the low areas of the valley. The spaces were still there, but now they were devoid of trees, long since cut for firewood.

On the right side of the valley, in the low ground, stood a small Orthodox church. Its once small graveyard was now a mass of wooden grave markers. The graveyard looked pristine with its blanket of snow. The sorrows buried there were hard to imagine.

It all looked so peaceful. The scars made on the ground by the impacts were covered in snow, and from a distance the city's buildings did not show the ravages of war. For a moment I could see why the Winter Olympics had been held in Sarajevo. It was a beautiful city.

My musings were drawn back to reality by the sight of the Olympic skating arena. There it sat, ripped and torn open, barely recognizable, destroyed by Serb gunners because it had been a symbol of peace and brotherhood.

I heard the crunching of footsteps in the snow behind me. A fellow was making his way down the street, his eyes downcast, as if he was feeling the weight of another day on the scrounge, or maybe not wanting to make eye contact. As he came near I caught him off guard: "*Dobro jutro*—good morning."

"*Dobro jutro*," he replied with a smile.

Maybe my greeting would make a difference in his morning. Maybe he'd have a good day. I started down the hill, placing my feet in the footsteps of my fellow early-riser. I felt alive, almost cheery—maybe it was the contrast the new snow offered, or maybe deep down I knew this would be the last winter of the war. Maybe it would soon be over.

## A BIG DAY

Strangely enough, living in Sarajevo meant that I was in a vacuum when it came to knowing what was going on in the peace process. I monitored the BBC World Service news daily, but got no details or feel for any progress actually being made. Goran and Mama, on the other hand, caught every bit and detail on the local news. In retrospect, I realize their need for peace was a lot more intense than mine. I would leave in six months, whether there was peace or not.

The Dayton Peace Accord was signed on December 14; amazingly, there was electricity in the city that day. I found out later that the electricity, gas and water for Sarajevo were part of the accord. During supper, Goran, Mama and I discussed what else the peace would bring. Goran was noncommittal: "Time will tell." The longer it lasted, the better the chance for a real, lasting peace: he pointed out that during the war there had been exactly thirty-six ceasefires. Some had lasted months, but most only a few hours. Would this one be any different?

Goran said that Bosnian television would be covering the signing live, via CNN, and we must watch it. So after supper we retired to the living room and settled in front of the tube, where various people talked about the significance of the accord. Goran translated for me and said that in essence they were all talking heads, fillers, until the CNN broadcast began.

We sat and waited for the real news. Goran and Mama, smoking and sipping on *fildjans* of strong coffee, were lost in their thoughts. I didn't say much; this was their moment. Goran said, "This is a big day, Fred." He repeated this several times. I knew that if he could express his feelings in English, he would have said more than "a big day."

CNN was broadcasting the news from Paris, where the European Union had pressured the U.S. to have the signing take place. Fucking Europeans, they did fuck all to end the war and now they wanted the symbolism of the signing ceremony in Europe—Paris, of all places! What bullshit! All the players were there, the leaders: Tudjman, confident and arrogant; Milosevic, basking in the limelight of the international media, acting the peacemaker, not the war criminal that he was, and Izetbegovic, sad and seemingly out of place—he would have his peace but not justice.

Mama sat on the end of the sofa, staring, legs crossed, arms folded across her body and a hand cradling her elbow, cigarette in her fingers. Her eyes looked sad, her face tense. She was lost in her thoughts. She averted her eyes every time Milosevic or Tudjman was on the screen. Mama hated them more than I could have imagined.

Goran sat on a footstool, leaning forward, eyes locked on the television screen, cigarette poised near his lips. It was as if he were afraid: *It's over. What do we do now?*

"Fred, big day," Goran said again. "Big day."

I sat in silence, watching these men sign the paper that would end the war. There were no tears of joy. Goran and Mama looked tired; they had made it, survived, when so many had died. But still we drank a toast to this Big Day. Then Goran flicked the channel to Serb TV—no coverage, only a couple of talking heads discussing art or farming or something, purposefully oblivious to what was going on in Paris. Goran said, "Fred, this is Serbia." Those words summarized his views on the war and its peace.

I was exhausted. I excused myself and went to bed. That night I slept the dreamless sleep of a dead man. I wanted my life back.

## GOODBYE SARAJEVO, HELLO ZAGREB

After having spent seven months in Sarajevo with the UN, I was now to move over to the NATO Implementation Force (IFOR) as a liaison officer with the Canadian-led brigade in the north of Bosnia, centred on Bihać. (UNPROFOR was slated to end in early January 1996 and to be replaced by IFOR.) Our UNMO team began to dismantle in mid-December 1995.

I missed most of the farewell gatherings because I had managed to get home on leave for Christmas. I surprised Janice, who was not sure if I would be home for the holidays. Although I don't remember much about those two weeks, I do know I was overwhelmed by the lights, the noise and the pace that everyone was moving at. My head was still in Sarajevo, and would be for some time to come. Janice, Ben and Erin made the best of having me back home, and yet my mind was on returning to Bosnia. I should have realized that something was wrong—especially when, as I sat in the airport with Janice, I felt calm and could hardly wait to get on the plane.

I made my way back to Sarajevo to help close out our team site and spent a good couple of weeks with Max and Ronnie. The day eventually came to say goodbye to the family I felt I had become a part of. The day was sunny and clear as we stood in the driveway of Goran's apartment. Goran was bundled in a sweater, as was Mama, in a new sweater Janice had sent her from Canada. They both looked tired, yet I could see hope in their eyes—they had survived. I felt guilty leaving them; in fact, I felt guilty about my time in Sarajevo. I wondered whether I had done enough as I looked at the window that Tameo used to lean out of to ask me the time. Collie sensed the sadness and continually nuzzled Goran's hand for a comforting rub. It was time to go. We hugged, smiled and said our goodbyes in English and Bosnian, and I promised I would return someday. They waved as I turned the car onto the street. I was headed for Zagreb.

Zagreb was a blur of UN inefficiency; we just dumped our cars in a compound and picked up our pay and a medal from the clerk at UNMO HQ. There were no parades or farewells, which was fine with us; we just wanted to be clear of the UN, to get the next five months over with and go home. I made my way to the Canadian Multi-National Brigade (CMNB) headquarters in Coralici, Bosnia, and met with the other liaison officers, most of whom were UNMOs that had arrived with me back in July 1995. I found out I was going to work with the British battle group in Ključ, about 120 kilometres south of Coralici. I was up early the next day and headed off with my driver to meet up with the Queen's Royal Hussars Armoured Regiment, who were bivouacked in a field about fifty kilometres north of Ključ. My trusty driver for the next five months would be Corporal Baird, of 1 Canadian Signals Regiment. Strange how I cannot remember his first name—it was always "Corporal." He had an uncanny ability to point out the absurdities of some of the things we and the contingent were required to do. He was also very good at sensing my moods, especially when I was quiet. Corporal Baird would never try to spark up a conversation when I was quiet; he just left me to my thoughts.

The Brits were a joy to work with; I liked them from the beginning. They were an eccentric bunch but very professional, and with a relaxed way of going about their mission. Our mission was to implement the Dayton Peace Accord decisions and timelines, with force if necessary. The accord was to be implemented on various timelines. For example, by "D+90" all heavy weapons (those with a range of ten kilometres or more) were to be placed in cantonment sites, which would be regularly inspected by liaison officers such as me. There were timelines for disbanding military units, for ensuring freedom of movement on roads, for returning prisoners of war and repatriating the dead to their families. So my next five months had the look of being quite busy, which suited me just fine.

I was glad to be away from the Canadian HQ, which was very large for a brigade; there were plenty of people with not enough to do other than jerk us around. I was happily dug in with the Brits and was authorized to move in with G Company 2 RCR in the destroyed carpet factory that became Camp Maple Leaf. I was overjoyed to find out that a company from my old battalion was one of the rifle companies in the British battle group. The OC, Colonel Denis Thompson, used my experience and gave me free rein in my day-to-day work.

The former warring factions were keen to adhere to the Dayton timelines for two reasons: they were tired, and for the most part were glad the war was over; and almost all of the international monetary aid was tied to complying with the timelines. I worked with several Bosnian and Serbian liaison officers and had access to all of their commanding officers. As the timelines were met, the changes in the town and villages in our area of responsibility (AOR) became very apparent. We moved ahead with such things as re-establishing schools and medical clinics and rebuilding infrastructure. After experiencing the horrors of Sarajevo, it was refreshing for me to see kids going to school, gardens being put in and smiles widening on people's faces.

It was not all peaches and cream. The destruction and ethnic cleansing in our AOR were considerable. We found several mass graves. Houses had been systematically looted and destroyed. Livestock that could not be herded, such as pigs, were shot and left to rot as the Serbs withdrew to their side of the Inter Ethnic Boundary Line (IEBL). All of the farm machinery had been removed to the Serb side, which placed farmers in a dilemma when it came to getting crops in for spring. Wells had been poisoned with dead bodies, and motors for pumps had been removed so that the basic human need for water could be denied. In the Sanica River, which ran behind our camp and where the Canadian Engineers had their water purification unit, bodies floated by for the first month we were there. Some were caught in the limbs of trees along the river, stuck there after the river rose and subsided in the spring. No attempt was made to recover the remains of these unfortunates. The Sanica River in the spring is a very fast-moving river that cuts through a mountain pass with steep cliffs on both sides. The bodies in the trees and stranded on rocks were on the far side of the river, and it would have meant risking one's life to recover them. To deal with the sight, the troops resorted to naming the corpses. "Skippy" stayed stuck in the trees the longest; eventually he broke in two and fell into the river.

The former warring factions were separated by a zone of separation (ZOS) with an inter-ethnic boundary line (IEBL) running down the centre. Only NATO could enter the ZOS; any parties from the former warring factions had to be escorted. NATO patrolled the ZOS vigorously, day and night. These patrol routes had been all cleared of mines but not of the dead. The IEBL had been the front line when the war ended, and with a two-kilometre ZOS on either side of it, there were bound to be bodies that had not been recovered prior to the withdrawal of the forward units from the IEBL.

The patrols encountered bodies along all the patrol routes, and we kept a register of their locations in hopes that there would be a recovery agreement soon. To keep focused on their patrols, the troops also began giving these bodies names. "Chesty" was a barrel-chested dead Serbian lying beside a road junction. He and his mates had been ambushed while trying to flee to the Serb side late in the war. Their van took a rocket-propelled grenade hit and plenty of small-arms fire. The remains of three of them were still in the van, burnt and in pieces, and a spine and a rib cage lay in the debris outside the vehicle.

It looked like Chesty had survived the grenade and made a run for it, but that he and another mate had been cut down by small-arms fire.

"Gord" was a body in a field full of gourds on one of the patrol routes. Early in the tour, a journalist accompanying a patrol had got excited and thought they had stumbled onto a mass grave. The troops told him that those skulls in neat rows were actually sun-bleached gourds. For the soldiers who patrolled these routes daily, the bodies were just another part of the landscape of war. But the journalists were a bunch of war pornographers with cameras, attracted by the sensationalism of war. It seemed that all that the journalists were looking for was the story that would win them the Pulitzer Prize. It was different for the soldiers: they could picture themselves lying dead on a battlefield.

Sometime in May a buddy and I, along with our drivers and an interpreter, accompanied the "Bosnian knacker van" into the zos to recover some Serbian bodies buried on the battlefield. The Bosnians did not have body bags, and they would not have used them on Serbian dead anyway. At one body exchange the bodies were in cardboard boxes, blankets and tarps—neither side showed any respect for their enemy's dead. Here, NATO supplied the body bags and the Bosnians supplied the excavators, in the form of four reluctant Bosnian privates with spades.

The Bosnian fellows were an interesting crew—older men who had been wounded during the war and were now part of the body-recovery efforts by both sides. We had been up there a few weeks earlier to locate the grave and knew that the bodies we would be recovering were Serbian. The day was hot, and none of us relished cracking the grave open again. The first time the shovels dug into the earth, the stench of putrefying flesh put us all into gag mode. We dug just enough to identify the boots of the dead as Serbian boots.

The sunny sky over the lush green field did not make our task any less gruesome. The dead were not buried deep, and we found four or five bodies piled on top of each other in the same grave. Gagging and retching, we bagged them and carried the bodies to the knacker van. We had no protective gear, no gloves, no masks or protective suits like you'd see on csi. I didn't give a shit anyway; it was just another piece of the aftermath of a gruesome war. When we arrived back at camp, among the clean people, we stank the place up. We quickly stripped our clothes off, turned our gear in for laundry, and then showered and scrubbed to get rid of the reek.

## TESTING THE RULES OF ENGAGEMENT

An incident during a liaison visit to a Bosnian brigade HQ brought home to me how distant and unrealistic our Ottawa bosses were. One morning I picked up my interpreter and, with Corporal Baird, headed to the village of Sanica, where I was to discuss with the brigade commander our progress in meeting one of the timelines. Corporal Baird remained with the vehicle, and I and the interpreter went inside. Waiting for me in the commander's office were the brigade commander, his second-in-command, the operations officer and the brigade mullah (a Muslim learned in theology and sacred law). Everyone seemed in a fair mood, and formal introductions were made. I had met everyone else before, except the operations officer. Then I introduced my interpreter, and I could see that their interest quickly turned towards him. They realized he was Serbian. *Fuck*. Here I was in a room with four Bosnian soldiers and a Serbian interpreter. I had assumed that the head interpreter always made sure the Bosnians never worked the Serb side, and vice versa.

The operations officer focused on the kid, who was all of eighteen years old. "So you are from Prijedor. Did you fight in the war?"

"No, I was too young."

"Sure, too young."

"Did you know the so-and-so family?"

"No."

"I thought you said you lived in Prijedor."

"I did, but I didn't know everyone."

"On what street did you live?"

I could sense the situation heating up. They had placed their hands on their side arms, and the kid was terrified; he knew things were getting out of hand. I was not going to let this go any further, so I drew my pistol and held it by my side. Their eyes shifted to my unholstered pistol as I stepped between them and the terrified boy.

"We will meet again tomorrow," I said as I backed towards the door, pushing the kid behind me.

Once out the door, we beat a hasty retreat to Corporal Baird and got the fuck out of Sanica.

Now I was angry. "Why didn't you tell me you were Serb? You knew we were going to a Bosnian army unit."

"You didn't ask. Anyway, I was a student during the war."

"But you wear the blood of those who did fight and kill Bosnians!"

I said no more as we made our way back to camp. But when we arrived I headed right to the senior interpreter and tore a strip off her ass.

So, how does this incident relate to Ottawa? It is in Ottawa, at National Defence headquarters, where the legal idiots who write our rules of engagement (ROE) park their asses. They also decided who had protected status and listed them on our ROE cards: people such as journalists, international policemen and diplomats. Being on the list allowed us to use deadly force, if necessary, to protect them. You'd think that an interpreter hired from the local population would have protected status, but he didn't. So in that room, with four armed and pissed-off Bosnian officers, the only thing I could do was to put myself between them and the interpreter, thereby making me the recipient of any threat and allowing me to defend myself. And, in the process, protect the interpreter. Assholes in jackets and ties thousands of miles away were writing the rules that put my life at risk. Amazingly, it took a few months for the system to respond and to have interpreters put under protected status in our ROES.

Time flew by, and my tour in Bosnia was coming to an end. By July 7, 1996, I would have a year "in country." Ottawa ordered that none of the former UNMOS would spend a minute over one year in theatre. By this time I knew I was being posted from Edmonton back to 2 RCR in Gagetown. My departure was anticlimactic. It consisted of a quick trip through brigade HQ in Coralici, where the chief clerk gave me a "wound stripe" for my neck wound as I got in the van that would take me to the airport. It seemed that the year had raced by; but when I looked at the wound stripe I thought, *That day in Sarajevo when I was wounded seems a lifetime away*. And maybe it was.

# FIRST FLASHBACK

**AN OVERCAST, DAMP EVENING** after several days of rain, and everything looks and feels grey. My memory is so bad that I often forget to eat. It's not until my gut aches that I realize I need food. My days have no beginning, middle or end, and I have no sense of time. All the markers—morning, lunch, supper, bedtime—are blurred by the confusion and anger that has taken hold of me. Depression paralyzes me mentally and physically; everything is an effort and has no purpose. I am locked into the past; there is no today or tomorrow, just memories and fear. I must eat, not just drink coffee and ingest fat pills from Tim Hortons. I need food! Pizza will do, so I drop in at The King of Donair pizza shop on King Street, across from "Tim's," for a slice of meat-lover's to clog my arteries. I settle on a stool at the counter that faces the window. I gnaw at the rubbery, tasteless slab of pizza, watching the people outside move about with a sense of purpose. Purpose—I wish I had some. I close my eyes and feel so tired and miserable. Will this end? I just want my life back.

When I open my eyes I am no longer in the pizza shop. I'm standing in the doorway of a building in the UN Protected Area of Goražde. It's 1995. Goražde is a small island of humanity surrounded by the sea of the Republic of Srpska (the Bosnian Serb area during the war). I am caught up in my first flashback. All my senses are abuzz; the air feels damp and cold as it was in October when I first went to Goražde. I can smell the wood smoke, the burning garbage and the sour, overpowering smell of urine and excrement. My body contracts, my muscles tense in fear of being in a very dangerous place. I have no idea I'm flashing back; in my mind I am there. The scene around me is just as it had been years ago. There is the burnt-out tank, the pharmacy with its front covered by logs, and a dirty Red Cross flag draped over them in an attempt to play on the sense of humanity of the Serbs who have surrounded the town. I am afraid and terrified. What am I doing here? Where are my UNMO teammates? Why are those Bosnian soldiers ignoring me? Fuck it's cold, I can see my breath, yet there is no snow and the people I see are dressed lightly. My shoulders are hunched, and I can feel the pain in my neck, mostly from stress but also from shrugging my shoulders up in an attempt to get my helmet to cover the vulnerable nape of my neck. This is such a miserable place, fifty thousand people cowering like rats, waiting for the Serbs to attack and finish their agony. Maybe a bullet in the head would be better than their miserable existence.

Still not realizing that I am caught up in the short circuit in my brain that has dropped me here, I feel the tension easing as I realize I've returned to a familiar place. Compared with my life at home and at work, this is actually comforting. It's a release of tension and a trip to a place where I was in my element. It was a life-and-death way of living; no grey, just black and white, life at its simplest, just trying to survive a war.

The door bangs, my head snaps towards it as I watch someone enter; I'm back in the restaurant. I feel exhausted and confused. What the fuck has happened? I leave my food and step out onto the street, not believing that I am in Fredericton. All is normal; people are moving about on this mild fall evening. Where the fuck have I been? I wander aimlessly around the downtown streets, trying to rationalize not so much *what* I experienced, but *why*. The only thing I know for certain is that I will tell no one. Only crazy people can travel into the past.

# PART TWO

# PTSD

I said horrifying things without knowing it until I got a reaction. My laugh sounded bitter and derisive even to me. When people asked me the simplest questions about myself I became cool and remote. Lonesome as I was, I made damn sure I stayed that way.

TOBIAS WOLFF, *In Pharaoh's Army: Memories of the Lost War*

Operational stress injuries (OSIS) are as much a reality for CF personnel today as they were during the Second World War. In fact, operational stress injuries have always been a reality of military service. In the past, an OSI was called "shell shock" or "battle fatigue." Regardless of the name, operational stress and trauma injure the mind and spirit, and those injuries can be as fatal as any physical injury.

DEPARTMENT OF NATIONAL DEFENCE (CANADA), *"The Reality of Operational Stress Injuries"*

Whenever I turned on the tap water, all I could see was blood gushing out. I would stare at it until it looked like water before drinking or taking a shower.

ISHMAEL BEAH, *A Long Way Gone: Memoirs of a Boy Soldier*

## 12 | **Home Sweet Home**

**C**OMING OUT of Bosnia in 1996 was not the release from hell that I thought it would be. My transition from Bosnia back home to Edmonton took less than twenty-four hours. I felt lost when I arrived home. I knew I had changed. I was having nightmares; I was jittery and angry. I was mentally exhausted and terribly bored.

Janice and I moved back to Gagetown in the summer of 1996. I had been posted to my old infantry battalion. It was great to be back; so many familiar faces and old friends to connect with. One of the battalion's rifle companies had also just returned from a six-month tour in Bosnia and was back to work by the time I moved in.

An opportunity arose for me to tell someone how my year in Bosnia had been. It came in the form of a questionnaire being administered to the soldiers of G Company by the base social work office. I tagged along and took part in the survey, which consisted of about 150 questions on the subject's (my) mental health. Some of the questions seemed strange ("Do you like fire?"), but for the most part I could see from the wording of the questions and their repetitive theme that they were trying to get inside my head.

So I finished the survey, turned it in and waited for the results. And waited, and eventually forgot about it until the subject came up over coffee with some other fellows who had taken the survey. No one had heard the results, or if there even were any results to be considered. So I called the social work office and inquired about how I had done. I asked if the questionnaires had been corrected or evaluated; they said that they had. I asked how I did on the questionnaire, and was put on hold while they went to check. When the phone snapped back to life the voice on the other end said, "We would really like to see you." I thought, *Interesting, after almost two months, and only after I inquired, did they realize I was special.* It was as if they were required to *ask* us on paper how we were doing, but not required to *tell* us how we were doing. For them, it was simply a paper exercise that had no link to the mental health of the soldiers.

I was infuriated, and this just added fuel to the anger and resentment that had begun to boil in me since my return. No one gave a fuck! I booked an appointment with one of the social workers and tried to quell the rage I felt towards those who had never seen the face of war.

I was referred first to a military social worker and then to a military mental health nurse. The social worker asked questions that would become the standard. Now, I can't fault him, because military social workers deal with family problems, depression, alcohol abuse, et cetera. I did not fit the mould, because the mould had yet to be made. Regardless, I felt angry because I knew they did not understand, and if they didn't then I would not open up to them. In my mind, they were the enemy: the people that are referred to as *them* and *they*.

In the end, the social worker did convince me to see the military mental health nurse. I figured that, being military, she would understand. Not likely. In fact, the meeting was quite amusing. I was to find out that for some time to come, whenever I related some of my experiences to health care professionals—whether they were doctors, psychiatrists or psychologists—they would be amazed. They found it hard to believe that I had experienced so much in Bosnia, especially Sarajevo. Even those in the military who I would confide in were doubtful about what I had experienced. I had no parallels that I could draw from the real world to convey what I had experienced. It's as if all they wanted to hear were the sensational horrors, the "war porn." But my experiences and memories consisted of more than just war porn.

Suffice it to say that my visit to the mental health nurse was almost a waste of time. However, the nurse knew that sooner or later I would have to be properly assessed to find out what was going on with me. She offered to have me sent to the National Defence Medical Centre in Ottawa to see a psychiatrist. I immediately declined, because in my military mind there was nothing wrong with me that some rest back in the "real world" couldn't cure. How wrong I was. I was not properly assessed for another four years. In retrospect, maybe it wasn't the right time. The thing that I do regret is the pain I caused in those four years to those who were close to me. I can never make up for that. As for the questionnaire, I have no idea where it went or if it had any effect on my quest for help.

### RAGE AND EMBARRASSMENT

Anger was my drug of choice, my upper. It would energize me, albeit with negative energy. It seems strange, but the exhaustion following an angry outburst was what I really looked forward to. Being angry takes an awful lot of energy, to the point where, when the inevitable explosion came, I had nothing left in me. I could then slide away embarrassed, confused, apologetic and exhausted. I could rest because I was spent. I could talk and be human because the wall of anger had been blown away by the outburst. But I knew the wall would be rebuilt; brick by brick, trying to hold back the rage burning inside me.

There was a large element of self-control intertwined with my anger. As a soldier I had been trained to be always in control—if you lost it, you died. In fact, my section commander back in 1971 had a saying: "Panic, and you lose your section." Those words are still with me. So whenever I lost control of my anger, I would be left with a strong feeling of weakness and embarrassment.

I could not pick and choose the place and time of these explosions. I always feared that the outburst would come when I was not somewhere safe, like at home, or in the field instructing young officers. Then the outbursts in the field would be taken as me giving a blast of shit in an attempt to motivate a group of aspiring officers; angry field instructors were common. In fact, when I did explode in the field it was because some young officer had jeopardized his life or, worse, the lives of his soldiers.

I feared my road rage, which could be triggered by the most trivial things. I was hell to be with in a vehicle. I just couldn't let someone else's driving mistakes go. I would rave on and on and be set off for the day because someone didn't use his signal light. Janice often used to ask me if she could drive just so that she would not have to listen to me rave. I can now relate my road rage to danger and over-protectiveness—danger being the threat of an accident and overprotectiveness relating to the people in my vehicle. It was never about my safety, but about Janice and Erin being safe. They were usually the unfortunate passengers and recipients of my tirades. I scared people, and I know they avoided me because they did not want to deal with me and my anger.

Janice was very concerned about what could and probably would happen if one of my explosions was physically directed at someone. Whenever I went out by myself, she worried that she would get a call from the police or the hospital. If I drove into town for a coffee at Tim Hortons, Janice usually knew that I would be gone for an hour, and if I was late all manner of fears would plague her. Had I cornered someone with my road rage? Was my narrow sense of right and wrong being tested?

Janice's fears were almost realized one day when I drove into town to return some rented videos. I was in one of my "flat" states, when I would feel nothing, no highs or lows; in army terms, my GAFF ("give a fuck factor," concern about the day-to-day necessities of life) was zero. I arrived in the busy parking lot at Jumbo Video; its busyness ruffled my nerves. As I was pulling into a parking spot, I noticed several teenagers standing around the car in front of me. This group of teenagers would have gone unnoticed by me had it not been for two of them arguing. The boy was about eighteen, with a shaved head and muscle T-shirt. He was fit, tanned and full of attitude. He had an image and was busy maintaining it, and at the moment it was being focused on a pretty blonde girl. She stood there as he played gangsta.

Big deal, and maybe it was just a bunch of kids sorting out their Friday night plans. But I happened to catch the look in the girl's eyes and saw fear, the kind of look I had seen in women, children and the elderly in Bosnia. Her eyes penetrated the black hole in my soul and drew out the rage and anger that lived there.

All of my senses were focused on the young punk. He was no longer some well-off suburban kid playing out some image he had picked up from an MTV video. He was one of the many cocky, young Serbian militia I had faced at checkpoints; pumped-up on alcohol, carrying an AK, being the boss because they carried a gun. My rage was building. He now wore camouflage pants and shirt, and the surroundings had changed to a checkpoint. He was threatening a woman. My fists clenched, my breathing and heart rate rose; my eyes were burning a hole in that little fuck. The trigger had been pulled and I walked towards him not caring about the outcome, just relishing the satisfaction I would feel while pounding the living shit out of him. I could feel myself smiling as I stepped towards my target.

The young woman made a move, turned and got into another car, and my target told her to fuck off as he entered the car beside him. *Crack*, like a rifle shot, my trance was broken as their cars left the parking lot. I was left standing, confused and spent. I stayed there until a car moved into the vacant spot where my target had been standing. I had come close, very close.

I never went into the video store; I got into my car and just sat there as my injured brain tried to sort out the reality and the potential consequences of my actions. Images of Sarajevo ebbed and flowed in my consciousness.

## A FAREWELL TO RONNIE

My first year back home was marked by a number of anniversaries: being wounded in the July 17 shelling the previous year, the Market II shelling, the NATO air strikes and so on. Christmas of 1996 arrived with a shitload of memories (and guilt). My situation at home in Canada was physically great, but memories of Sarajevo haunted me. I really missed everyone I had made friends with there, especially my UNMO teammates.

To make contact with them and the family in Sarajevo, I decided to send everyone a Christmas card for 1996. I wrote a short note to each of them and hoped they would do the same. Most did, and I enjoyed reading about how they were doing and that all was well. But not until sometime in March 1997 did I receive a reply to my card to Ronnie Denyft. His son wrote, on behalf of his mom, that Ronnie had died as a result of a heart attack in Sarajevo in the fall of 1996. I was stunned; I couldn't believe that Ronnie, our pillar of common sense and experience, was dead.

Ronnie had retired from the Belgian army after returning from Sarajevo in 1995. Before leaving, he told me he was looking forward to retirement and to being a grandfather to his recently born grandson. At that time I envied him. I thought Ronnie would make the best of his retirement and told him that I hoped to visit him someday. But Ronnie, like many of us, was an adrenalin junkie and within a few months he was back in Sarajevo as a European Community monitor, doing work very similar to what we had done as UNMOs. I found out that he had died before he hit the ground in a compound in Sarajevo. I guess the city finally got him.

### DEBUT AT THE NATIONAL DEFENCE MEDICAL CENTRE

People, friends, were beginning to notice. Janice certainly knew that something was very wrong, as did my daughter Erin. My anger and rage were at times out of control. My sleep was minimal and filled with nightmares, paranoia, startle responses, anxiety, fear and flashbacks, spinning around me. I felt I was caught up in a vortex that I couldn't escape. The tough soldier deep down knew he couldn't handle it, but he would not admit it. *There's nothing wrong*, I assured myself. *It'll go away.*

We had deployed to the field for a training exercise in the spring of 1997, and by chance I had a bunk right next to our battalion medical officer, Dr. Roy Lilly. Roy was a nice guy. He was more doctor than soldier, which in some ways is a good thing. One evening we were sitting on the edge of our bunks gabbing, and I must have been feeling comfortable because I let it drop that I had been having problems sleeping since my return from Bosnia. I think that Roy knew more about me than I did, and he delicately coaxed me to talk. It felt great, because he just listened and I felt trustful because I knew he had never been on a mission, which meant he had nothing to compare my experiences to.

I don't know how long we gabbed, but I felt relaxed and that our talk had been beneficial. Roy admitted that he was just an M.D., but he could recommend sending me to Ottawa for a psychiatric assessment. Again, the image thing came up. I did not want anyone to know, especially my peers. Roy said that he could inform the CO I was going to Ottawa to have my wounded neck looked at by a specialist, that any report would go directly to him and that he'd only discuss the report with me. "Deal," I said, and committed myself to the trip.

It wasn't long before I was booked to see a National Defence Medical Centre (NDMC) psychiatrist who was a civilian. On the day of my appointment I headed for the Fredericton airport wearing my summer tans, service ribbons and paratrooper wings. I was fit, my shoes were gleaming . . . I was a proud soldier. I was amazed that I would fly up to Ottawa in the morning, see the psychiatrist at 1300 and fly home at 1700 with the cost to DND of $1,600. I arrived in Ottawa on a beautiful late spring day and grabbed a cab to the medical centre. This centre, in its day, had been the main fully staffed hospital for the whole of the Canadian Forces. Time and budget cuts, however, had whittled it down to the size of a clinic, with a few specialists and researchers occupying some space. It had a worn-out 1960s feel to it. The paint colours, furniture and layout hinted at its age, as did the vacant rooms and hallways.

I had a coffee in the snack room and noticed a few stares, because an infantry officer was not often seen at NDMC. The soft cushy feeling of the place irritated me, and I felt that everyone who looked at me felt that I must be weak if I was here. I cleared out of the snack room, went to the floor for psychos and found the office of the doctor I would be seeing. Like a good soldier, I was early. I tried to relax by pacing the hallway.

My scheduled 1300 appointment time came and went. I figured Doc was just a bit slow in returning from lunch. But 1315, 1330 and 1345 slipped by, and then finally at 1350 this overweight, scruffy gentleman wandered down the hall with a toothpick in his mouth, gingerly picking parts of his lunch out of his teeth. This guy was already batting zero on Fred's getting-pissed-off-and-angry scale. I was the only one in the hallway sitting across from his office door and he ambled by, opened the door, walked in and closed it, without a glance in my direction. So I figured he'd be sorting out my file, getting things squared away for my appointment. I waited and waited a bit more, then even more, and I finally thought, *Fuck this, I've got a plane to meet soon.* I got up and knocked on his door.

"Come in. Yes?"

"Captain Doucette, Fred, 1300 appointment with you." I tried not to lose it while thinking, *Great, he's a slob, he's late and he's a civvie!*

He beckoned me into his office. I picked a chair and sat down. The doctor had my medical documents in front of him and was flipping through them. "So, how are things going?"

I began my well-rehearsed confession of how I was feeling and what I had experienced. He still wasn't looking at me. I was already thinking what a waste of time this was. He was doing the "document flip" as I spoke, giving me the odd "Yes, uh huh, umm," then out of the blue asked me if I was going to put a claim in against the Crown. And was I thinking of hurting anyone?

Within fifteen minutes of coming through the door I had clammed up. All my symptoms were at a boil. *Just get me out of here.* But I was still the well-trained, disciplined soldier, so I sat and boiled and said nothing. The doctor, still absorbed in my medical file, stopped flipping and said I had failed the heart stress test in Edmonton. I had to be removed from the treadmill test before completing the first level.

"I never had a heart stress test."

"Really."

"I couldn't even tell you what it is."

He opened the ARCO fastener that held the paperwork together to show me the date of the test and revealed the top of the document. It showed that someone with a name similar to mine had failed the test. So here was some poor bastard's heart test results filed with my medical documents. I wondered if he was still alive. That sort of summed up the whole visit: all fucked up and a waste of time. Total time with the psychiatrist was forty minutes. I was livid. I got up and said, "Goodbye." And I left.

A sad side to this trip was that as I was leaving, I bumped into Chief Warrant Officer "Hodgie" Hodgson in the hallway. He was supposed to be in Bosnia as the regimental sergeant major of 1 RCR, so I was surprised to see him. We had served together, and he had lived down the street from me when we were posted to Edmonton. His wife was with him here. She remained seated and looked grim. Hodgie told me he was back for a few tests, nothing major; they just wanted to check something out that they couldn't check in Bosnia. I asked him how the tour was going and how the battalion was. He said all was great and he was looking forward to getting back. I told Hodgie that I had a plane to catch, shook his hand, wished him luck and said goodbye. As the elevator doors closed, I watched him turn and walk back to his wife. Then I saw a sign over the door behind him: Department of Oncology. Hodgie would be dead in a year, not long after being presented with the Order of Military Merit in his bed at his Petawawa home. Governor General Adrienne Clarkson helicoptered in to confer the award on him.

As I sat in the taxi, my mind was on Hodgie. He was a soldier's soldier, and he was dying. I felt weak and ashamed of having made this trip just because I was having head problems. I convinced myself that time would heal my problems. I would waste no more time on the medical world.

## FROM BAD TO WORSE

I returned home from Ottawa angry, bitter and disgusted. It had taken a lot out of me to come to the decision to actually go to Ottawa and see a shrink. But all the trip did was confirm my feelings of abandonment by the system. I was even more angry. I vowed I would never trust "the system." It did not understand and it did not care.

Janice had pinned her hopes for me on this trip. She was looking for some kind of answer or, better still, a solution for whatever was eating away at me could be brought to light. All she got was an energized, angry, bitter and raving man. I didn't care what she felt, and I didn't care how anyone else felt. If they could not understand, then it was their problem, not mine.

Much later, Janice told me that during my black days she felt despair and loss. She said it was as if the Fred she knew had died, and now she had no idea who the person was that had replaced him. It was impossible for her to avoid or ignore what was going on with me, and being a loving and caring wife of twenty-five years she tried to help. But she couldn't, and her trying to help me only angered me more. In my mind, if she didn't understand, no one understood.

Janice never feared me; but she did fear *for* me, especially my explosive anger. If I came home late from work or disappeared for a few hours, she worried. Had I lost it? Had I exploded and taken out my rage on someone? Where was I, what had happened?

Our home was not a home for me; it was my hiding place and became my prison. My ravings and angry outbursts were always followed by apologies. But my apologetic words were hollow. When would the next explosion occur? Janice had given up trying to figure out what initiated these explosions. My wife loved me, but she did not like me.

Work became therapy for me. Work was a safe place, a familiar environment for me to go and hide for eight hours of the day. I kept hoping that one of my peers would notice the changes in me and ask, "How are you doing?" No one did. I was just a crusty old captain, one of the "bitter and twisted" group. What they did not know was that my bitterness did not come from being passed over for a course, a posting or a promotion. They just did not know what I had been through. I felt that some of them had an inkling because they had also served in Croatia and Bosnia, but maybe they were dealing with their own demons. Deep down I felt that they were too afraid to admit their fears to anyone, just as I was also afraid to let them into my secret nightmare. My life, my need to live, had stalled. There was no purpose, no reason for me to keep living. I did not have the guts to end it myself, but I wished and prayed for someone or something to just end it for me.

I still was not sleeping. My nights were filled with dreams, faces, sounds, smells, sweat, fear and pain. I had no short-term memory; all was caught up in the memories of Bosnia. I forgot to eat. Janice would keep me on track, almost force me to eat. My body ached, my headaches kept recurring. My neck hurt constantly and my ears rang. I felt and looked like shit. I wanted to go back to Bosnia, to the black-and-white, life-or-death simplicity of the monster that is war.

### ORANGE TARP

An orange tarp lay on the side of the road as I drove to work. I spotted it from about a kilometre away. It was hard not to see the tarp against the dark shadows of the ditch. As I closed the distance between me and the tarp, I drifted into a flashback. I was in the hills just outside Goražde. The sky was grey and overcast, and it was hard to tell if the clouds would offer up snow or rain. I wanted a thick blanket of clean white snow, to cover everything like a fresh coat of paint and hide the images of war.

There on the road was a frayed plastic tarp. I slowed down and at the last moment braked hard, swerving to avoid it, then came to a stop just beyond it. I put the Land Cruiser in park and got out. The air was fresh and heavy with moisture. I took a deep breath and felt my shoulders tense up and my fists clench. I turned around to face the bundle. A breeze played with the tattered ends of the tarp.

I reached down and grabbed the frayed edge of the tarp with both hands, and with my back to the bundle I walked away. Whatever was inside was heavy; I could feel the tarp unrolling behind me. Suddenly there was no more resistance. The tarp had come loose and was flapping in the wind behind me. Although I was upwind, I could smell the rotting flesh. I turned around and let go of the tarp. The wind grabbed it and settled it into the ditch. With the tarp gone, my eyes came to rest on a mother with a child bundled in her arms.

I told myself, *Take in the details.* The bundled baby couldn't be more than a year old. Its face was pale white, and thankfully its eyes were closed, sunken deep into their sockets. The fingers of the mother's hands were splayed open, as if trying to cover every part of her child. Her feet were bare; she looked to have a couple of dresses on, and her head was wrapped in a blue-flowered shawl. The shawl framed her face; its splash of colour was a stark contrast to her pale white face. Her eyes were frozen open, and I couldn't break her deathly stare. She seemed to look into my soul. *I'm sorry, fuck, I'm sorry, just stop staring!*

I was stopped at a street light. How'd I get there? The tarp on the side of the road had sent me on one of those trips I could no longer control. My jaw was clenched, my shoulders ached and I had a white-knuckle grip on the steering wheel. A blaring horn broke my trance. "Fuck you, asshole!" I yelled at the face in the car behind me. My guilt changed to anger as I tramped on the gas and accelerated, cursing and swearing. *No one gets it and no one cares!*

Whenever I think back to that day on the road outside of Goražde, the guilt I feel for only being able to bundle them back up into the tarp and place them on the shoulder of the road is overpowering. It consumes me for days. And added to the guilt is the anger I feel when I remember the Serb soldiers at the checkpoint, who with a shrug said: "Wow, you found a body in Bosnia. How special. We'll get right to it and bury it with all the dignity it deserves. Now fuck off, UN asshole."

The bundle was gone when we made our return trip to Sarajevo.

### NATIONAL DEFENCE MEDICAL CENTRE, AGAIN

Nothing mattered at work. If I was not interested in something, I just didn't do it. A fine example was during the Quebec ice storm of 1998. I was battalion transportation officer and was responsible for moving six hundred men, their equipment and about one hundred vehicles. When we were called out to deploy to the Montreal area, I managed to write a movement order on two pages of foolscap. Normally a movement order is quite a piece of paperwork, far more than two pages..I didn't care. We marshalled all the vehicles, sent them off in packets of five and six, and that was it. There were two refuelling stops, and everyone ended up in the location in twenty-four hours—proof that a lot of the military paperwork is for the untrained. The fellows in the battalion were well trained, and I trusted and relied on that training. Lo and behold, it worked.

At home I was becoming more and more of an explosive jerk. My outbursts were more frequent and much more vicious. They would set the tone for the day regardless of when it happened—six in the morning or six in the evening, from that point on I would be miserable until I went to bed. I remember, once, having a screwdriver fall off the ladder when I was working in our garage. I raved at it as if it had planned to fall. My ranting was so loud and angry that Janice and Erin thought someone was in the garage with me, but they were afraid to find out what was going on.

Sometime after the ice storm I was approached by our medical officer, and we talked about my first trip to Ottawa and the utter waste of time it had been. I knew that something was wrong and that I was spinning out of control. So, with a promise from the doc that something would come out of this one, I agreed to try again.

It was early spring when I flew to Ottawa. I was put up in the Kiwanis Motel, next to the Ottawa General Hospital. I thought that at least they weren't too worried about having me stay in this place with all these civvies. I was concerned that my dreams, which could be quite loud, would upset the civvies staying at the motel. I walked a lot while waiting for my appointment time, and I stayed away from the military hospital to avoid meeting anyone I knew. The stigma attached to anything regarding mental health in the army is really cut and dried: soldiers with problems between their ears are weak and should be punted out of the army before they infected other soldiers with their weakness. So I roamed along the Rideau Canal well into the night, and then crept back into the motel and sat in my room until dawn. I couldn't sleep. Tomorrow I would have to admit I was weak.

My appointment was set for 0900. I was on time, and so was the psychiatrist. For about two hours we talked. No. She asked questions and I answered them. There were a lot of yes, no, maybe, I don't know and I guess so answers on my part. When I did describe some of the horrors I had experienced or witnessed, the doctor looked at me in amazement and disbelief. She could not imagine those things happening to Canadian peacekeepers—Canada never sent its "peacekeepers" into harm's way.

At about 1100, I was administered a questionnaire of about five hundred yes/no questions, which I guess could determine my mental state. I went through it quickly, once again picking up the pattern of the questions. It was the same questions presented in five different ways, but with the same point and hopefully the same answer from the person doing the questionnaire. I was finished just before lunch and was told to come back around 1400 for a chat. I headed outside for a walk and ended up in the cafeteria of the Ottawa General Hospital, where I sat down and ate a sandwich. I felt that everyone was looking at me and judging me. I didn't stay long and found a bench outside in the sun, relaxing there until I had to go back to see the doctor.

At 1400 I was seated in the doctor's office, waiting to find out if I was crazy or going mad. The doc said that I had done what most combat arms soldiers do: I had minimized my symptoms. If on a scale of 10—1 being great and 10 being horrible—I was asked to rate my sleep, I put down a 3 when in actual fact it was 10. She said that until I was honest and let out how I was really doing, I could not be properly assessed, let alone diagnosed. So the ball was back in my court. I thanked her for her time, and she wished me good luck. *Fuck it*, I thought. All I had to do was get a grip on things and toughen up, and all would be fine. I could handle this. *I'm a rough, tough soldier.*

## PICKING UP THE PIECES

Janice was getting tired of my outbursts. I was not a very likable person. The only place that I seemed to fit in was at work, but that lasted only eight hours out of twenty-four. Only when the battalion deployed to the field could I actually relax, feeling the muddy ground, smelling the diesel fuel, hearing the noise of activity and enjoying the simple camaraderie of the world of soldiers. It was a great place to vent the stress that was building up in me. I could yell, run and fight either in the training or on the sports field, and it felt good to let out some of my aggression and anger. I could feel the stress bleeding off. I felt calm; I was in my element in an organization that was always training for war.

I was blessed with good leaders during this time: Major Ken Butterworth, Major Bill Pond and my commanding officer, Lieutenant Colonel Doug McLean. I don't know if they sensed anything wrong with me; if they did, they chose to leave me alone. In 1998 my battalion was warned that it would be deployed to Bosnia in January 1999, to serve with the NATO Stabilization Force (SFOR). So once again I would be returning to Bosnia. I felt calm and content in the knowledge that I would be going back to familiar places. I had to see the changes and progress that I hoped had come to Bosnia since I'd left in 1996.

During the summer of 1998, I had enjoyed some space. Most of G Company had been tasked out to various jobs at the infantry school as instructors, drivers and so on. There were only about a half dozen of us left in the company, which meant plenty of PT (physical training) on our own and shorter days at work. By August the company had reformed with Major Pond as the new company commander, and with three new platoon commanders. We had just finished three weeks of leave and were adopting the configuration that company would be in for the training and deployment to Bosnia. G Company had also taken over the Immediate Reaction Unit task for the Maritimes, which meant we were on eight hours' notice to move anywhere the government felt there was a need for us.

On September 2, Swiss Air flight 111 crashed into the ocean just off of Peggy's Cove, Nova Scotia, with no passengers surviving. We knew this meant we would be deploying to Peggy's Cove, and deploy we did. Major Pond and Company Sergeant Major Bob Girouard left immediately. After we were "bugged out" (recalled to duty), I and the rest of the company were to follow in a few hours. As usual, all of the battalion resources swung into action, launching us to the area of the disaster. By midnight we were on the buses heading towards one of Canada's most popular tourist sites. It had now, in a matter of hours, become a place of sorrow and disbelief.

We drove through the night. The buses were quiet; most of the soldiers slept, and those who didn't talked in hushed tones. I know we all were wondering what we would be doing. The crash site was on water and the navy was securing it, so the only task we could expect was to recover debris from the coastline. I say "debris," but we all knew there would be the personal effects of passengers and human remains to deal with.

We rendezvoused with the oc on Highway 103 near Hammonds Plains and moved to an area of the coast between Blandford and Bayswater. This length of shoreline was closest to and about eight kilometres from the crash site. Our mission was simple: we were to search the shore and recover anything that related to the crash. I felt apprehensive, not sure what I'd do if we discovered any bodies or parts thereof. I already had seen many bodies in Bosnia, but for some reason, in my clouded mind, these would be different. I thought: *At least they won't stink, because they're freshly dead.*

Our grisly task went as well as could be expected; the company scoured the coastline for two days. I was safely located in the command post with our medic, drivers and signallers. A freezer truck was parked nearby for the human remains. The troops found debris, personal effects and human remains. What was really hard to handle were the photos from wallets, the disposable diapers and teddy bears. These items, simple as they were, linked us to the last moments in the lives of the passengers on that flight. We knew that the Pampers and teddy bears meant there had been children on board. There were some scratches on our hearts when the realization hit that a cross-section of humanity had died in that crash.

After scouring the beaches for two days and recovering all that was there to recover, we were relieved by an artillery and reserve unit. We moved into a militia armory in Halifax for a shower, a hot meal and a session with our Critical Incident Stress Debriefing (cisd) team. These were our peers—corporals, master corporals, sergeants, warrant officers and officers who were trained in debriefing troops after a critical incident or operation. It is not rocket science. These fellows separated us by rank, took us to separate rooms and in groups debriefed us. They encouraged us to talk about what we had seen, not bottle it up.

I thought the whole process was bullshit. I failed to see how it would or could help. As far as I was concerned, all went well; there was no need to talk, and we wasted two hours talking. At about 2200 we boarded our buses and fell asleep. We arrived back at Base Gagetown around 0400. My ailing 1978 Chevette would not start—a fitting end to a successful mission.

### RETURN TO BOSNIA

The fall of 1998 was spent training for our deployment to Bosnia in January 1999. The pre-rotation (roto) training had evolved over the past several years into a three-month program that attempted to cover every possibility or situation we could face in Bosnia. The weapons training and the first aid made sense, but the rest was a long checklist of crap. What did not make sense was that we were trained soldiers being tested on the things that were our bread and butter, such as manning checkpoints, patrolling, establishing observation posts, cordons and searches and so on.

What pissed me off, as well as the others who had been to Bosnia, was that no one was testing the clerks on typing, the mechanics on vehicle maintenance, the cooks on cooking; yet here we were, being put through endless training. It was as if we were required to do this training so that desk soldiers in Ottawa could tick the items off of a list and declare us operationally ready. Most of us who had previous tours overseas felt this training requirement was a "cover your ass" list for Ottawa, a list that could be used to point the finger at the soldiers if anything went wrong. I could hear them now: "We can't understand what happened! They covered that on the pre-roto training, it must be their fault." Ass-covering had been elevated to an art after the Somalia inquiry and the disbandment of the Canadian Airborne Regiment.

And I was bored to tears and angry about the approach being taken to our upcoming tour. For example, Ottawa paid some high-priced help from the Pearson Peacekeeping Centre to brief us on negotiation skills. Christ, it was a farce! They talked about negotiating techniques that could be used at a level far above what we would be required to conduct. What we needed to know was how to negotiate concerns at the ground level, things like how to sort out refugees returning to a village, the use of roads by the locals, opening the schools and so on.

All I wanted to do was get on the plane and go. We were trained well enough to do whatever we would have to do. Deep down, I also felt that a break from the home front for Janice and me would be good. I thought I would get better. I'd be able to purge the demons and return a happy, healthy Fred.

Christmas break was anticipated by all; we were all tired of the training. Then Christmas day brought tragedy to our family. That afternoon Ben, Erin and I drove to Fredericton to pick up Erin's friend Terri and have her over for supper. It was a gorgeous sunny day. After picking up Terri, we turned for home, taking the Trans-Canada Highway. At the top of a hill, a car heading towards us suddenly turned left onto a side road and hit us head on. I broke my right foot and left hand. Ben put his hand through the windshield, and Terri injured her arm and elbow. But worst of all was Erin. Her hip was broken, her scalp torn and her nose peeled back. We all ended up in the hospital.

Janice was at home at the time of the accident, preparing Christmas supper with my sister Marie, when she got my call from the hospital. It is strange how one thinks in time of duress; but I remember telling her to take the turkey out of the oven so that it would not burn. It was a very upsetting scene that greeted her at the hospital. Here was her whole family, with various unspecified injuries, in the emergency ward. Other than Erin, we had been very lucky. Ben and I went home later that evening, Terri remained in the hospital for a few days, but Erin was in for two weeks. She had surgery on her hip and plastic surgery on her head and nose. To this day Erin still has problems from nerve damage where her hip broke and with her jaw, which was hyper-extended by the impact. I was a few weeks away from leaving for Bosnia.

# SNIPER VICTIM

**I WAS TALKING WITH** my daughter, Erin, about my battle with
my demons because she too seemed to be going through a rough
time. Perhaps she experienced a bit too much during her teen years in
Edmonton. Erin told me that she was coming to grips with her own
demons, but she was frustrated, ashamed and afraid to ask for the help
she needed. Janice and I wanted to help take away some of the pain and
fear, to help Erin rise above the depression that seemed to cloak her.
But our words seemed to fall on deaf ears. It hurt to see Erin so down
and so hopeless; all we could do was be there with unconditional love.

As Erin was talking about her concerns I was listening intently,
wanting to take on some of her pain, when I suddenly blurted out
something about trying to help someone who was bleeding from a
gunshot wound. I said something about sticking my finger in the bullet
hole in the side of his chest. I exhaled deeply and looked into Erin's eyes,
which not surprisingly were registering shock and confusion. I had let
my shield down and was caught off guard. My body reacted by kicking
into one of my practised grounding drills, deep breathing. But it was
useless. I was back in hell.

That summer day in Sarajevo in 1995, a young man was slumped
against the wall of a building. He had pulled up his shirt and was
staring at the hole in his side, about six inches below the right nipple.
Blood, a pinkish red, was flowing in a rhythm with his breathing, which
was strained and heavy. His face was pale and drawn in pain; he was
already in shock.

Our eyes met. His dark brown eyes were wide with shock and surprise. They were burning a hole in me. He knew he was dying. *Everyone is dying in this fucking war,* I thought. But I said nothing. I knelt down beside him. His blood was pooling under his ass. I took care to notice where the blood was; I didn't want to kneel in it, because I had only three pairs of combat pants and had no way of cleaning them. *His life blood flowing out of him and I don't want to get blood on my pants.*

By now I had seen so much death that I didn't care. He was in no pain, and he would soon die and be free from this hell on earth. I placed one hand on his shoulder and my other hand on his wound. The blood was warm as it oozed out from under my palm and between my fingers; it wouldn't stop. I was alone because everyone had fled the scene once the sniper had dropped this fellow. What could I do? I had no more dressings or bandages, so I rammed my middle finger in the hole like a plug and pushed my fist against his ribs. *Christ, there's a lot of blood here.*

All the time I was yelling "Help, fuck, someone, help!" But fear kept them away. The Serb snipers knew that rescuers would be coming and providing them with fresh targets. I wondered if those cocksuckers were watching me, a blue-helmeted UN idiot kneeling over this guy yelling for help. I was not afraid, but my anger seethed as I imagined them watching, laughing and sharing a drink of *rakia* over their latest kill.

*He's still breathing.* I was still yelling, but then I heard the reassuring growl of one of the Sarajevo "miracles on wheels": a VW Rabbit taxi cum ambulance. It roared up the street under the cover of buildings and stopped in the shadow of one, shielding it from the view of our tormentor. The driver and his mate jumped out and, without hesitating, ran over and grabbed the fellow by his ankles and under the armpits—as I trundled along, with my finger still stuck in his side. The hatchback was open. We laid him in sideways; one of them pulled my finger out and produced a large bandage. He pressed it to the wound. Then he jumped into the open hatchback, straddled the wounded man, and off they roared in a cloud of black diesel smoke.

I was left standing there, my hand dripping blood which was still warm, yet already becoming sticky as it began to coagulate and dry.

Somewhere nearby there was a loud explosion as another shell landed in the dying city. The sound broke my trance and snapped me back to reality. *Get the fuck out of here.* I sprinted down a narrow side street to get away from the scene. Panting, I stopped and crouched next to a pile of debris that was once a building. My heart was pounding and my breath coming in gulps. There was an acrid taste in my mouth. I looked at my bloody hands, reached down and grabbed a handful of plaster dust. The fine dust clung to the blood like a glove. I kept rubbing my hand in the dust to get the blood off. I had to forget those eyes. All the time I told myself the fellow would live. *Of course he lived. They all lived happily ever after.*

I left Erin sitting in the room, dumbfounded. I made my way to the kitchen, tense and confused, already at a loss about what I had just said. Erin had stepped on a land mine: a memory that had receded but not disappeared, that was just waiting for some unfortunate to uncover it.

# 13 | Returning

AS A RESULT of the car accident and the injuries I'd received, I feared I would be left behind in Canada. In fact, I should have been kept back. But I rested as much as I could and returned to work in pain, letting on that all was fine. I flew to Bosnia on January 19, 1999, doped up on anti-inflammatories and painkillers. I spent the first few weeks popping pills and lying on my bunk in pain. One day the contingent doctor noticed me hobbling and grimacing, and he asked what was going on. I told him the truth; he thought I was mental. He told me to report to the medical section, where I was given cortisone injections into the injured muscles and stronger anti-inflammatories. I was also given valium for sleep, which I never took for fear of its effects on my ability to do my job.

The medical intervention worked; I began to mend physically. However, my head was still fucked up in Bosnia. By fucked up I mean I was content, happy and generally at peace with my demons. But I did not socialize, except at meal times. I went to a small gym regularly and burnt off the excess energy I seemed to have. My "give a fuck factor" was low. When it came to my work as the second-in-command of G Company, the company pretty much ran itself.

To help alleviate my low GAFF, I would take a vehicle and driver and cruise around the Bosnian countryside. The drivers must have thought I was strange, because I said little and just took in the countryside. It felt good to be in familiar places, to see the people going about their daily chores and to witness the rebuilding that had taken place since the end of the war. But even those escapes became boring, because this was not the area I had served in during the war.

## SARAJEVO, AGAIN

By July I had just returned from my leave with Janice. We'd met in Paris and had a grand time roaming around France, Belgium and Holland—a great break after five months in Bosnia. The Bosnia tour had a month to go, and then I would be home again.

Living in the same camp as the Battle Group Headquarters was not a place to spend your whole tour. The camp was full of many bored people with not much to do. As our days in Bosnia wound down, I was quite pissed that I had not been able to get back to Sarajevo. Another officer who had served in Sarajevo submitted a memo to the co requesting permission for him and me to visit Sarajevo. We were refused. I could not figure out why we could not go; after all, the National Support Element sent a vanload of their personnel to Sarajevo each week to sightsee and shop. The negative answer did not deter me; I wrote another memo and had my knuckles rapped for the tone of my words. Still no. I was beside myself: just a few hundred kilometres away were some dear friends, and I wouldn't be able to see them. I had expected the refusal, so I was already planning an unauthorized trip. Fuck the orders.

I was glad to be serving in G Company with Bill Pond as the oc. Bill was always looking for any tasking that would bring us together as a company, so when a security tasking came up for the Balkan summit in Sarajevo, he quickly volunteered G Company. When Bill told me of the tasking, my anger immediately disappeared. I was filled with the anticipation and excitement of going back to Sarajevo. We would be working with a multinational task force, securing the city. Our part of the mission was to man the inner cordon around the Zetra Stadium. This was a high-profile event; Bill Clinton, Tony Blair and even our own Jean Chrétien would be flying in for the day. A few days after we received orders, we were off. Bill Pond brought me along on the advance party. I normally moved with the main body, but he told me to hand that job over. I think he wanted to make sure that I got to Sarajevo. (I'd also make a pretty good guide.)

The trip was quick: the roads were clear and the weather was balmy. We stopped at a few cafes en route, and I felt as if I were on holiday. Once in the city, we made our way to the new American camp in Butmir, just west of the airport. The United States was helping to establish a new Bosnian army with training, equipment and this huge base. We linked up with our American counterparts and got settled into our accommodation, then checked out the amenities of the camp, which had several cafes, two PXs and a large kitchen with pretty good food.

I was eager to get into the city. I wanted to track down Goran, Mama and Zoran. I was also keen to see the changes that must have taken place since the war. Acting as a tour guide, I navigated our way through Dobrinja, which had changed radically. This part of the city had been a constant combat zone throughout the war. At first I was a bit disoriented. All the streets were open and all the barricades were gone. These had been my reference points when we roamed the city in '95. I was excited but a bit apprehensive, because I knew that some places would elicit brutal memories.

The streets were busy with people who looked healthy and contented as they went about their business. We made our way through the old town and then down Tito Boulevard, past the site of Market I and II, past the place where I had helped the sniper victim. We then drove up to the Zetra Stadium, where the summit was to be held. My mind was pumping out the memories at a pace that had me dumbfounded. I think that Bill and Company Sergeant Major Bob Girouard were wondering: for someone who had such a strong connection to this city, I had very little to say.

But in fact I had so much to say that I did not know where to begin. I was caught up in a kaleidoscope of images. When we came to a stoplight I glanced out of the window and was snapped back to July 17, 1995. We were sitting at an intersection where I had been wounded. I was not prepared for the impact that this place had on me; everything closed in, and my senses were on hyper-alert. The light changed, and as we moved off I said: "This is where I almost died in '95." My voice must have given away that I was in some distress. No one said anything; we just drove off in silence. Once we were clear of the site I said, "Let's go and check on my old friends."

I directed the driver to the narrow street I had walked down so often. It was on this street that I had found "the finger." We came to a stop at my old digs, and I told them to "give me a few minutes" as I got out of the vehicle and headed up the driveway. I was giddy with the anticipation of seeing Mama and Goran as I made my way up the stairway to the landing where their apartment was. I paused, took a breath and knocked on the door. The door opened. I did not recognize the man who answered, and I could see over his shoulder that the apartment was not the same. "*Dobar dan*, Goran Mehmebegovic," I said. The man must have seen both the puzzled look on my face and the uniform, and realized that I had lived there during the war. In Bosnian he told me that they now lived on Tito Boulevard and that Goran ran a little convenience store there. I must have looked disappointed, because he then said that he had their telephone number and would call them. I thanked him profusely as he led me to the phone and made the call.

He had been joined by his wife, who offered me a seat in what had once been the kitchen. The little wood stove was gone, and so was the familiar round table. It seemed strange to be in a familiar place that held so many memories, yet physically the place had changed so radically. The apartment had been renovated into what we would call an "open concept." Gone was the kitchen and the tiny parlour where we had watched the Dayton Accord being signed live on CNN. The renewal of people's lives had made its way into the apartment: *Get rid of the past by moving on.*

I snapped out of my reverie when the man handed me the receiver and said "Anna." I took the phone. "Hello, Anna. My name is Captain Fred Doucette, from Canada. I lived with Mama and Goran during the war."

"Yes, I know who you are," she replied. Anna spoke perfect English, a result of having been a refugee in Norway for almost four years. "They have spoken about you and Einar often. I am sorry to say, but Mama, Goran and Zoran are on holiday on the Adriatic coast."

"How are they?" I asked.

"They are all doing well. Their health is fine and life is good for all of us, now that we have been reunited."

My disappointment was replaced with an upswell of happiness on hearing that they were all doing well. Anna gave me their mailing address, and I told her that I would write and that someday I would visit not as a captain but as Fred: "Tell them that I am fine and that I miss them."

"I will. Thank you for being so kind to them during the war. And thank you for calling."

I stood there in the old kitchen, the dial tone buzzing in my ear, locked in a trance of years gone by. I could feel myself smiling as I remembered the happy times I'd spent here by the candlelight. I handed the receiver to the gentleman and thanked him for his kindness. As he led me back to the door, I glanced over my shoulder. I could see all my friends from '95 sitting around the table, laughing and joking, making the best of a miserable time.

Bill and Bob had waited patiently for me. I thanked them and told them where my friends were as I got into the vehicle. The last six months had all been crystallized in that two-minute call to Anna. I had found what I had returned to Bosnia to find. They were all right—Christ, they were on holiday at the oceanside, enjoying the sun and the peace they so deserved. They had survived the war and had reunited with their family. I felt that they had returned to a life they could only have imagined before those dark days of fear and despair.

My sixth tour was coming to an end. I had made it to Sarajevo and had found the answers I was looking for. I had no idea that it would be my last tour.

### SECOND RETURN FROM BOSNIA

I can't remember my return from Bosnia. I do remember the excitement and anticipation of the flight timings and manifests being announced. Which meant you knew exactly when you would be on your way home. I knew I wasn't ready to come home yet, because I gave up my early-departure seat to one of our platoon commanders who had been married for less than a year. I ended up staying in Bosnia for several more days. Janice was not pleased, but I was indifferent to the tour ending and my return home. I was confused and my head was fucked.

I landed in Moncton because the Fredericton airport could not handle a 747. Tim Hortons coffee and doughnuts were waiting for us, compliments of a grateful lady who approached Tim's and had them donate goodies for the arrival of each flight. The two-hour bus drive to CFB Gagetown was quiet and filled with the snores of soldiers who had been on the move for over twenty-four hours.

The brightest spot in my return was seeing Janice at the drill hall. It is difficult to explain the joy and comfort that seeing her brought to my restless, troubled mind. And being in her arms was like a tonic. My return leave was a whirlwind of visits, especially to my son Ben's place in Petawawa, where Terri, Erin's friend and now Ben's wife-to-be, was pregnant with their first child. It amazed me how in a space of a couple of years he had joined the army, had met Terri and was on his way to being a father. Life moves so fast—even faster if you can't put the brakes on to slow down and enjoy it. Erin was on the mend from the car accident, but her injuries to her hip and jaw would continue to cause pain. Her plans for continuing university had been derailed, and in the end she enrolled in a one-year media graphics/design computer course.

After the happiness of returning home wore off, I retreated into the depths with my demons. Returning to work was anti-climactic: we reformed the battalion and I moved to Kilo Company as the company second-in-command: same job, same old shit.

I was chosen to be part of a NATO training cadre that would go to Poland and train Polish, Romanian, Ukrainian and Latvian soldiers in peace support operations. There were about thirty instructors, drivers, store men and support soldiers who would be in Poland for two or three weeks. It was great to be back in a foreign country, especially one with so much history, particularly from World War II. I had a chance to visit Hitler's headquarters, where he commanded his forces during the invasion of Russia. It was also at this headquarters that the attempt to assassinate him took place. It was strange to stand were Hitler had stood on that fateful day. I also visited his most infamous legacy, the Auschwitz death camp. It is impossible to imagine the suffering that occurred in this place.

The training we gave to the troops was well received, and it was interesting teaching through an interpreter. I did not take advantage of the local bars and kept mostly to myself, except for going out for a late supper at a local eatery in the small village that lay just outside our compound. I had a meal with some of the locals, and felt quite at home there. It reminded me of the meals I had shared in Sarajevo.

But in fact I was feeling worse. I couldn't sleep, I was explosively angry, my short-term memory was gone and I forgot to eat. When it came to work, I just didn't care. My uniform was a mess, my hair and moustache were beyond regulation length and I just didn't give a shit. When I think back, I can't figure out why I wasn't taken to task over my attitude.

I was planning to request a one- to two-year posting as an UNMO to the Middle East. I was hooked on the adrenalin of the UNMO work, even though 98 per cent of it was routine and boring. It was the 2 per cent that I craved. I also missed the camaraderie of the UNMO teams.

The trip to Poland came and went, as did the remainder of the fall. We crept slowly towards the Christmas block-leave period. Then, around the first week of December 2000, my dad's health slowly took a turn for the worse. He was frail, eighty-one years old, and was admitted to the Miramichi hospital with respiratory problems. We all feared the worst. We visited Dad often and spent some nice times with him. He was never a big man, all of five feet six inches and 140 pounds, and with his illness he looked smaller and frailer in his hospital bed.

When we were alone, Dad told me that he was dying. I countered with a "No, you're not," which was more for me than for him. I had lost my mom ten years earlier, and now I knew I would have to say goodbye to my dad.

Janice was with me as we said goodbye. Janice is a strong woman; I know she kept her emotions in check for the rest of us, but she was feeling intense pain. My mom and dad really meant the world to her. Then she left me alone with Dad for a few minutes, and I cried—in sadness, but also in happiness for what he gave me, a sense of both responsibility and humour. I told Dad that I loved him for the first time in my life and thanked him for his part in my life. Four of us were with him when he gasped his last breath in the early morning of December 23. I still miss my mom and dad and often allow myself to be caught up in my memories of them. Sometimes I cry out of happiness and love for them.

My depression sank to greater depths with the death of my dad. I questioned the purpose of my life, and I asked a higher power to just end it all for me because I didn't have the guts to do it myself. I may have thought that no one noticed my depression and lack of interest in my work, but they did. I found out later that there was a move afoot in the battalion to move me into a base job for a rest. My OC recommended that I be posted to the engineering school as the infantry instructor. It was a safe, quiet job, and being the only infantry officer at the school would mean that I would be left alone. So on January 21, 2001, I was posted from the battalion to the Canadian Forces School of Military Engineering, about five hundred metres from the battalion lines where I had begun soldiering thirty-one years ago.

At the school I was in charge of the combat training section. The section ran itself. I deflected the shit that came from higher up, which allowed the fellows to do their job. Having been in a war, I stressed combat survival and brought realistic training to the young soldiers and officers. Unarmed combat, bayonet fighting and a variety of PT enhanced the training. I had a feeling that some engineers, who are a laid-back bunch to begin with, must have thought I was some kind of zealot. My focus on combat survivability for the soldiers would come to haunt me later on.

My macho self-image was still very much in control. I was still denying both to myself and to Janice that anything was wrong with me. Janice stood by me through my moods and explosive anger. At times I wondered why she put up with me; *she would be better off without me*, I thought. On this roller coaster ride through hell the thoughts of being alone or dead came and went, but thankfully they never hung around for long. But Janice told me that being around me during those dark days was like walking on eggshells, never knowing what would set me off.

I hit the wall in the spring of 2001. Janice finally had seen enough. And she was exhausted. She said, "Fred, you really need help. This can't go on much longer."

I agreed. No more tough soldier. I was hurting, and I desperately wanted help. I did not care who knew; I would spill my guts to whoever would listen. I saw a military doctor, who referred me to the social work office so that they could refer me to Halifax for a proper assessment. At the social work office I had my first taste of "professional" incomprehension and indifference. I was visiting a social worker, who asked me how I was doing. I listed several complaints, one being my emotional state and how I could be driven to tears by the smallest thing. In an off-hand way, he said that this was because I was getting old.

I felt like ripping his heart out and shitting in the hole, but instead I told him to sign the paper and let me go. *What a fucking asshole*, I thought. But then I realized that he was just a small wheel in a big machine, and I was now determined to find out what was wrong with me.

### PSYCHIATRIC ASSESSMENT, AND THERAPY BEGINS

I left for Halifax on a beautiful June morning. I felt both calm and curious about what would transpire at the Operational Trauma Social Support Centre (OTSSC). I arrived at the base in Halifax in the early afternoon and checked into my accommodation. Being a good soldier, I found out where the OTSSC was and took a drive over so that I would know how to get there. I didn't want to be late in the morning. I ate supper in the Naval Officers Mess, then went for a stroll to collect my thoughts and kill some time. I went to bed early, but I could not sleep. The heat, the city noises and the pending assessment combined to keep me restless and awake. I fell asleep eventually but was awakened at about 0500 by a crying baby. I looked out my window and across the street at a bus stop. There, a young mother sat with her baby. I watched them and wondered where they could be going at such an hour. I lay down in bed again for a while, then got up, showered and shaved.

When I went down for breakfast I was dressed in my uniform, pressed and with all the bells and whistles, and received quite the once-over from everyone when I entered the dining room. I was an army guy on a navy base—a bit of an oddity. I ate and drank too much coffee, but I had time to kill before my 0900 appointment for my assessment. When I finally got there I kept telling myself to hold nothing back and spill my guts.

The assessment was quite simple, but it took two hours to complete. It was mainly questions and answers. My answers were rated on a scale of 1 to 10, 10 being the worst. I felt exhausted by the time I finished and went straight back to my room, closed the curtains and lay down. I was to report back the next morning, when I would be seen by the psychiatrist who would give me the results of the assessment.

I had a lousy sleep and was up early. I felt anxious as I made my way back to the clinic, all the time hoping that the assessment would tell me what I "had." Sitting in the waiting room, sipping on an over-brewed bitter coffee, I tried to look cool, calm and collected. Promptly at nine I was called into the doctor's office. The room was dark and decked out with all of the things you'd expect to see in a psychiatrist's office. I sat on the couch. The psychiatrist and I gabbed a bit about how I was, what I thought of the assessment and so on. She said that the assessment had given her enough information to diagnose me as suffering from severe, chronic post-traumatic stress disorder (PTSD). She quickly added that I could be treated with medical help and psychotherapy and that I could, with hard work, become healthier.

It was as if a load had been lifted off my shoulders: what was going on with me had a name, and it was treatable! The doctor explained that medication would take the edge off things and help me sleep. I had only one concern: after my encounter with the military social worker in Gagetown, I did not want to participate in therapy with anyone related to the military. She assured me that she would make arrangements for me to see a civilian therapist in Fredericton. I thanked her and went directly to the base pharmacy to have my prescription filled. I felt happier than I had in years, even though I was one sick puppy.

I phoned Janice from a pay phone and told her what had transpired. She too was relieved, elated, in fact, that I had finally reached out for help that was sorely needed. My therapy began in June 2001 in Fredericton. I don't remember being anxious or nervous before my first appointment with my therapist, who I will call Debra. Debra's office was on Queen Street, across from the Legion, in a four-storey office building. The day of my first appointment found me sitting in the busy waiting room. Again, here I was in uniform, being stared at by others in the room. I was relieved when Debra came out, introduced herself, offered me a coffee and led me to her office.

Here I was finally ready to face my demons. Our first appointment was not what I expected: it was an introduction to what lay ahead for me. Debra explained that the therapy consisted of three unequal parts. First, education and stabilization. Second, dealing with the demons, "the dark side." Third, reviewing or confirming the first part. The hour went by quickly; we set a date for the next appointment, and I left feeling hopeful and optimistic about where I was headed with my illness.

One of the demons I had to face was the dilemma that all Canadian infantrymen face: we are trained to destroy the enemy yet are employed as peacekeepers. All those years of training as soldiers seems a waste. Peacekeeping mandates put us in situations that we have never trained for. The results of our continued training and conditioning over many years cause some of us to crack, especially when we know we are not being supported or respected by our leaders and by the civilian population in Canada. In the Canadian Forces there is a general feeling of bitterness and anger towards those both in the military and in the civilian world who are totally out of touch with what we do on peacekeeping missions.

I have read and listened to experts who say there are situations or conditions in a person's upbringing that may influence a person's susceptibility to PTSD. I guess that anyone who looks back on his or her upbringing can find situations that could be interpreted as a sort of preconditioning that might have left them vulnerable to psychological trauma.

I've often tried to remember how I handled stress during my time in Bosnia. During my time there I must have felt its mental and physical warning signs. What I did recognize was an overall feeling of doom that was always foremost in my thoughts. At times I felt I had a heavy weight on my shoulders. Situations and circumstances would pull these feelings to and fro, making for some really confusing moments.

Now that I was in therapy and would be required to attend regular appointments, I felt that the commandant of the engineering school, Lieutenant Colonel Tattersall, and my immediate bosses should be made aware of what was going on with me. I did not think they would think less of me if they knew about my PTSD. The commandant was very understanding about my illness, and we talked for almost two hours. Even though he had never been on a mission, he seemed to have more insight and understanding of the significance of operational stress injuries (OSIS) for returning soldiers than did most of those who had been overseas. My OC, Paul Davies, assured me that whatever I needed to get healthy was mine for the asking.

### PROGRESS, WITH SIDE EFFECTS

My medications kicked in about three weeks after I had started them. I had been told that although they would take the edge off, there could be side effects. And there were. When I first woke up my eyes saw movement with a strobe, or whirling, effect; I could not shit; I had the sweats, or, better still, "I'm on fire" hot flashes and I felt stoned until about midday. I used to have to sit on the edge of my bed until my eyes calmed down. Then I would sit on the toilet and grunt and groan as if I were shitting a watermelon, and all I'd produce were a few grape-sized pellets.

I drove Janice crazy with my hot flashes (and still do) by either freezing her out of the house or driving around in December with the car window down. Being a typical soldier, I tried to tough it out. I put up with the medication for about a year. Janice frequently suggested that I should try another antidepressant, as there were many on the market with fewer side effects.

I finally brought up the side effects with my doctor after she informed me that I would have to have my blood checked regularly. Toxins from the medication might be building up in my liver. Something else to think about: *With this crap, I'll be nice and mellow when I die from liver failure.* The doctor then sent me to see a psychiatrist, who immediately switched me to a new antidepressant, explaining that prescribing these meds was not an exact science.

After I helped to screw up the transition from the old medication to the new by not reading the instructions properly, things began to settle down. I could shit, and had no more strobe-effect wake-ups, but my hot flashes are still with me. (Janice humours me when I sometimes have a hot flash, reminding me that this is what women go through with menopause, and much more. So "toughen up!")

My medications were finally sorted out and working. Meanwhile, fortunately, my doctor found another medication that sorted out the nerve damage to the right side of my face—the result of the shelling incident in Sarajevo. Until she found the silver bullet, my face was palsied and twitching, my right eye watered, the right side of my mouth drooled, the roots of my hair hurt and my jaw would lock open at the most inappropriate times.

For the first year of my therapy, things seemed to ebb and flow: some sessions showed progress, others were benign. I was still battling with my tough-soldier self-image. I always went to my sessions in uniform and continually told myself, "There is nothing wrong with me." This, despite the fact that I had already admitted that there was. The old "toughen up and take the pain" loop kept running through my head. When I didn't doubt my illness, I'd practise using the coping skills that Debra was teaching me. I had developed some coping skills on my own, but they were really rough and ready. For example, to deal with my fear of crowded places, such as the local mall, I would not go to the mall and avoid crowds. By doing this I thought I was coping, but really I was exhibiting another symptom: avoidance.

The key was to practise and test my new skills. "Grounding" was one of the important skills. By grounding myself, I was putting myself in the here and now. For instance, at the mall I would tell myself, *Fred, you are in Canada. It's Saturday, and you are at the mall in Fred-*

*ericton. There will be people, noise, kids. All the sounds and movement are normal and you are safe.* And over time, this worked. My brain eventually made a new pathway to that grounding mantra. The panic still occurs, but now it takes only a few milliseconds to ground myself.

The breathing and relaxation techniques were also a great way to gear down whenever I began to feel stressed. I had a routine before bed: I'd stretch and do a series of breathing exercises, and they worked. Now, however, my problem was not getting to sleep but staying asleep. Debra taught me how to distance myself from what was happening in my dreams. It may seem odd, but the first time it worked for me I woke up and thought, *Christ, it works.* What I had done was take myself in a dream and move off to become the spectator of what was happening to me in my dream.

The dream that I first had success with was one about being totally helpless. In the dream I had been captured along with some other soldiers, and the Serbs had us lined up against a wall. They were roughing us up and threatening us with weapons, and all we could do was stand there and take it. There was no fear, just anger at not being able to do something. We were under their control because they had the guns. At one point during the dream I could hear myself saying, "This is fucking bullshit." Then *boom*, I was off to the right flank on the road, watching myself being fucked around by the Serbs. That's when I said to myself, "It's a dream, Fred. Wake up!" Next thing I knew, I was awake in my bed at home. I was elated that I had made a decision that got me out of a bad situation, even though it was a dream.

During the first year of my therapy I began to realize that I was slowly regaining some control over my life. But just getting to therapy began to cause me some grief. I had to cut loose from work at one-thirty and race to Fredericton. I'd arrive agitated and not mentally ready for the sessions. It was then that my "give a fuck factor" kicked in and I decided to start leaving at midday. This gave me time to go home, eat, change and make my way to Fredericton. At work, no one cared that I was gone for Wednesday afternoons; if they did, I didn't notice. Arriving not stressed out, and wearing civilian clothes, made a difference in the session. I was more relaxed and ready for whatever the session brought out.

The path the therapy took was quite subtle and to me seemed disorganized. Being military, I expected therapy to progress in stages, with a definite beginning, middle and end. Not until a few years later did I realize that the path was controlled and measured not by me but by Debra. She would coax and steer the session, allowing me to vent and rave but always subtly easing me back on course. (That's why Debra was the therapist and I was the client.) There were a few occasions when I would avoid and steer away from persons, places or events that really bothered me. To come to grips with those demons, I would tell Debra before the end of the session to ask me about this and that. For instance, I'd say, "Ask me about children next session," and sure enough, at the next session Debra would bluntly say: "You want me to ask you about children. So, what about them?" I then felt that I had a reason to let out some of the demons because someone asked me about them. There were times between sessions where I would make notes, and before the end of the next session I would give them to Debra and say, "Let's talk about this next session." These questions and notes seemed to work.

On a parallel course with my mental health, rehabilitation was the administration action that would eventually lead to my release from the army on medical grounds. All personnel in the Canadian Forces have a medical suitability category, which is based on factors such as hearing, eyesight and so on. Your health in these factors is measured numerically, with 0 or 1 being good and 4 to 5 being poor. A 4 or 5 in any category in all likelihood requires a review of your medical category (Med Cat). So, while I was in therapy I was placed on a six-month temporary medical category (T Cat) for geographical (G) and occupational (O)—what is called a G404, which meant that there were severe restrictions on my employment as an infantry officer as well as on where I could be employed. The technical aim of the T Cat is to restrict employment under specific categories, to allow a person to mend. For me this meant no employment outside the local area, and I had to be available for medical appointments—in my case, therapy.

This may sound like a caring way to treat your employees, but in a lot of cases, especially with mental health, it is the route to ending your career. The T Cats are six months in duration and during the six months your progress is monitored by a doctor. At the end of the first six months, if you have recovered, your T Cat is removed and you return to work. If you are still ill, another six-month T Cat is initiated and you carry on mending. Administratively, you can only be awarded two back-to-back six-month T Cats, after which your medical file is sent to National Defence Headquarters in Ottawa. There it is reviewed, and a decision is made on your future in the Canadian Forces.

Herein lies the problem with a mental injury versus a physical injury. With a physical injury, say, a broken leg requiring surgery, there is the incident, the injury, diagnosis, recovery, physiotherapy and a return to work. With a physical injury there is a predictable amount of time between incident and return to work, and a six-month T Cat is sufficient time to mend.

With PTSD, however, although recovery follows the same path, there is a great difference in recovery time. For example, if the incident is the recovery of bodies of dead women and children, the injury becomes apparent with the onset of symptoms; diagnosis occurs when the soldier comes forward and admits he is hurting; and recovery, at best, requires two or more years of therapy; then, hopefully, there is a return to work. It can be easily seen that two or even three six-month T Cats will not be sufficient time for a person with PTSD to be properly diagnosed and treated. So your file ends up in Ottawa, where it is reviewed, and in all likelihood you are awarded a permanent category (P Cat), G404, the proverbial kiss of death for your career.

The umbrella that covers your future service is "universality of service," a list of duties and requirements all Canadian Forces personnel must be able to do and meet, regardless of trade or rank. The catch-all in the universality of service is that all personnel must be able to deploy outside of the country. As a result, "No deploy, no employ."

It is well known in the Canadian Forces that universality of service is not universal. It depends on your trade and where and who you work for. If you are an infantryman or combat engineer in an operational unit, you must be fit and ready to deploy; there is no time or space in these units for you to mend. On the other hand, if you are a clerk or driver at a static base unit, there is the time and space in these units for you to mend and return to work.

My case was an odd one. I had two T Cats, with an administrative mix-up of a few months between the two, which meant that my file went to Ottawa after fifteen months instead of twelve. To its credit, the system offered me accommodation: if a commanding officer was willing to accept me with my medical limitations, then I could remain in the Canadian Forces for three more years. I was offered a few jobs, one being recruiting, which I thought was humorous because of my mental state. I was definitely not a good ambassador to influence young people to join the Canadian Forces. I could see myself buzzed on medication, fuelled with anger, telling people to stay away, get a job, enjoy life as a civvie.

## A NEW LIFE?

My therapy had now been going on for almost two years; I knew I was getting better, but I had not experienced that "Eureka, I'm cured" moment. Around June 2002 I asked Debra, "How will I *know* when I'm better?" She was very cunning. She answered my question with another question: what would I be doing this summer. I said that Janice and I had planned to drive to Montreal to visit family and then to Ottawa to visit my son, his wife Terri and Ethan, their son. Debra's next question brought the last years of therapy together: "Would you have been able to plan and think about the future last year?" And there it was, my Eureka moment. A year earlier, I couldn't think of what I would be doing in the next hour; there was no planning for the immediate future then, let alone thinking one month ahead. Now I had a future; my life was back in that moment. I told myself, *I am in control, I have a life.*

The realization that I was getting healthier was fantastic. All of the work that Debra and I had put into my therapy had worked. It was as if the cloud that had been following me for the past several years had disappeared. So, feeling the need to challenge my new mental fitness, I proposed that I would not have any weekly sessions for July and August. I did not want to end up being dependent on those sessions. I felt mentally stronger than I ever had. All the bits of the puzzle had fallen into place, and I wanted to get on with my life.

A few months earlier, in April, I had attended an information-gathering session presented by a couple of gentlemen from Ottawa. I cannot remember what they were gathering information on; I did, however, have a chat with Major Jane Livingston, who had been the co of the surgical unit in Bosnia in 1999. She knew I'd been diagnosed with PTSD and was facing release from the Canadian Forces soon. Major Livingston asked if I would be interested in attending a briefing on peer support for those suffering with an OSI. I thought I could spend the afternoon sitting in my office staring at my computer or at the base medical clinic listening to a briefing on something that caught my interest. I met Jim Jamieson that afternoon after his presentation on a project that was co-sponsored by DND and Veterans Affairs Canada (VAC), called the Operational Stress Injury Social Support (OSISS) project. Jane had put the bug in his ear about me: my service, my injury, my recovery and imminent release. Jim asked if I was interested in going to Montreal for an interview with the project manager to determine whether I would be interested in and capable of being the OSISS Peer Support Coordinator for New Brunswick.

Things were moving fast, and I needed time to absorb the fact that people were looking at me as being out of the army in the near future. The job offer was a shock. I told myself, *It's over. Your soldiering days are over.* Until now I had felt that I would get healthier and carry on soldiering; I still had a few years to serve. But my safety net was being pulled out from under me. I never thought I would end my career on a medical release. Deep down, I knew that I was no longer in control because my temporary category had marked me as "unfit," and it was just a matter of time before I was a civvie. I told Jim that I would get back to him, and, with my head reeling, I thanked Jane for her confidence and headed home to tell Janice about what had happened.

From the beginning of my therapy, Janice had been my confidant in trying to make sense of what was going on in my therapy sessions.

Janice helped me to deal with my demons. She noticed the healthy changes in me early on in my therapy, and told me more than once that something good always comes from a bad situation. She suggested that I would feel the need to help others once I had regained a solid footing. Janice encouraged me to write my feelings and experiences down, and she gave me the space to work through my confused state of mind. So, when I told her of Jim's offer, she said: "There it is. Almost as if you were meant to become ill, recover and go out and help others through their pain and horrors of their battle with an OSI."

I was not so confident. In fact, I had not come to terms with my impending release from the military. I could not believe that it was coming to an end with a medical release for a mental illness; I had a lot of thinking to do before I could commit to anything.

In April 2002, I was asked to go to Montreal for an interview with Major Stéphane Grenier, the creator and manager of the OSISS project. The start-up of the project would be in three phrases, with four peer support coordinators being set up every four months until there were twelve across Canada. The mission of the project was first to establish, develop and improve social support programs for Canadian Forces members and their families who were affected by operational stress, and then to provide education and training in the Canadian Forces community that would create an understanding and acceptance of OSI and, in time, eliminate the stigmas attached to it.

My interview with Stéphane was not a formal one. We shot the shit for a couple of hours and then went out for supper. I was not sure what I was getting into, but I did understand that we, the injured, would be helping others with OSI. Regardless of how my trip to Montreal and the interview went, there was a stipulation that dampened my enthusiasm: "If funding is authorized," I would have the job. Pondering my future on the return flight to Fredericton, I did not put much faith in the funding being available.

That summer tested my ability to cope without regular therapy. Janice and I travelled to Petawawa to visit Ben, Terri, Ethan and Amos, their most recent arrival. We had a great time with the grandbrats. The boys were a constant source of joy and happiness to us; their innocence and joy in life were irresistible. Ethan and Amos made me feel alive.

After my leave was over, I returned to work and conducted the infantry training portion for new engineer officers. I always enjoyed instructing and passing on my knowledge, and I felt this would be a good way to end my time in the army. It was at this time that I was offered "accommodation": the army would retain me for three years with my injuries, if the co agreed. But for some reason, the commandant of the engineering school would not accommodate me. It was his right to refuse, and the reason for the refusal was never explained to me. And to this day I still resent his decision. The commandant of the infantry school, Lieutenant Colonel Mike Pearson, did, however, offer to accommodate me. I was thankful, but I sensed that my next three years would be at a desk in some administrative job. I felt that if I could not lead or teach soldiers, then I should part ways with the army. I needed time to think and decide whether or not I would accept accommodation.

Now it was September. I needed time to create some space and think about my future. I was fifty and had served for thirty-two years. I decided to take a couple of weeks off to visit my younger brother Larry, who was living outside Philadelphia. During that trip I decided that my army career was over. I felt good about my service and what I had achieved. But I was angry about how my service would end. I did not want to just hang on, grasping at the bone the system had thrown me; even the word "accommodation" left a sour taste in my mouth. I had not chosen the time and place to end the most significant part of my life; some faceless military bureaucrat a thousand kilometres away in Ottawa was forcing my hand.

The drive to my brother's place took two days and coincided with the first anniversary of 9/11. There were tributes, eulogies and music geared to commemorate what had happened a year ago. I felt relaxed and at peace as I drove, and reflected on my life and my service to my country. I felt a pride that had eluded me for the past several years, and some anticipation and excitement about starting a new chapter in my life. I decided not to fight my release or accept accommodation before I reached my destination. The relief of having made that decision, and realizing deep down that it was the right one, lifted a great burden from my mind. I rationalized my decision by telling myself that if I could not lead or train soldiers, then I was finished and had to move on.

When I got back to work, I wrote a memo to the commandant stating that I would not request accommodation and that I wished to be released within a month. I dropped the memo off at his office and returned to my office to check my email and voice mails. One of the voice mails was from Stéphane: "We have the funds to hire a peer support coordinator in Gagetown. Do you want the job?" So, five minutes after putting in my memo saying I wanted to be released, I'm offered a job. It was over; I would no longer wear a uniform. To dispel any rumours surrounding my release, I decided to email the people I had served with to explain my situation. Call it a pre-emptive strike—I did not want to hear anyone saying, "He left because of the stress" or "I heard Fred flipped out and was thrown out of the army." In the end, I sent out about a hundred emails, and to my surprise many people replied with words of support and thanks for my service.

I wore my uniform for the last time at the trooping of the Queen's Colours for 2 RCR. I had arrived in 2 RCR in 1971 at the CO's change of command parade, and now I was leaving at another parade. There are no words to describe how I felt the years had raced by. I had never thought that I would leave the army on a medical release; I had always looked forward to the day when I would decide to retire. But deep down I knew that my years were numbered, regardless of the PTSD. I was less physically able to do the job; my bones and joints ached, and I dreaded going to the field. Hard soldiering is a young man's job. Even though I did well in the jobs I was put into, I knew that the fuel was running out. So I moved on to a job that would keep me near the army but no longer as a part of it.

Janice would not let my thirty-two years of service pass unrecognized. She planned a retirement party and invited my close friends and family, including Larry, who came up from the United States. It was great to see so many friends and to enjoy their company and accolades. I realized again how indebted I was to Janice for her thoughtfulness, kindness and love.

My farewell from the Canadian Forces, to whom I had given over three decades, was done prior to a combined mess dinner at the Engineer School. The commandant said a few words as we gathered in the hallway before going into dinner. I said "Thanks," and left it at that.

My regiment bid me farewell at the officers regimental birthday mess dinner, where goodbyes are said to officers leaving the RCR. My good friend and brother officer Bill Pond spoke on behalf of the regiment. His words were kind and heartfelt. As I stood there, I felt proud to have served as a soldier and officer in such a fine regiment. When I was given the floor, the words I had penned for the occasion seemed insufficient to convey the feelings I had. How do you sum up three decades of service, other than saying that you will miss them and the RCR and the "Brotherhood of Arms": *Pro Patria*—For Country.

## BECOMING A CIVILIAN

In late October, I went to Ottawa for a couple of weeks' peer support training. It was very interesting, but I still was unsure of exactly what I would be doing. I simplified everything by telling myself that I had to be there for the soldier and the veteran. I had to be non-judgmental, to listen to and care about where they were at. It felt odd to go to work in civvies; the uniform had been such a big part of my identity. And the work was very unconventional—very little office work, with the main access to me being on my cell phone. I put the word out as best as I could, and allowed the peers to gravitate to me—which they did, and in droves.

Most of them needed someone to validate their experiences and their present situation. The key to the program was to point the soldier or veteran towards professional help. Our program mantra is *Listen, Assess and Refer.* Many professionals balk at the "assess" part of what we do. I explain it to them like this: first, listen actively and sincerely. Then, assess: "Have you seen a doctor about this?" And last, refer: "You should see a doctor." I try to point the soldiers and veterans in the right direction and be there for them when they need me.

The job has been very rewarding. I have seen many soldiers and veterans get healthier and move on with their lives. At the same time, I feel sorry for the fellows who are still serving and have the injury but choose not to seek professional help because they fear being labelled and perhaps being released from the armed forces. It will be a long time before the system will consider an OSI an honourable injury, one that is treatable and is not a sign of weakness.

It has been five years since I hung up my uniform. I'm still on medication today. My antidepressants are low-dose, but my medication has remained the same. During my medical release, the doctor informed me that I would probably be on medication for the rest of my life. My response was, "I don't care if I have to take a suppository the size of a beer bottle—three times a day, so long as if it works, I'll take it!"

My son Ben has been to Afghanistan four times; several of my friends have been killed or wounded over there. One of those to die over there was my dear friend and all-round nice guy, Bob Girouard. He and his driver were killed by a suicide bomber near Kandahar, Afghanistan, in November 2006. Bob had achieved the rank of chief warrant officer and was the regimental sergeant major of 1 RCR when he was killed. His death sent a shock wave through the RCR and the armed forces, reminding us once again that in war no one is safe, regardless of rank.

The army is still overworked; there is no rest in sight, and our program continues to see the casualties from our old and now new battlefields. The public support for our troops in Afghanistan is phenomenal, unlike the situation with our involvement in Bosnia. It makes a big difference to know that your country is behind you when you are deployed to these tense and dangerous trouble spots.

The OSISS statistics show that 80 per cent of the OSI casualties are in the army and that 80 per cent of those casualties are from the war in Bosnia. The solution is simple: if we send our soldiers to do our bidding, then it is our responsibility to take care of them. That is what soldiers want; they do not want to be discarded like an empty casing and left on the battlefield to disappear into dust.

# THE PUMPKIN

**JUST WHEN I THINK** I have control of my thoughts and memories, *bang*, my world comes crashing down. The trigger this time came after Halloween. Most Halloween pumpkins end up in the garbage, but some fall into the hands of teenagers who drop them from rooftops and bridges or kick them to pieces just for the joy of seeing them explode. I was heading home after a busy day at work, my thoughts on the quiet evening ahead. I rounded one of the four traffic circles in Oromocto, and there it was, by the curb—a pumpkin. It had been bashed open and had a jagged, gaping hole the size of my hand. The interior of the pumpkin, visible through the hole, was grey to black, and as I passed the darkness of the hole drew me in.

I was no longer looking at a pumpkin but at the head of a man splayed out on his back, mouth open, empty eye sockets looking skyward. He had been shot in the left temple, and the bullet had exited the upper part of the back of his skull. The energy released by the bullet had blown off a piece of his skull the size of my hand. The head looked surprised. Its mouth was open as if its last words were "Oh, fuck." I knew there had been no words or warning when the bullet blew the back of the man's head off; just blackness, silence and death. Whatever had eaten his eyes had also cleaned out what was left of his brain, leaving a grey-black interior. I had always imagined the head as a pretty solid part of the body, but in fact it is such a fragile container for our brain.

With the image of the hole in this guy's head racing around my head, I passed the innocuous pumpkin and drove home. I don't remember the drive.

A fucking hole in a pumpkin had brought this on. It took about a week before the memory began to subside and I stepped out of my cone of silence. I felt the shits—exhausted and confused. It was just a goddamn pumpkin by the roadside. What will it be next? A Christmas wreath, a Valentine heart?

# 14 | Sunshine Diner

I HAVE BEEN off work for the past two weeks, using up some overtime from last year. I had planned to travel west to Ontario to visit my brother Larry, who had moved back to Canada from the U.S., and stop in Ottawa to visit Terri, Ben and the boys. At the last minute I decided to hang at home and get some projects done. However, Mother Nature thwarted my plans for outside work with rain, snow, wind and cold, so I've painted the living room and put down new carpeting.

The "for me" time has been spent in long coffee breaks and the occasional breakfast at the Sunshine Diner. It is nice to be here between the peak times, 0700–0900 and 1130–1330; it is a lot quieter and the service is quicker (not that I am in any hurry). On the days when it has been sunny, I find it difficult to work. The sun feels so good on my winter bones. For some reason I have been staying up late at night, which makes for a slow rise in the morning. It's not that I am sleeping in, because I wake up at my normal time; but I just lie there in a half-comatose state, staring at the ceiling. I don't like doing that and feel guilty when I do—guilty for what, I don't know. Maybe these feelings are a warning that I have to have my shit together when I retire from this job. I really don't want to waste my time, but I also want to be able to relax and not feel guilty for doing so.

My PTSD has been at bay for some time now, but in the past few months I've been concerned about my moods. I really notice the effects when I forget my medication. Within six hours I have a terrible headache and feel anxious and tense in my chest and gut. The meds work, but I feel a bit off balance even when I'm consistent with them. It's as if the spark is gone, and I'm worried that I'm not giving a 100 or even an 80 per cent effort to the troops. That lack of drive comes with a heavy dose of guilt: I'm earning a fair wage, but I feel that I'm not earning it. My coping and grounding skills seem to be in a continual "test" mode.

Fear can pump you up or pull you down; the extremes are amazing. It's the roller coaster ride between extremes that wears you down. In a perverse way I miss the rush, the changes in adrenalin flow. My life and my soldiering are pretty sedate, yet maybe that is for the good—you tend to live longer that way. Lately, it's as if the "triggers" are surfacing closer and closer to my memories. I used to pride myself in the knowledge that I could resist the demons at a distance, yet recently they've been popping up in my face. Maybe I've been overconfident, too cocky. Even as I write these words I feel a knot of tension building at the base of my neck and down between my shoulder blades. I will have to talk this one out with Debra and see if there are any reasons why I feel the way I do about work.

I have gotten into the habit of doing an assessment of my mental health. I can happily say that on a scale of 1 to 10, my life is about an 8.5. I feel contented and very happy, and what stress I do have is work related and quite manageable. And, speaking of work, my work with OSISS is very rewarding and satisfying. Most of the soldiers and veterans I deal with want help and want their lives back. Their problems really vary: from being suicidal to just having administrative problems with Veterans Affairs or National Defence. At least the positive outcomes have been noticed by VAC and DND, and the program is now part of the mental health support network for soldiers and veterans.

The effort put into changing soldiers' attitudes towards OSIS is moving forward, albeit slowly. It will take a generation of soldiers admitting to OSIS before an OSI is considered an honourable injury and one that you can treat and recover from. My plan is to stay with OSISS for as long as I can, or until I burn out. At that point, I will move into retirement and slow the pace of my life down. I am looking forward to the flexibility of being retired. I want to travel, do woodwork and probably take some guitar lessons. I am planning for one of my trips to be back to Sarajevo and to have a reunion with Mama, Goran and Zoran. I miss them as if they were family; I guess they are.

PTSD is the illness that keeps on giving. Nothing is safe, everything is a potential trigger. One sunny Saturday morning, as I drove into Fredericton, I passed the Agriculture Canada research farm. There, on a forward slope in one of their fields, was a large patch of disturbed soil. *Boom*, I was off. A vision of the mass graves I had seen in Bosnia returned. It was so vivid against the tan colour of the dead grass, this dark patch of earth, this dot on the landscape. These types of patches meant that ten or twenty people were gone, never to return. By summer's end, the grass would grow in and nothing would be left to mark their grave. Some of these graves are lost, never to be found, leaving the living to wonder and to hope that all is not lost.

Thinking about that dark patch of earth brings on feelings of anger and frustration that I have lived with for several years. *I don't like it*. I must go and get into the sun and try and force the demons to leave.

THIS BOOK, which began as a small daily journal, grew to become a way for me to expand on my experiences and memories of Bosnia. I did not realize that "talking to the paper" would be therapeutic, but some of my demons have been laid to rest in these pages. I hope that the writing has also honoured all those who were caught up in the Balkan war.

With my experiences as a soldier behind me now, I realize that life is short and that you have to make the best of each day. I miss the uniform and the camaraderie of the army, but at the same time I feel lucky that my transition to civilian life was filled by my job with OSISS. To be able to help soldiers and veterans work through an OSI is humbling yet rewarding. It has taken me several years to realize that I was a good soldier and that my battle with PTSD is not a weakness; I now know that I can wear my medals with honour on Remembrance Day. *I do not care to remember, but I will not forget.*

And that's my story. Take care, all the best. *Pro Patria.*

# Acknowledgements

I SERVED MORE than three decades in the army and I have had the privilege of serving with many great soldiers who I would call my friends. During my service I was also exposed to many different kinds of leaders, from corporals to generals. I watched and learned and adapted bits and pieces of their styles, and developed my own. I will allow the following people to figure out their influences on me as friends, leaders or, better still, both: Ralph Beek Sgt (Ret'd), Joe Bennett wo (Ret'd), Capt "Ranger" Ron Bertin, Ross Bradley Maj (Ret'd), John Bragg Cpl (deceased), LCol Ken Butterworth, Wayne Cardinal mwo (Ret'd), Mark Chapman Capt (Ret'd) , LCol Howie Coombs, Tom Defaye MGen (Ret'd), mwo Denis Deveraux, Maj Mark Douglas, LCol John Fife, cwo Bob Girouard (deceased), Col Rick Hatton, Maj Russ King, LCol Steve Nash, Larry Hulsman Capt (Ret'd), Maj Dave Lambert, Col Doug Maclean, Paul McNally Maj (Ret'd), BGen Greg Mitchell, Maj Keith Osmond, Len Piercey Cpl (deceased), Maj Dave Price, Maj James Price, Maj Bill Pond, Maj Dave Schultz, Russell Scott Sgt (Ret'd), Maj Roger Sheppard, Stu Short mwo (Ret'd), Col Jim Simms, Maj Glenn Sylvester, Col Denis Thompson, Wayne Walker Sgt (Ret'd), Maj Steve "Pinkey" Whalen, and last but not least all of the soldiers I have ever had the privilege of serving with or leading.

The Royal Canadian Regiment has a proud history of service to Canada. It was my home for many years and I feel honoured to have served with such a great regiment. To those who serve in the ranks of the RCR, you have done your regiment proud and written your place in history. May the RCR continue to serve Canada with quiet efficiency, pride and spirit, always up to the task and "never passing a fault."

To the veterans and staff of the Operational Stress Injury Social Support Program, who make a big difference in the lives of our veterans and soldiers suffering from operational stress injuries: LCol Stéphane Grenier, Jim Woodley, Maj Mariane Lebeau, Kathy Darte, Lisa Murphy, Dr Don Richardson, Jim Jamison, Juan Cargnello, Johanne Isabel, Francine Gagnon, Sophie Richard, Al Payment, Vince Tytler, Liz Atkins, Cyndi Greene, Greg Prodaniuk, Janet Bennett, Sandra Guenther, Mike Spellin, Michael Mathieu, Ross Macdonald, Tom Martineau, Marvin Burr, Patrick Sudrau, Michelle Keddy, Anne Prefontaine, Johanne Couture, Bob Danis, Christian Marquis, Pierre Trepanier, Jennifer Fairbank, Shawn Hearn, Dave McCardle. Thank you for caring, take care and all the best.

My Fredericton friends with the Blue Helmets: Fred Leblanc, Fred Gallant, Marcel Richard, Ron Richard, Thom Joordens and John Lomax. I thank you for your camaraderie and honourable service in the pursuit of peace.

I owe a great debt of gratitude to Dr Diane MacIntosh, Debra Bourque, Paytra Schurman-Smith and Robin Geneau, who all played a part in my recovery and my return to the world of the living.

I owe a great debt of gratitude to my publisher, Scott McIntyre, for his confidence and enthusiasm and for his interest in soldiers and what we do. A heartfelt thank you to my editor, John Eerkes-Medrano, for his astute editorial probing and suggestions; you were a joy to work with. Scott Steedman and Susan Rana at Douglas and McIntyre, thank you for making the process interesting and user-friendly. My longtime friend Emelie Hubert, you saw the potential of my words from the beginning—thank you for the encouragement and support.

My immediate and extended family have cared and supported me throughout my life as a soldier, with letters, calls and just plain caring. Mom, Dad and Eva, Neddy, Larry, Marie, Vickey, Alain and all of the Doucettes, I thank you. The Wiper clan, I honour you for caring and having a proud history of military service. Ben and Erin, you have given me joy and love since birth. Theresa and "the boys" Ethan and Amos, you have added to the joy of being alive. I love you all.

I do not know where I would be today if it were not for Janice, who has been by my side through sickness, health, good times and bad. There are no words that can express my gratitude for your staunch support as we made our way through my years as a soldier. When it comes to this book your encouragement, proofreading, typing and suggestions about what readers want to know were invaluable. Thank you.

FRED DOUCETTE
*Lincoln, New Brunswick · Sept 2007*

# Index